THE CREATION OF WEALTH

J. N. TATA
1839-1904

'He was above all a patriot,
who made no public speeches.
To his mind wealth,
and the industry which
led to wealth,
were not ends in themselves,
but means to an end,
the stimulation of the latent
resources of the country
and its elevation in the
scale of nations.'

—The Times of India
13 April 1912
on the occasion of the
unveiling of the Memorial
Statue of J.N. Tata in Bombay.

The Creation of Wealth

The Tatas from the 19th to the 21st Century

R.M. LALA

Foreword by
J.R.D. TATA

Epilogue by
RATAN N. TATA

Illustrated by
MARIO MIRANDA

PENGUIN
VIKING

VIKING

Published by the Penguin Group

Penguin Books India Pvt Ltd, 11 Community Centre, Panchsheel Park, New Delhi 110 017, India

Penguin Group (USA) Inc., 375 Hudson Street, New York, New York 10014, USA

Penguin Group (Canada), 90 Eglinton Avenue East, Suite 700, Toronto, Ontario, M4P 2Y3, Canada (a division of Pearson Penguin Canada Inc.)

Penguin Books Ltd, 80 Strand, London WC2R 0RL, England

Penguin Ireland, 25 St Stephen's Green, Dublin 2, Ireland (a division of Penguin Books Ltd)

Penguin Group (Australia), 250 Camberwell Road, Camberwell, Victoria 3124, Australia (a division of Pearson Australia Group Pty Ltd)

Penguin Group (NZ), cnr Airborne and Rosedale Roads, Albany, Auckland 1310, New Zealand (a division of Pearson New Zealand Ltd)

Penguin Group (South Africa) (Pty) Ltd, 24 Sturdee Avenue, Rosebank, Johannesburg 2196, South Africa

Penguin Books Ltd, Registered Offices: 80 Strand, London WC2R 0RL, England

Originally published by IBH Publishers Pvt. Ltd, Bombay 1981 (1st edition 1981, 2nd edition 1981, 3rd edition 1992)

This edition first published by Penguin Books India 2004

Copyright © Jamsetji Tata Trust 1981, 2004

Typeset in *Perpetua* by Mantra Virtual Services, New Delhi

Printed at Saurabh Printers Pvt. Ltd, Noida

To
Sharokh Sabavala
who opened
for me
the world of Tatas

Books by the same author:

Encounters with the Eminent (1981)

The Heartbeat of a Trust (1984)

In Search of Leadership (1986)

Beyond the Last Blue Mountain: A Life of J.R.D. Tata (1992)

The Joy of Achievement: Conversations with J.R.D. Tata (1995)

Celebration of the Cells: Letters from a Cancer Survivor (1999)

A Touch of Greatness: Encounters with the Eminent (revised and enlarged) (2001)

*There is a difference
between making money
for oneself and creating
wealth for others. This is the story of a House
that has created wealth
for a Nation. It is the story of struggle,
anxiety, adventure,
achievement.*

An unfinished story . . .

CONTENTS

Acknowledgements   xiii

Introduction   xv

SECTION A—1874 to 1991

Foreword   xxv

Preface   xxix

Part One—The Spirit of Adventure

1. The Man and His Vision   3

2. The Steel Saga   20

3. Impulse to Learning   37

4. A Lamp is Lit   47

5. The Taj Mahal   54

6. A Breath of Fragrance   63

7. Those Mad, Mad Days   70

8. Wings for a Nation   75

9. Treasures from the Sea   85

10. The Cult of Excellence   91

11. Cup of Awakening   100

12. Dreamers and Performers   106

Part Two—Ripple Effects

13. On Industry   115

14. Beyond Business   137

15. On People   172

16. Creating a New Industrial Culture   183

Part Three—The Facts

17. How Do Tatas Function?   191

SECTION B—1992 to 2003

18. Liberalization: Challenge & Response   209

19. Dramatic Turnarounds   221

20. Planning Ahead for Success   229

21. Growth Points for the Future   233

22. Some Performers   241

23. Tata Philanthropy—Vision,   253
    Compassion, Attainment

Epilogue   266

Appendices

A Tatas at a Glance   275

B Chairmen of Tatas from 1887   276

C J.R.D. Tata—Guiding Principles   277
   Ratan N. Tata—My Business Values

D Key Business Sectors and Tata   279
   Companies

E Firsts in Labour Welfare   284

F Tatas and Sports   286

G Directors of Tata Sons Limited   290

Index   29

ACKNOWLEDGEMENTS

The author wishes to acknowledge his thanks to Mr Ratan N. Tata for the epilogue; Dr Jamshed J. Irani, who encouraged him to re-issue the book; to Tata Sons executive director R. Gopalakrishnan for his cooperation, and to other officials of Tatas who have given inputs in their respective fields of operation.

Thanks are also due to Mrs Villoo K. Karkaria, who has gone beyond the call of duty as a secretary and lived into every aspect of the book.

INTRODUCTION

Not many books are in demand twenty years after first publication. *The Creation of Wealth* is. First published in 1981, the last and the third edition was published in 1992. The book ended at a watershed for Tatas as well as for India, for in March 1991 Ratan Tata took over as chairman of Tata Sons, and in July the same year Manmohan Singh announced the policy of liberalization. In the intervening period between then and now, 2004, there has been a sea change in the industrial scenario from the world of controls to globalization.

The book was first written at a time of controls when the hangover of state capitalism was still there. *The Creation of Wealth* portrayed what private enterprise could do.

It is an account of how the foundation of India's industrialization was laid by Jamsetji and his heirs. The book evokes an era so different from today's business world. That was a world of adventurous men with undaunted hearts who dared to accomplish things for the sake of the country and not just the bottom line.

Their sights were set high; their gaze often distant. This book recalls Sir Dorabji Tata and party exploring for iron ore in Chanda District, central India, in a bullock cart, where tigers roamed and even their tea had to be prepared in soda water!

It is hard to imagine in today's power starved India that in the 1920s, Tata Hydro-Electric Company, in order to sell its power to mills, had to offer to buy their old boilers from the owners to convert the mills to electric power.

JRD launched civil aviation at a time when flying was a rich man's sport and he had the vision in 1932 that it would knit India close together. Later, he launched Air-India

International as Asia's first international airline in 1948.

Tata Chemicals too had its romance of cracking the secret code of making soda ash which only a handful of companies abroad had the monopoly of. Soon thereafter, struck by years of drought and under cloud of a closure, it survived under the leadership of Darbari Seth, changing the water connections to sea water wherever possible and defying the prophets of doom that it would shut down.

We now live in prosaic times. It is not only industry that is changed; it seems men's motivations and circumstances have changed too.

A book is like a personality. It is of one piece

When the economic scenario has drastically changed, to revise the contents of the 1992 edition would only serve to reduce the effectiveness of the pre 1992 narration. What I have chosen to do for the reader's benefit is to keep the original edition in **Section A** and added developments between 1992 and 2003 in **Section B**. In Section A I have deleted only two chapters from the original edition: 'A Little Leaven' and 'Tata Assets'. They are not only outdated but confusing in the context of 2004. I have, however, in the footnotes, updated essential statistics in the 1992 edition and only occasionally deleted a few lines. This procedure will make for smoother reading.

Section B covers the liberalization era 1992-2003.

'Liberalization: Challenge & Response' is a bridge-chapter that enables the reader to make the transition from the past to the present. It seeks to give only a broad picture of the Tata group's meeting the challenge of the changing scenario.

Significant developments of the decade 1992-2002 in select Tata companies are covered in the chapters in this section. The earlier edition gave facts that were known to me then. New facts have come to light in the last decade, especially on Sir Ratan Tata Trust. For Sir Dorabji Tata Trust I have updated briefly the developments of the last decade. (The chapter 'Tata Philanthropy: Vision, Compassion and Attainment' needs to be read along with the section Tata Trusts in 'Beyond Business' in the previous edition to get a more complete picture.)

I hope this arrangement will enable the reader to get an integrated view of the Tatas, capturing the romance of the early days as well as the challenges of the present and Tatas' response.

In 1991 JRD announced that the Tata Central Archives would be founded. The archives were inaugurated in the year 2000 by Ratan Tata. Located in Pune behind the Tata Management Training Centre, it portrays the history of Tatas which synchronizes with the industrialization of India. It has aroused the interest of many other companies who have benefited from its expertise. It has a magnificent exhibition hall and a replica of the office room of J.R.D. Tata.

Not only does a foundation have an endowment. A company too can endow itself with certain principles and values—or have none! Jamsetji believed in being fair to all stakeholders. He said in 1895, 'We do not claim to be more unselfish, more generous or more philanthropic than other people. But we think we started on sound and straightforward business principles, considering the interests of the shareholders our own, and the health and welfare of the employees the sure foundation of our prosperity.'

In 1924 when Tata Steel was at its lowest ebb with no money to pay the workers Sir Dorabji Tata risked his entire personal fortune of Rs 1 crore (about Rs 90 crore of today) to get a loan from the State Bank of India for a public limited company to save the name of Tatas.

In 1979 when I started writing *The Creation of Wealth*, in reply to a question J.R.D. Tata observed: 'What would have happened if our philosophy was like that of some other companies which do not stop at any means to attain ends . . . If we were like other groups we would be twice as big as they are today. What we have sacrificed is a 100 per cent growth,'

and firmly he added: 'But we wouldn't want it any other way.'
Perhaps it is relevant to give only two instances at this point.

In 1967 Darbari Seth of Tata Chemicals at Mithapur
prepared a unique fertilizer project related to the resources
and needs of India that would ultimately have culminated in
a solar-cum-nuclear power agro-industrial complex. The
Prime Minister, Indira Gandhi, flew to Mithapur for a
presentation of the project, which appeared to thrill her by
virtue of its conceptual grandeur and the vital role it would
play in India's development. Unfortunately, some people
around her objected to supporting Tatas.

In subsequent years the imports of fertilizers went up from
a few hundred to a few thousand crores. Foreign companies
benefited and Indian enterprises did not! Who lost more—
Tatas or India? Some indication of the loss to India is from
our import figures of fertilizers:

1975–76 Rs 592 crore
1985–86 Rs 1436 crore
1995–96 Rs 5628 crore

In 1960 Mercedes-Benz were so pleased with the quality
of production of their trucks in India that they were willing
for Tatas to manufacture the Mercedes-Benz 180D model in
India. Sumant Moolgaokar, the builder of Telco, told the
author in 1960, 'I gave keys of six Mercedes-Benz cars to
K.B. Lal and told him that you use these six cars for one year
and at the end of it you can decide whether you want to give
us the permission to manufacture it.' Mr Moolgaokar added
that one of these cars was used by Krishna Menon. A year
later the six keys and cars were delivered back to Tatas. It
seems there was no reply from the government.

Where would India have been today if we had got the
technology of Mercedes-Benz in the 1960s?

When Sweden was at the height of its power in the 17th
century and had the audacity to take on Russia, the chancellor

of Sweden, Count Axel Oxenstierna, in a letter to his son, 1648, wrote: 'Thou dost not know my son, with how little wisdom the world is governed.'

Even with all this the reader will find in Appendix A 'Tatas at a Glance' where Tatas stand today.

As J.R.D. Tata wrote the foreword to the last edition in January 1992, I thought it appropriate to invite his successor Ratan N. Tata to write the epilogue of this edition. Who could be more suitable than he who has given leadership and direction to the group in the last turbulent decade and more? He has graciously obliged.

Some details of his eleven years as chairman and his strategy are covered in the chapter 'Liberalization: Challenges and Response'. The epilogue gives a view from the top, a human record of what it means to head India's largest industrial group—the steps he took and why, the exhilarations and the disappointments. Reading business newspapers we tend to forget that behind each group or company is a person. With him 'the buck stops.' What is it like to be on this lonely height? He writes the epilogue with candour and sincerity.

What about the future?

'Whoever succeeds Ratan Tata, one thing is clear,' said *Indian Express*, 29 December 2002, 'the future trajectory of Bombay House has been decided.' It has to do with I.T., telecom, cars but old war horses are not being neglected, especially Tata Steel. 'With TCS, Tata Tea, Tata Steel and Tata Engineering (Telco) all showing signs of moving ahead confidently, Ratan Tata can justifiably claim to have left an indelible impression on one of India's most important industrial groups.'

Looking ahead Ratan Tata concludes his epilogue with the words: 'I would hope that my successors would never compromise and turn to soft options to meet their ends, and never allow the Tata group to join the growing number of companies in India which have shed their values, forgotten about their integrity, and closed their eyes on maintaining ethical standards. If Mr J.R.D. Tata was able to uphold the values of the firm and if I have been able to carry on that tradition through my tenure, I hope the future generations in Tatas will recognize these traditions as being critical to the fabric and the fundamentals on which our group was built and grew so successfully for over a century.'

Also a part of the fabric of Tatas has been the human touch. In the rush of modern business life and the pressures of survival, some tough decisions have to be taken, but one hopes that the human touch—the respect Tatas have accorded to human dignity for over a century—will never be lost.

Ratan Tata speaks of JRD's business ethics. One of India's best known tax consultants, Dinesh Vyas, says that JRD never entered into a debate between 'tax avoidance' which was permissible and 'tax evasion' which was illegal; his sole motto was 'tax compliance'. On one occasion a senior executive of a Tata company tried to save on taxes. Before putting up that case, the chairman of the company took him to JRD. Dinesh Vyas explained to JRD: 'But Sir, it is not illegal.' Softly JRD said: 'Not illegal, yes. But is it right?' Vyas says not in his decades of professional work had anyone ever asked him that question. Vyas later wrote in an article, 'JRD would have been the most ardent supporter of the view expressed by Lord Denning: "The avoidance of tax may be lawful, but it is not yet a virtue."'

Ratan Tata has been faithful to these standards. JRD could foresee it. He said: 'I knew what Ratan's strengths were, and I was totally convinced that he was the best man to succeed me—not only because of his abilities, but also because he totally shared my sense of values.'

Jawaharlal Nehru when he came to Jamshedpur for the Golden Jubilee of Tata Steel, said of Jamsetji Tata: 'When you have to give the lead in action, in ideas, a lead that does not fit in with the very climate of opinion, that is true courage, physical or mental or spiritual, call it what you like and it is this type of courage and vision that Jamsetji Tata showed.'

In the present climate of the country and the business world, Tatas are once again called upon to give that lead.

In the emerging scenario of the business world they represent a beacon light. A few other such lights are also beckoning business. In the years to unfold one hopes there will be a festival of such lights to lead India to wealth and prosperity.

1 February 2004   *R.M. Lala*

Section A

1874 to 1991

FOREWORD

Books written on the history of large industrial or business concerns usually suffer from a lack of credibility or reader interest, or both. I am glad that Russi Lala has successfully avoided both these pitfalls. Not only has he narrated the Tata story in a highly readable form which arouses and maintains the reader's interest in what might have been a dull subject in less skilful hands, but he has brought out into the open important and controversial issues which needed to be clarified in the context of the great changes in thought and attitudes towards the world of industry and business that have taken place in the past fifty years or so, not always for the better.

Jamsetji Tata and his sons were products of an era in which bold and adventurous men made large fortunes by exploiting the scientific discoveries and inventions of the nineteenth and early twentieth centuries of steam, electric power, railways, and the motor car, amongst others. In the process, but only incidentally, they advanced economic development, in their own country, and throughout the world.

While he shared the spirit of enterprise and the boldness of such men as Rockefeller, Krupp, Leverhulme and Ford, Jamsetji Tata, as the book clearly brings out, was of a special breed. Having made a substantial fortune from trading and the textile industry, he could have rested on his laurels or concentrated on making more money. Instead, he saw that under the exploitation of colonial rule his country was being bypassed by the industrial revolution which was rapidly transforming Europe and America. He knew that before the advent of steam and electric power India had, for a thousand years or more, been the most industrialized country in the world, a pioneer and a leader in the manufacture of cloth, iron and steel, ships, and many other products, not to speak of its eminence in mathematics, astronomy, architecture and philosophy. Surely, he thought, the creative and productive genius of such a people could be made to flower again if given the tools which modern science and technology had provided to the people of the West. With that object in view, he decided, almost single-handed, to launch India on the path of modern science and industry and to risk his fortune in the process. That the great projects which he conceived and his sons carried through were successful is less important than the motives with which they were launched, than also the sense of social consciousness and trusteeship which Jamsetji inculcated in his two sons and my father, R.D. Tata, and which have continued to this day to inspire and guide his successors and, through them, the management of the various enterprises which they promoted. This book brings out well the remarkable extent to which this process has continued to survive for nearly a hundred years and has become characteristic of the Tata group, even after the abolition of the managing agency system in 1970 had set all the companies in the group managerially adrift.

Where Russi Lala has perhaps failed in completing or rounding off his task was in neglecting to seek out and criticize, where due, any weaknesses or failures of the firm: for instance, its remarkably consistent propensity, perhaps unavoidable in any pioneering and risky venture, for getting into difficulties in the early years of new projects, ultimately retrieving them by enormous and prolonged effort backed by a dour determination not to admit failure. Thus Tata Steel, Tomco, Tata Chemicals and Telco, amongst others, had to go through such initial struggles for survival on the way to ultimate success.

The firm has also been criticized at times for not being enterprising enough in diversifying into new fields. I personally believe it reflected not so much a lack of enterprise as the impact of two forces on the firm's policies and progress:

on the one hand, an unwillingness to compromise certain principles but for which, in the licence and permit raj in which private enterprise has had to operate in our country for the past forty years or so, growth and diversification would undoubtedly have been greater; on the other hand, long, perhaps too long, adherence to the belief that Tatas' principal role was to develop basic industries, as a result of which they are today more vulnerable than others to government controls, and even to nationalization.

In this third edition of Lala's book, I find of special interest the chapter on the creation of a Tata industrial culture. In this chapter, Russi Lala has spelt out how the sociological aspects of Tatas' activities have widened with each succeeding generation. First, Jamsetji's concern for his workers at a time when capitalist enterprise in the West could be pretty brutal. His son Dorab invited the well-known socialists Sydney and Beatrice Webb to Jamshedpur to organize the social services of Tata Steel. By the nineteen sixties when Tata Steel and other Tata companies could, by and large, be considered as having fulfilled all reasonable obligations towards their employees, I, along with most of my colleagues and the managements of Tata companies felt that their sense of responsibility should extend beyond the immediate surroundings of the companies' factories and townships, to the people living in surrounding areas. To give formalized expression to such widened feeling of public responsibility, I arranged, incidentally with total support from the directors and managements of all Tata companies, for their Articles of Association to be amended so as to make such extended social responsibility a written part of each company's commitment to society. On my regular visits to Jamshedpur and other industrial areas served by Tatas, it always heartened me to find evidence of such added commitment, thus reaching out to our less fortunate fellow beings in other areas and providing them with some part of the quality of life enjoyed by our own employees elsewhere, which, alas, is so often lacking in our country.

I believe that the social responsibilities of our industrial enterprises should now extend, even beyond serving people, to the environment. This need is now fairly well recognized but there is still considerable scope for most industrial ventures to extend their support not only to human beings but also to the land, to the forests, to the waters and to the creatures that inhabit them. I hope that such need will be increasingly recognized by all industries and their managements because of the neglect from which they have suffered for so long and the physical damage that the growth of industry has inflicted, and still inflicts, on them.

In congratulating Russi Lala on the initial and well deserved success of his book, I hope that the young people who read it will find in it some inspiration in pursuing successful careers in which the knowledge that they are contributing to the country's progress will be one of the most satisfying rewards.

Bombay
1 January 1992

PREFACE

Ten years have passed since this book was first written. It has since been published in Hindi, Gujarati and Marathi. There was a demand for a third edition but demands of my job as well as the pressure of other writing made me put it off for some years. In a way I owe this edition to the initiative of a Japanese scholar, Professor K. Kurozawa, an authority on Indian economics and the president of a university in Kobe, who had the conviction that the book should be published in the Japanese language. Moved by his conviction I said 'Yes' to revising it, little knowing what it would entail. I thought the main task would be to get the statistics updated and latest developments of ten years incorporated. When revising the book I found it was not so simple. Companies and Tata-founded institutions had grown so much that the chapters had to be substantially rewritten or added to. The Tata Institute of Social Sciences had almost doubled in size and outreach within the span of a decade, while the Tata Memorial Hospital has considerably expanded its own facilities during its golden jubilee 1991-92. Companies that were once tender have firmed up; while a company like Titan Watches which was a dream ten years ago is now a household name.

Throughout history there have been two categories of people—those who create wealth and those who consume it. This century has given rise to a new category of people whose passion is to control the wealth others take the trouble to create. To consume or control wealth needs little qualification. To create wealth is a different proposition. Through the study of one leading industrial house this book takes a look at what it takes to create wealth for a nation.

The word 'wealth' is derived from the old English word 'weal' which means well-being, happiness, prosperity, welfare. In its larger context it embraces 'the welfare of a country or community; the general good.'* The English expression 'the public weal' or 'commonweal' has its counterpart in French 'le bien publique' and in Latin 'bonum publicum'. It is significant that the Japanese publishers of this book, Simul Press, got the point and entitled their edition *The Creation of Wealth and the Use of It.*

If words and slogans could create wealth, the streets of India would be paved with gold. It takes more than that. A nation's wealth comes out of vision and hard work; out of anxious days and long unrewarded nights; out of courage that is ready for sacrifices; out of values cherished and battles fought for them; out of a compassion for human beings. To what extent have some of these qualities found expression in the moulding of the House of Tata?

The wealth created by an industrial house is to be measured not only on the basis of its balance sheet but also in terms of its skilled manpower, its advanced technology and its ability to conduct satisfactory industrial relations. Even more so in terms of its ripple effects on a nation's life. A good part of this book is devoted to the ripple effects.

When working on this revised edition I asked J.R.D. Tata what he reckoned were the significant developments of Tatas in the last decade. He noted particularly the growth of Tata Steel, Telco, Indian Hotels and Tata Tea.

This sent me to the highlands of Kerala where one morning, driving past a tea plantation, we noticed three elephants who stood still beside a boulder as in a photograph—their asphalt skin merged with the colour of stone. Shortly after, we came to the ibex, endangered elsewhere but merrily multiplying under the protective umbrella of the officers of the Tata Tea and the forest guards

* *Shorter Oxford English Dictionary.*

of the neighbouring sanctuary and national park. The tea estate officer who took us round was even more proud to be one of the eleven Tata Tea Voluntary Wildlife Guards than of the fine tea he was growing. He was preserving nature's wealth which J.R.D. Tata refers to at the end of his foreword.

In the previous two editions I had briefly touched on Tata Oil Mills, one of the pioneers in the field of soaps. To cover it more fully I went to Cochin, the site of its first factory. Alongside the factory, the backwaters of the Arabian Sea lie still as a lake in the morning mist. The fronded palms provide the skyline. In the quiet of that morning one could only utter the Psalmist's verse:

He leadeth me beside the still waters;
He restoreth my soul.

If the backwaters are peaceful, the test track of Telco was anything but peaceful. Driving a new model unseen by the public was a joy despite the bumps.

A return visit to Jamshedpur, the hub of Tatas' industry, was a further revelation. Ten years ago it was the companies who assisted in rural work. Now some individuals, irrespective of their company's help, go to the villages for social work. They too, and not management alone, are contributing to a new industrial culture of care. It deserved a fresh chapter.

Further south, at a meeting of the court of the Indian Institute of Science in Bangalore the speaker was Dr Raja Ramanna, chairman of the council of the institute. Though he was then Minister of State for Defence, he took an active interest in the institute because, he said, a nation's strength lies in the quality of research of her scientists and not only in the preparedness of our armed forces. He made a pertinent point. This institute established by Jamsetji Tata and nurtured by successive generations is, said Dr Ramanna, 'an island of excellence' in the academic world of India. But we cannot be satisfied with that, he noted, and enquired of the Court members: 'How do we reach out to the other academic institutions so they too can attain excellence?'

The plantations of Tata Tea, the factories of Jamshedpur, the educational institutions founded by Tatas, can all these go forward from being 'islands' to becoming the radiating points of excellence in the country?

This book is an attempt to capture 100 years of industrial activity within a little more than 200 pages. It lays no claim to being a critical analysis but will I hope provide the background material for anyone writing on Tatas, or for that matter, on Indian industry. Perhaps reading about these institutions and companies may inspire some readers as well as remind those working in Tatas, that theirs is a national adventure.

This revised edition was completed on the eve of the far-reaching liberalization introduced by Dr Manmohan Singh, the Union Finance Minister, in 1991. The heavy hand of control that has inhibited the growth of Indian industry is now lifted. The future should be very different from the past.

Bombay   *R.M.L.*
21 January 1992

Part One

The Spirit of Adventure

1

THE MAN AND HIS VISION

When you have to give the lead in action, in ideas—a lead which does not fit in with the very climate of opinion, that is true courage, physical or mental or spiritual, call it what you like, and it is this type of courage and vision that Jamsetji Tata showed.
                                                          —Jawaharlal Nehru

In 1858 the British Crown stood forth in name and in fact as the ruler of India. After the failure of the uprising of 1857, a vast subcontinent lay still and submissive. The decades to follow were to mark the high noon of British imperialism. In that period, the geographical expression known as 'India' received two benefits: unification of the country into a stable political entity and a railway system that sought to make the subcontinent a single, viable economic unit. Writing of this period in his *Discovery of India*, Jawaharlal Nehru notes: 'Slowly India recovered from the after-effects of the Revolt of 1857-58. Despite British policy, powerful forces were at work changing India and a new social consciousness was arising. The awakening of India was two-fold: she looked to the West, and, at the same time, she looked to herself and her own past.' Indians began to ask themselves why a foreign power had gained such supremacy over their ancient land. Was it because the culture of the West was superior to their own? Or was it because modern science and technology gave Europe a lead? A new class of Indians was rising, eager to learn English and to benefit from the study of western ways and methods which Lord Macaulay was offering.

The year that Macaulay left for England, 1839, Jamsetji Nusserwanji Tata was born in a family of Parsi priests in

Navsari, Gujarat. At the age of fourteen he came to Bombay, and at seventeen he joined Elphinstone College from which he passed out a couple of years later as a 'Green Scholar', the then equivalent of a graduate. The love for literature and books he then acquired was to last him throughout his life. He was fond of reading Dickens, Thackeray and Mark Twain. After initial trading ventures in the Far East and Europe, he started in 1868—at the age of twenty-nine—a private trading firm with a capital of Rs 21,000.

He and his associates obtained a contract to furnish supplies required by the expeditionary force of General Napier in Abyssinia. The share of the profits was sufficient to launch him on his career in textiles. His earlier visits to Manchester had stimulated his desire to manufacture cotton goods. He bought an old oil mill in Bombay in partnership with a few friends, converted it into a textile mill, managed it himself and within a couple of years made it a going concern. He sold it at a profit two years later. There were, at that

The Empress Mills—Intermediate Fly Frame, 1894

time, about a dozen textile mills centred in Bombay, which was known as the 'Cottonpolis' of India. Jamsetji Tata decided to plant his new mill where the cotton came from. He picked on Nagpur in central India, and took advantage of the railway system which had, by that time, moved to the area.

The company he floated in 1874 with a capital of Rs 1,500,000 subscribed by his friends and himself, was named The Central India Spinning, Weaving and Manufacturing Company. On 1 January 1877, the day Queen Victoria was formally proclaimed Empress of India, the Empress Mills was inaugurated. Jamsetji had bought, at a low price, marshy land near the Nagpur railway station and had proceeded to fill it up. A local Marwari banker, asked to subscribe to its shares, refused to back a man who was wasting gold by sinking it into the ground. The gentleman lived to admit that 'Tata had not put gold into the ground but had put in earth and taken out gold.' Jamsetji was to launch another textile mill before he stepped on the scene of history as one of the great builders of modern India.

Jamsetji was a nationalist long before this word had any real significance. He was present, for instance, at the founding of the Indian National Congress in Bombay in 1885, and gave generously to its funds. His nationalism, however, was not narrow. It was, like Tagore's, rooted in his love for humanity, arising out of his passionate love for his own land to which he harnessed the creative forces of his genius. Every day of his life, therefore, became a day of preparation for that time when his country would be in charge of her destiny. When he surveyed the untilled industrial field of India he perceived the benefits it could gain through science and technology. Not only did he grasp the full significance of the industrial revolution of India, but his clear mind spelt out the three basic ingredients to attain it. Steel was the mother of heavy industry. Hydro-electric power was the cheapest energy to be generated. And technical education coupled with research was essential for industrial advance. This may be obvious to

us today, but it was not so a century ago to a nation subjugated to a colonial economy. In Jamsetji, India had found a man of ideas with the ability to translate them into reality.

Wisely, he concentrated his energies on implementing these three imperatives of industry. Upon these objectives he brought to bear the resources of his wealth and experience, the prestige of his name, and that rare gift only few can command—the full-hearted devotion of his colleagues.

An English observer, Sir Stanley Reed (later Editor of *The Times of India*) described him as a sturdy figure whose 'voice was sonorous and rather harsh; he conveyed to my mind the impression of the energy and force of a man of action rather than that of an industrial seer.'

His day began fairly early in the morning. At times he went for a short walk along Bombay's sea-front and after that would drop in to see his friends. At breakfast he presided at the family table, often joined by relatives and friends. He then read and wrote for a while till he went to office at midday. After office, at 6 p.m. he would go for a drive in his horse-carriage—later in his car—or play cards and converse at the Elphinstone Club. On his return he enjoyed his dinner. Good food was one of his two indulgences; the other was a voracious appetite for knowledge, which he constantly fed with reading. The curator of the Calcutta Botanical Museum, an authority on Indian plants, came out of Jamsetji's room one day staggered at his knowledge of botany. 'I learnt several things from him,' said the curator. When an epidemic of bubonic plague was at its height, Jamsetji put aside all else and worked on the history and treatment of different plagues with a view to preventing the spread of infection. One day he had lined up his household staff for inoculation, when Colonel Hormusji Bhabha, Inspector-General of Education for Mysore State arrived. The bewildered colonel was immediately recruited by Jamsetji as a candidate for inoculation. Everyday Jamsetji spent a couple of hours in undisturbed contemplation and reading in his study.

A young Englishman, Norman Redford, who paid several visits to Jamsetji, records that on evening drives in his horse-carriage, Jamsetji and his colleagues would talk of schemes, schemes, and more schemes. 'Never,' records Norman Redford, 'did I see Mr Tata impatient or intolerant, nor did I ever see him critical of others' shortcomings.' When Jamsetji died *The Times of India* said that 'he was not a man who cared to bask in the public eye. He disliked public gatherings, he did not care for making speeches, his sturdy strength of character prevented him from fawning on any man however great, for he himself was great in his own way, greater than most people realized. He sought no honour* and he claimed no privilege. But the advancement of India and her myriad peoples was with him an abiding passion.' The same paper spoke of Jamsetji's 'quiet, strong, stern, unselfish

* He had declined a baronetcy.

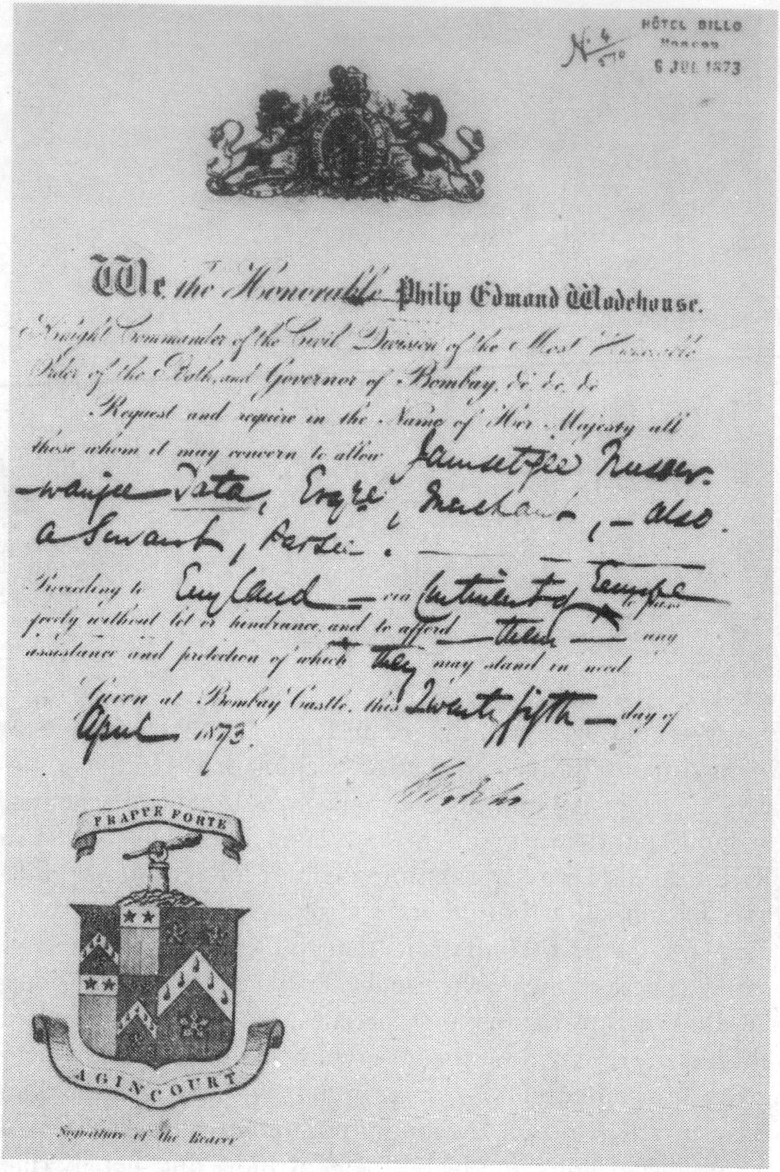

HÔTEL BILLO

6 JUL 1873

We the Honorable Philip Edmond Wodehouse.

Knight Commander of the Civil Division of the Most Honorable Order of the Bath, and Governor of Bombay, &c. &c. &c.

Request and require in the Name of Her Majesty all those whom it may concern to allow Jamsetjee Nusserwanjee Tata, Esqre., Merchant, — also a Servant, Parsee. —

Proceeding to England — via Continent of Europe to pass freely without let or hindrance, and to afford them every assistance and protection of which they may stand in need.

Given at Bombay Castle, this Twenty fifth day of April 1873.

FRAPPE FORTE

AGINCOURT

Signature of the Bearer

Travel document of J.N. Tata

The Empress Mills, Nagpur

determination to pursue his calling.'

Jamsetji's mind spanned almost every area of human endeavour though he is remembered for his three great nation building projects and the famous Taj Mahal Hotel. He was never short of schemes. He had plans to construct a huge circular building where the Prince of Wales Museum stands today in Bombay. He wanted it to house an ice factory that would cool offices in the circular building. This was long before Carrier invented air-conditioning.

Jamsetji not only knew his country well, he knew the world as few other men of his time. In his youth, he had travelled to China and the Far East as well as to Europe and the Middle East. In later years he covered North America. He repeatedly visited Europe and America for industrial exhibitions that first became fashionable in his days. He took advantage of these journeys to study steel plants, coal mines and factories abroad. George Westinghouse encouraged him to visit the Niagara Falls to study hydro-electric generation of power.

Wheresoever he toured, whatever good he saw he wanted to bring its benefits to his country. He introduced to India foreign trees and plants which he personally cultivated at his estates in Panchgani, Bangalore and Ootacamund. While in France he made a study of the cultivation of the silkworm, and when he visited Japan in 1893 he invited the Japanese to experiment in sericulture. He picked on Mysore for climatic reasons. The Japanese discovered that silk was once a flourishing industry of that state and that Jamsetji had selected the right place. The silk industry was revived in Mysore. Similarly he chose the Sind area to experiment with the growing of long staple Egyptian cotton. He gave detailed instructions to a number of people how to grow and experiment but, alas, the experiment was not successful.

He opened a park at Navsari, his home town, to house exotic animals. On one of his last visits he imported a pair of Italian greyhounds and white peacocks for breeding.

The textile mill at Nagpur became Jamsetji's laboratory.

He looked after every little detail of its growth. Here he tried experiments in technology and labour welfare never before attempted in India. To conserve the new company's capital, he purchased in Britain low priced equipment and, consequently, his yarn turned out to be of inferior quality. He replaced it with the most up-to-date American machinery, ring spindles, till then untried even by the mills of Lancashire. In the future, nothing but the best was to be good enough for him.

The excellence of his new plant was matched by his care for the workers. He installed the first humidifiers and fire-sprinklers in India. In 1886, he instituted a pension fund and, in 1895, began to pay accident compensation. He was decades ahead of his time and miles ahead of his competitors. The Empress Mills experiment showed that not only profits but people mattered to him.

Emboldened by these early successes, he decided in 1886 to buy a mill that had proved to be the graveyard of many reputations. This mill in Bombay had spacious acreage, but the unit itself was ramshackle. At forty-seven, Jamsetji took on the challenge of making a 'sick' mill healthy. Humorously he called it 'my rotten mill', not realizing at the time what a back-breaking task he was taking on. This second unit, called 'Svadeshi Mills' to mark the first beginnings of the swadeshi movement, was massively supported by Indian shareholders who cheerfully invested in Jamsetji's, by now, rising reputation as an industrialist. But two years later the mills failed to pay a dividend. A shipment to the Far East was rejected. Rumours circulated. Share prices toppled to a fourth of the original. The name 'Tata' was at stake. For the first—but not the last—time, a member of the Tata family risked his personal fortune for saving a public company. Banks refused Jamsetji an overdraft when he offered to pledge his family trust. Jamsetji revoked the trust, liberated his capital, sold some Empress Mills shares and pumped more of his capital into the Svadeshi Mills. As soon as the shareholders learnt of this, the shares firmed up again. By an amazing display of personal energy, and by bringing the best of his staff from the mills at Nagpur, he pitchforked the Svadeshi unit into the top bracket of the textile industry. Within eight years, Svadeshi Mills cloth fetched the highest prices and was in demand in the Far East.

Even as he battled for the survival of his industry, he was not too busy to think of the health of his workers. As polluted water was a cause of illness, he installed a water filtration plant and arranged for sanitary hutments. A grain depot was opened, followed by a dispensary, provident fund and pension schemes. In those early years he also introduced a system of apprenticeship. At that time, of course, there was no academic training in textile technology; so he urged graduates to study books from the mill library.

In the 1880s, it was the practice of all managing agents to charge a commission on production or sales, irrespective of whether the mills made a profit. Jamsetji pioneered the principle that a commission of five per cent to ten per cent would be levied by the managing agents only on profits. Half a century later, the Indian Companies Act of 1937 turned his pioneering principle into the law of the land. One of his early biographers wrote: 'Had he no other title to recognition, his conduct of the mills would suffice.' But much more was to come from his fertile genius. Successful in two textile ventures, his name trusted by the public, contemporaries said that Jamsetji would multiply his wealth by adding to his textile units. He and his staff had the know-how to do so if he so wished. Instead, he chose the unknown path to give India steel, hydro-electric power and technical education of a high order. Something had happened to Jamsetji. The nation had become his business.

In 1902, five years before the site of the steel plant was finally located, he wrote from abroad to his son, Dorab, of what his dream city of steel should look like:

> Be sure to lay wide streets planted with shady trees, every other of a quick-growing variety. Be sure that there is plenty

'Earmark areas for Hindu temples . . .'

'. . . Mohammedan mosques . . .'

of space for lawns and gardens. Reserve large areas for football, hockey and parks. Earmark areas for Hindu temples, Mohammedan mosques and Christian churches.

Jamsetji had seen it all in his mind's eye.

In 1904, three years before the steel plant site was discovered, Jamsetji died at Bad Nauheim in Germany. In his last days, he urged his cousin R.D. Tata and close members of his family to carry forward the work he had started: 'If you cannot make it greater, at least preserve it. Do not let things slide. Go on doing my work and increasing it but if you cannot, do not lose what we have already done.' They not only continued but expanded his work. Others reaped, but he sowed.

Success or failure was not a major issue with Jamsetji. He did what was needed to be done in an environment which was not usually favourable to him. He respected Britain for its liberal traditions but it fell to his lot to fight British imperialism wherever it stunted the industrial growth of his own country. For years he waged a war against the P&O Line which charged excessive freight for Indian exports to the Far East. He started, with Japanese collaboration, a rival shipping line. In the freight war P&O finally offered to carry cotton freight free to the Far East; the exporters failed to support Jamsetji and he had to close the Tata Line. But he did fight.

It was a struggle for his successors to set up a steel plant and get under way the hydro-electric projects. It was also a battle to establish a university of science for which Jamsetji had offered his properties worth Rs 3,000,000—a staggering sum in 1898. The then Viceroy, Lord Curzon, was 'rather lukewarm' to this project. But for Jamsetji it was the key to India's modernization.

The British authorities were convinced that students who would pass out from this university of science would not find employment because 'India had no industries'. The Secretary

'. . . and Christian churches.'

of State wrote to Lord Curzon that as the British had not given the green signal to the university plan, Jamsetji would probably divert some of his endowment to his other projects of steel and hydro-electric power. Some of Jamsetji's close friends too poured cold water on the scheme. A lesser man meeting with such discouragement would have withdrawn the offer. Jamsetji was sore, but so clear was his conviction that he would not abandon the project. He simultaneously proceeded with his steel and hydro-electric projects. For him it was not a case of either/or. At sixty, he knew time was running out, but he had put his hand on the plough and he would not turn back.

What followed was the story of India's leap from the Middle Ages to the threshold of the 20th century.

2

THE STEEL SAGA

Do you mean to say that Tatas propose to make steel rails to British specifications? Why, I will undertake to eat every pound of steel rail they succeed in making.
—Sir Frederick Upcott,
Chief Commissioner for the Indian Railways.

At the age of forty-three in 1882, Jamsetji read a report by a German geologist, Ritter von Schwartz, that the best situated deposits of iron ore were in Chanda District in the Central Provinces, not far from Nagpur where he worked. The area named was Lohara, after the iron ore deposits nearby. In the vicinity, Warora had deposits of coal. Jamsetji is believed to have visited Lohara himself and obtained specimens of Warora coal for testing. He took a consignment of coal with him and had it tested in Germany. The coal was found unsuitable. The mining terms offered by the government were too restrictive and Jamsetji gave up the project. But the idea of giving India a steel plant abided with him.

For the next seventeen years Jamsetji maintained a book of cuttings on minerals available in India. A steady flame burnt in his heart before blast furnaces were to be lit in Jamshedpur. In 1899 the Viceroy, Lord Curzon, liberalized the mineral concession policy. The same year, Major R.H. Mahon published a report on the manufacture of iron and steel in India. Mahon said that the time had come to establish an iron and steel works on a considerable scale. He suggested that the Jharia coalfields in eastern India would provide the necessary fuel. For iron ore he suggested Salem district in the South, Chanda district in the Central Provinces, and Bengal.

The next year, Jamsetji was in England seeing the Secretary

of State for India, Lord George Hamilton. Hamilton had respect for him. The idea of the steel plant which Jamsetji unfolded sparked the imagination of the British statesman. Jamsetji said he had first thought of the idea as a young man. Now he was sixty and blessed with more than enough for his needs. If he undertook this project it would be for the sake of India. Could he expect the support of the government, Jamsetji enquired. Hamilton assured him and wrote accordingly to Lord Curzon.

Speedily Jamsetji instructed his office in Bombay to obtain prospecting licences, and proceeded to the U.S. himself. He wanted the best technical advice. He studied coking processes at Birmingham, Alabama, visited the world's largest ore market at Cleveland, and in Pittsburgh met the foremost metallurgical consultant, Julian Kennedy. Kennedy warned the enthusiastic though ageing Indian that even preliminary investigations would cost a fortune and there was no guarantee of returns. If, said Kennedy, a thorough scientific survey was made of raw materials and conditions, he would build the plant. He suggested the name of Charles Page Perin as the best man to undertake the survey. To Perin, Jamsetji went. Perin later described his encounter:

I was poring over some accounts in the office when the door opened and a stranger in a strange garb entered. He walked in, leaned over my desk and looked at me fully a minute in silence. Finally, he said in a deep voice, 'Are you Charles Page Perin?' I said, 'Yes'. He stared at me again silently for a long time. Then slowly he said, 'I believe I have found the man I have been looking for. Julian Kennedy has written to you that I am going to build a steel plant in India. I want you to come to India with me, to find suitable iron ore and coking coal and the necessary fluxes. I want you to take charge as my consulting engineer. Mr Kennedy will build the steel plant wherever you advise and I will foot the bill. Will you come to India with me?'

'Are you Charles Page Perin?' asked Jamsetji Tata

I was dumbfounded, naturally. But you don't know what character and force radiated from Tata's face. And kindliness, too. 'Well,' I said, 'yes, I'd go.' And I did.

Before Perin arrived, he sent his partner Weld to prospect for the raw materials.

Geologist C.M. Weld arrived in April 1903 and set out for exploration with Dorab Tata and a cousin Shapurji Saklatvala, who was elected to the British House of Commons. Chanda district was one of the finest for shikar. The trouble was they were not hunting for tigers but for iron ore. They travelled by bullock-cart. Clean water and food were difficult to obtain, they were often compelled to brew their tea with soda water. As days went by, the immensity of the task they had taken on began to dawn on the prospectors.

Weld was meticulous in his observations. Initially, iron

ore and limestone were found but Chanda district was short of the right type of coal. Even the iron ore was in pockets and not in continuous areas. So, sadly, the Chanda scheme was abandoned.

Weld was all set to go home and any businessman other than Jamsetji would have tried to cut his losses on an expensive consultant. But Jamsetji invited him to stay on, and explore for iron ore, coal and fluxes irrespective of location. Weld said that he then realized that Jamsetji was inspired by something far greater than the desire to merely amass a fortune.

The next signal came from an unexpected quarter at the very moment Dorab Tata went to tell the chief commissioner of Chanda district that Tatas had abandoned the prospecting at Chanda. As the commissioner was out, Dorab Tata aimlessly drifted into the museum opposite the Nagpur Secretariat, to await his return. There he perceived a geological map (in colour) of the Central Provinces. On the map, at Durg district, 140 miles from Nagpur, dark colours indicated heavy deposits of iron ore. To Durg did they repair.

As they climbed on the hills of Dhalli and Rajhara, their footsteps rang with the sound of metal. They were walking on a hill of the finest ore in the world—67 per cent iron. Coking coal and limestone were needed, and, above all, a steady supply of water. But water there was none. So they had to look elsewhere. Their labours were not wasted. Fifty years later those very hills were to furnish the ore needed for the steel plant at Bhilai.

Again the hand of fortune intervened. A letter arrived from an Indian geologist, P.N. Bose, who had originally marked the Durg area for ore. Now working for the Maharaja of Mayurbhanj, he had discovered rich iron ore in the state. It was within range of the Bengal coalfields and the ruler was keen to develop his state. In the wooded hills where elephants roamed and tribal Santhals eked out a precarious existence, the lofty Gorumahisani Hill rose to 3,000 feet. It was a superb storehouse of iron ore later estimated at thirty-five million tonnes, with an iron content of over 60 per cent. Other neighbouring hills were also rich. All the prospects were pleasing, but where was the water? A reservoir proposed had proved impracticable. The search went on. Early one morning Weld and his assistant, Srinivas Rao, plodded down a dry stream on their horses. It was heavy going through the sand. 'At length we came upon a sight which filled us with joy; a black trap-dike, crossing the river diagonally, and making an almost perfect pick-up weir. It seemed too good to be true.'

Weld and Srinivas Rao clambered up the river bank shouting with excitement. They found themselves close by the village of Sakchi near the meeting point of the two rivers, Kharkai and Subarnareka ('gold-streaked'), which, together never run dry. A couple of miles away was the railway station of Kalimati. They had come to the end of their search. Three years earlier Jamsetji had passed away at Bad Nauheim in Germany, but his dream was to outlive him.

Tatas had braved the jungle; now they had to brave the financial world. It was initially suggested that capital for such a large and pioneering project would have to come from the London money market. In 1907, the London market was passing through a bad patch and financiers in London also wanted to exert control if they were to invest.

Some faint-hearted souls said India would not be able to raise the considerable capital. Tatas decided to take the plunge into the Indian market, and issued their prospectus to raise Rs 1.5 crore* in ordinary shares, Rs 75 lakh in preference

shares, and Rs 7,00,000 in deferred, a total of Rs 2.32 crore.
From early morning till late at night people besieged Tatas'
offices in Bombay and within three weeks 8,000 investors
had subscribed. The hidden wealth of India surfaced for her
first great industrial adventure. From this amount of Rs 2.32
crore a steel plant of 1,00,000 tonnes capacity plus the
township was set up.**

Jamsetji's company had obtained concessions for iron ore,
rail freight, and had taken the risk and the burden of the
exploration. All the concessions were turned over to the new
Tata Iron and Steel Company for an allotment of Rs 15 lakh
worth of shares in the new company and Rs 5,25,000 out-of-
pocket expenses to be reimbursed in cash which Tata Sons
put in equity, adding Rs 4,75,000 of their own money. The
total Tata stake was Rs 25 lakh—about 11 per cent of the
total capital subscribed.

Between the two rivers, a city had to be planned. As the
jungles were cleared, in place of towering trees, steel chimneys
arose. At the same time, in another part a township grew.

Though the Maharaja of Mayurbhanj had given highly
favourable terms to Tatas, the local 'kings' of the jungle were

---

* A 'crore' of rupees is ten million; a 'lakh' is 1,00,000.
** In the 1980s, modernization of the Tata Steel plant of 2.1 million
tonnes cost Rs 1,000 crore, and an additional capacity of 6,00,000
tonnes will cost Rs 1,500 crore in the 1990s. This is not only a
measure of the new technology but also indicative of the fall in
the value of money.

less hospitable. Tigers killed two tribal labourers. An elephant driven frantic by the din of dam construction stampeded over a number of huts and flattened them. One night a bear crawled into the hut of the railway superintendent and delivered a cub under his table!

Erecting a plant of this nature in the wilderness was called by contemporaries 'a titanic enterprise'. Communications were slow; machinery was hauled over vast distances from home or abroad; labour had to be trained. There was then no pool of technicians or scientists at home to draw upon.

In the early stages, coal was not of uniform quality; designs of furnaces were found unsatisfactory. Even the German crew for the blast furnace was not up to the mark. Charles Page Perin was summoned again from America.

The chief commissioner for the Indian Railways, Sir Frederick Upcott, had earlier told Perin: 'Do you mean to say that Tatas propose to make steel rails to British specifications? Why, I will undertake to eat every pound of steel rail they succeed in making.'

On 16 February 1912, the first ingot of steel rolled on the lines of the Sakchi plant amidst much rejoicing. During World War I Tatas exported 1,500 miles of steel rails to Mesopotamia. Dorab Tata commented dryly that if Sir Frederick had carried out his undertaking, he would have had 'some slight indigestion.'

In December 1916, a confident chairman of the company was to speak to shareholders of: 'Bumper earnings; production 30 per cent above original design . . . ready and willing markets . . . order book full to bursting.' The success was intoxicating. An ambitious programme was taken in hand to expand the steel capacity by five times. The expansion programme ran into stormy weather. Spiralling post-war prices, transport and labour difficulties completely upset price calculations. It seemed the stars were conspiring to crush the fledgling enterprise. Japan was the largest customer of pig iron. An earthquake struck Japan and prices fell. The faint-hearted reeled under the misfortunes. One director suggested that the government be asked to take over the company. Thereupon R.D. Tata,* a cousin and colleague of Jamsetji, sprang to his feet, pounded the table and declared that the day would never come as long as he lived.

One day a telegram came from Jamshedpur that there was not enough money for wages. R.D. Tata and Sir Dorab Tata (who was knighted in 1910) struggled to raise funds. In November 1924, the steel company was on the verge of closing

---

* There were two Ratan Tatas—one was Ratan Dadabhai Tata, the father of J.R.D. Tata, who was related to Jamsetji. The other was Jamsetji's second son, Sir Ratan. When Tata & Sons was founded in 1887, the three original partners were Jamsetji, Dorab and R.D. Tata. Jamsetji's son Ratan, quite young at the time, was made a partner later.

R.D. Tata

down. Sir Dorab pledged his entire personal fortune of Rs 1 crore, including his wife's jewellery, to obtain a loan of Rs 1 crore from the Imperial Bank of India for a public limited company. It was touch and go whether the firm would survive.

Sir Dorab's readiness to sacrifice was honoured by providence. Soon, the first returns from expanded production came in and gave the company a breather.

Meanwhile, a new threat had arisen from the dumping of foreign steel. Thanks to Motilal Nehru and the Congress Legislative Party, the British government finally consented to impose protective duties on imported steel and paid a bounty on steel rails for three years from 1924.

Throughout this struggle for survival not one worker was retrenched. The shareholders went without a dividend for twelve out of thirteen years. There was a certain vision and spaciousness about the men and the times they lived in.

Just before the first ingot of steel rolled in TISCO in February 1912, R.D. Tata had told the shareholders: 'Like all infants this company will have its infantile ailments, its period of convulsions and teething as well as hours of smiles and caresses. It will be then that your courage and ours will be tested.'

His prophecy was to come true.

In October 1923, also speaking to the shareholders at the time of the great struggle and crippling shortage of money, R.D. Tata told them: 'We are constantly accused by people of wasting money in the town of Jamshedpur. We are asked why it should be necessary to spend so much on housing, sanitation, roads, hospitals and on welfare. . . . Gentlemen, people who ask these questions are sadly lacking in imagination. We are not putting up a row of workmen's huts in Jamshedpur—we are building a city.'

And in his last address to the shareholders in June 1925, a year before he died, he said, 'We are like men building a wall against the sea. It would be the height of folly on our part to give away any part of the cement that is required to make the wall secure for all time. That is why we and you have to use this money which we have made firstly to build up this great industry which we are making for India and we should not think of dividends until we have done that. Now let me come from the general to the particular—to this sum of Rs 64 lakh net profit which we have made this year and which we propose to use chiefly to strengthen our wall . . .'

R.D. Tata said about the profit they had made that year (after a couple of difficult years): 'We hold this money in trust for you—but you yourself hold it in trust for the Indian nation which has at great sacrifice given you in the shape of protection more than the whole net profit we have made.'

The upward swing came with World War II in 1939. The value of Tata Steel appreciated. Armoured cars were fitted with bullet-proof plates and rivets made by Tata Steel. They were called 'Tatanagars'. There was such pride when a report came from the Eighth Army in the western desert, that even when a 75 mm shell burst on one side of a 'Tatanagar', the metal plates buckled but were nowhere pierced, and the occupants were all safe.

After World War II, in association with Kaiser engineers of the USA—the plant which before the war expanded to a million tonnes—was further expanded to two million tonnes.

The mother of heavy industry in India, Tata Steel has spawned many children around herself in Jamshedpur—The Indian Tube Company (now the Tubes Division of Tata Steel), The Indian Cable Company, The Tinplate Company of India, Indian Steel and Wire Products (started by Sir Indra Singh), Tata-Yodogawa, Tata-Robins-Fraser, Tata Refractories and the biggest of all, Tata Engineering and Locomotive Company (Telco).

To get the plant moving in those early years took some doing. The general superintendent, T.W. Tutwiler, an American, was a terror. Beneath a ferocious exterior resided a soft heart. He fired people at the slightest provocation but hired them again gladly. He liked no frills. Every Christmas the directors journeyed to Jamshedpur ostensibly for the board meeting, but, it was said, really to please Tutwiler and play with him his favourite game of American poker. Till his last days in Jamshedpur, Tutwiler could never understand how Indians could beat an American at his own card game.

A chemical engineering graduate called Jehangir Ghandy went to Tutwiler for a job. When asked, Ghandy replied he would prefer to work in the laboratory. Tutwiler bawled out that he wanted no 'goddam booklearning' and asked him to report at the coke ovens at 6 a.m. the next day. Years later when Ghandy took over as the first Indian general manager, there were not many things he did not know. Not only steel but men were forged at Jamshedpur.

Tutwiler was succeeded by a genial Irishman, John Keenan. Keenan relates the story of a serious accident in the works when a ladle with 75 tonnes of molten metal crashed on the ground with a deafening sound emitting sparks and burning metal. The confused and frenzied shouts of men were heard above the inimical hiss of steam as red-hot metal hit puddles of water.

A Blast Furnace

Keenan could take only three of the injured men in his small car to hospital. He chose one who seemed to have a better chance than the others to survive and told his helpers to bring him.

The man shook his head in negation. 'Do not take me away,' he said. Turning his head feebly, the Hindu nodded towards the body of a half-burnt Muslim and spoke. *'Hamara bhai ko le jao'* (take my brother), he said clearly. The Hindu who was in pain and in danger of death remembered, not that the Muslim was of a different faith, but that he was his brother.

The company in its own captive mines and collieries, has a task force of 23,000 people, in addition to nearly 55,000 in the works and the township of Jamshedpur, at the Adityapur complex, the bearings plant at Kharagpur, and in the sales offices and stockyards of the marketing division around the country. In 1971, when the coal industry was nationalized the then minister, Mohan Kumaramangalam, left the mines of the company untouched because he wanted nationalized units to 'sharpen' themselves against the more efficiently run Tata collieries.*

A memorable day in the life of Tata Steel was the Golden Jubilee when Prime Minister Jawaharlal Nehru came to open the public gardens bequeathed to the city by the steel company. The prime minister was at his best. He gave perspective to the younger people, 'It is very easy for those of us who think in terms of today to belittle what has been done by those who preceded us, not realizing the conditions under which they lived . . . when you have to give the lead in action, in ideas—a lead that does not fit in with the very climate of opinion, that is true courage, physical or mental or spiritual, call it what you like—and it is this type of courage and vision that Jamsetji Tata showed and it is right that we should honour his memory and remember him as one of the big founders of modern India . . . We have our planning commissions but

* *The Economic Times*, 17 January 1979.

Jamsetji Tata formed himself into some kind of a planning commission and began his own—not a five-year but a much bigger plan.'

In 1978, two ministers of the Cabinet proposed nationalization of the steel company. The Tata Workers' Union first sent a cable of protest to the Prime Minister. They who worked in the plant, the mines, the collieries and in sales, all resolved on 7 January 1979, that nationalization would be detrimental to the interests of the nation and to all employees of the company. The government did not touch Tata Steel. In October 1979, the company celebrated fifty years of industrial harmony.

Until 1979, a good part of Tata Steel machinery was either twenty-five or fifty years of age. The government controlled the steel prices so tightly that government steel plants ran at huge losses to the public exchequer and Tatas barely avoided losses and gave a modest dividend purely by managing to work this old plant at over 100 per cent efficiency. There was no money for modernization, leave alone expansion. By 1980, the government realized its folly and partially decontrolled steel prices. Tata Steel went in for modernization with a modest programme of Rs 225 crore in Phase I. With further government relaxation of prices they went into Phase II of modernization of Rs 850 crore. Thus, over Rs 1,000 crore were spent to update the equipment. Expansion was to come later with a Rs 1,500-crore plan to increase the capacity from 2.1 million tonnes to 2.7 million tonnes of steel. Along with expansion it was decided to produce improved and special qualities of steel. Tata Steel is the first company in the private sector to touch Rs 2,000-crore turnover per annum.

Tata Steel has either started or revived a number of companies. Some of them are Tata Pigments Limited, Special Steels Limited, Tata Metals and Strips Limited, Ipitata Sponge Iron Limited and the Indian Steel Rolling Mills Limited. Others include Kalimati Investments Company Limited, Tata Korf Engineering Services Limited, Tata Timken Limited, Tata Davy

Limited, TATA MAN GHH Limited, Tata Korf Metals West
Bengal Limited, Kumardhubi Metal Casting and Engineering
Limited, Tata Aquatic Farms Orissa Limited, and Nicco
Corporation Limited (Steel Division). Such is the management
reputation of Tata Steel that when a plant gets 'sick' in, say,
West Bengal, its government appeals to Tata Steel to set it
right. Today Tata Steel operations are no longer limited to
eastern India but extend to western and southern India.

In 1984, J.R.D. Tata stepped down after forty-six years
as chairman. Russi Mody, who for fifty years made an
outstanding contribution to the company, especially in terms
of human relations, succeeded him as chairman.

A former vice chairman of Tata Steel, J.D. Choksi,
summed up the unique position of the company in the Indian
context. 'There are,' he wrote, 'certain corporations the world
around, which stand out from their fellows. They need not
be the largest or the most prosperous in their country or even
in their given field but their achievements and traditions are
epochal and in peoples' minds identify the trade or industry
to which they belong with themselves. They may be in trade
or commerce opening up new frontiers and new territories,
such as, for instance, the East Asiatic Corporation of
Denmark, or they may be established in one place in a basic
or key industry. The Tata Iron and Steel Company is such a
corporation. It is part of the geography and landscape of
India—as much a part of her as her great mountain ranges
and rivers.'

For generations to come such a company is to be held in
trust for the nation.

The Indian Institute of Science, Bangalore

3

IMPULSE TO LEARNING

*What advances a nation or community is not so much
to prop up its weakest and most helpless members, as
to lift up the best and the most gifted so as to make
them of the greatest service to the country.*

—Jamsetji Tata

The Presidency Universities of Bombay, Madras and
Calcutta had given India its first graduates with a
background of western education. In 1889, Lord Reay,
Bombay's popular governor, said in a convocation address
that education could no longer develop if universities remained
purely examining bodies. He called for 'real universities which
will give fresh impulse to learning, to research, to criticism,
which will inspire reverence and impart strength and self-
reliance to future generations.'

Such advanced learning was not available in India, so in
1892 Jamsetji endowed a fund for the higher education abroad
of deserving students. Some of India's early engineers,
surgeons, physicians, educationists, barristers and ICS
officials benefited from the endowment. Once the Indian Civil
Sevice was thrown open to Indians, Jamsetji was especially
keen that deserving Indian students should take advantage
of it. (Some years later, in 1924, it was calculated that one
out of every five Indian ICS officials had been a J.N. Tata
Scholar). But the progress of the early years was too slow
for Jamsetji's liking.

Writing to Lord Reay on 17 November 1896, he told the
Governor of Bombay that 'no more . . . fruitful results, can
be provided than (by) a national system of education.' He
continued: 'The efficiency of general education must depend,

in the last resort, on the efficiency of the highest university education.' In September 1898, Jamsetji announced an offer that was to astonish men of his day. He decided to set aside fourteen of his buildings and four landed properties in Bombay for an endowment to establish a university of science. His donation was worth Rs 30 lakh in those days, equal to over Rs 10 crore of today. It was half his wealth. The other half he left to his two sons.

His offer fetching an interest then of Rs 1.25 lakh a year was hailed in many quarters, but some of his fellow Parsis regretted that the wealth of the community was being diverted to a scheme from which few Parsis would benefit, when such wealth of the community could be used to give clothes, food, medical facilities and housing to Parsis in need. In reply to them, Jamsetji, in an interview, spelt out his views on philanthropy:

> There is one kind of charity common enough among us, and which is certainly a good thing, though I do not think it the best thing we can have. It is that patchwork philanthropy which clothes the ragged, feeds the poor, and heals the sick and halts. I am far from decrying the noble spirit which seeks to help a poor or suffering fellow-being. But charities of the hospital and poor asylum kind are comparatively more common and fashionable among us Parsis. What advances a nation or community is not so much to prop up its weakest and most helpless members as to lift up the best and most gifted so as to make them of the greatest service to the country. I prefer this constructive philanthropy which seeks to educate and develop the faculties of the best of our young men.

The proposal of Jamsetji was presented to the new viceroy, Lord Curzon, in 1898, the day after his arrival in India. The proposal was put to him by a deputation led by the vice-chancellor of the Bombay University. Typical of Jamsetji, he did not say much on the occasion himself but let the vice-chancellor, Mr Justice Candy, and others do the talking. Curzon was lukewarm, and had two major doubts about the scheme. The first was whether qualified Indians would be forthcoming for such advanced scientific training. Secondly, whether there would be employment opportunities for them in a country that had no industries worth the name.

To report on Jamsetji's scheme, the Secretary of State for India requested the Royal Society of England to send out an eminent scientist. The Royal Society selected Professor William Ramsay, the discoverer of rare gases (including helium and neon), who was later to be awarded the Nobel Prize. After a quick tour of the country in ten weeks Ramsay reported that Bangalore was a suitable site for such an institution. On Curzon's doubt whether the qualified students would come to the institute to be trained in scientific methods, Ramsay recommended liberal scholarships. Ramsay also indicated certain industries that could be developed in India. Later Curzon appointed a committee, consisting of the principal of the Roorkee Engineering College, Colonel J. Clibborn, and Professor David Orme Masson of Melbourne University to draw up 'a less ambitious plan' susceptible to expansion according to circumstances. The Clibborn-Masson Committee recommended Roorkee as a suitable area.

Meanwhile, Curzon was writing to the Secretary of State for India, Lord Hamilton, on 26 June 1901:

We are endeavouring to save Tata's scheme from the shipwreck which his ambitions and Ramsay's exaggerated ideas threatened it, and are asking the Committee (Clibborn-Masson's) to consider and submit a scheme under which the annual expenditure will be limited to £10,000; £2,000 of which will be provided annually by the Government of India for ten years.

It may be mentioned that Jamsetji's endowment alone provided £8,000 (Rs 1,25,000) a year. Curzon also wrote to Hamilton that his government would propose to create the institution on a more modest scale and then if Jamsetji declined it, the responsibility for destroying the scheme would be upon Jamsetji Tata and 'we shall escape the odium which would have been fully bestowed upon us.'

Jamsetji had hoped 'that corporations, the native chiefs, sardars' will gradually see their way to bountifully help such an institution. For this reason he insisted that his own name should not be attached to the institute. The Maharaja of Mysore did come forward with a generous offer of 371 acres of land in Bangalore for the institute, a gift of Rs 5 lakh for construction and a recurring grant of Rs 50,000 a year. But no other source of revenue came forward. The Curzon government was taking its own time and was concentrating on cutting down and controlling the scheme. Did Curzon comprehend fully that what Jamsetji was after was not just a university of science but a new 'national system of education'? According to the original plan proposed by Jamsetji, the university was 'destined to promote original investigations in all branches of learning and to utilize them for the benefit of India.'*

The original plan of Jamsetji included: scientific and technological education; medical and sanitary education, including research in bacteriology; and studies in philosophy and education (including methods of education), ethics and psychology, Indian history and archaeology, statistics and economics and comparative philology.

The canvas that Jamsetji was working on was too vast for his contemporaries to fathom, far less to accept. The largesse he had given for the institute was from his private account. To increase the regular income of the institute, he wished to levy and lay aside a certain commission from his business. His colleagues in business opposed him. Jamsetji must have felt hurt. Though he could have pushed through his idea, he graciously bowed to the desire of his colleagues

* Resolution of the Government of India, Home Department, No. 434-448, Simla, 27 May 1909.

and restricted his endowment to his personal wealth. Attacked by some co-religionists, denied co-operation from those he had inducted into his business, confronted with an arrogant Viceroy who could not understand the greatness of the giver or of his gift, any other man than Jamsetji would have withdrawn the offer. In fact the British reckoned that he would. Lord Hamilton, who had sympathy for Jamsetji, wrote to Lord Curzon in 1903: 'My impression is that Tata will drop his scheme and devote a certain proportion of his endowment to practical purposes in connection with electricity or the development of the iron industry.' But Jamsetji was not easily deflected from the accomplishment of his purpose. In 1904, Jamsetji added a codicil to his will urging his two sons not to use this money set aside for the university. If need be, he requested they may add to the university from the wealth he was leaving them. While the scheme was still being considered and a provisional committee was looking into it, Jamsetji died on 19 May 1904. Perhaps *The Times of India* (quoted on p. 9 more fully) was thinking of him and Lord Curzon when it wrote the following day that Jamsetji's 'sturdy strength of character prevented him from fawning on any man however great, for he was great in his own way, greater than most men realized.'

In the year, 1905, when Lord Curzon was on leave in Bexhill, he finally gave the green light to Dorab Tata, by agreeing that the government would meet half the cost. Dorab, who was educated at Caius College, Cambridge, and knew quite a bit about the West, wrote to a friend in India that year: 'One thing is certain. India is not ripe for the institute and I doubt very much that Britain is ripe.' In prophetic tones he continued:

If we make the effort to give India what she might have we shall have achieved something, even if the institute, when established, fails to answer our expectations. It is thus, I think, that the beginnings of all great reforms take place. The man who sows never gathers the fruit. It is left to somebody else at some remote date to make the tree bear fruit. All that the man who sows ought to be content with is that the tree should remain alive so that at some future date another might give it the right treatment and make it bear fruit.

'To give India what she might have' became the lodestar of the House.

A director was speedily appointed in 1906. When the vesting order came from the Government of India in May 1909, it was generously worded. The order which vested in trust the properties endowed by Jamsetji Tata, spoke positively of the enlightened promoter and donor. The order stated that 'the Governor-General in Council has no desire to associate himself intimately with the actual administration of the institute, or to claim a determining voice in the settlement of the lines of research to be followed and the methods of instructions to be employed.' The powers were vested in a Senate, a Court and a Council of the institute. To the credit of the British government and its successor governments of independent India, this autonomy of the institute and its academic freedom have been honoured. From its inception the institute is a tripartite venture of Tatas, the Government of India and the Government of Mysore (now Karnataka). In view of its national importance the Government of India bears the expenses.

The institute opened in 1911 with three major departments of General and Applied Chemistry, Electro-technology Chemistry and Organic Chemistry. Chemistry, which now is divided into several disciplines, in those days covered a very vast field. In the 1940s and 1950s aeronautical engineering, high voltage engineering, internal combustion engineering and several others were added. Today the institute has over thirty departments.*

The Indian Institute of Science, Bangalore, has occupied a

---

* In 2003 there are forty-two departments.

pre-eminent position in national life. The Council of Scientific and Industrial Research was established in New Delhi only in 1942 and India then set on the path of opening national research laboratories in the late 1940s and 1950s. The first Indian Institute of Technology opened at Kharagpur in 1950. Bombay, Madras, Kanpur and Delhi I.I.T.s came up by 1961. In the early years the institute at Bangalore focused on utilizing indigenous materials to benefit industry. The Mysore Soap Factory and Sandalwood Oil Factory were among the early beneficiaries. The origin of the hydrogenation industry can be traced to the work done by the Department of Organic Chemistry.

Like Tata Steel in Jamshedpur, the Indian Institute of Science in Bangalore has spawned many children. The Central Food and Technological Research Institute in Mysore, the Lac Research Institute of Ranchi and the National Aeronautical Laboratory in Bangalore are the direct offshoots of the Institute of Science. The institute also provided the nuclei for the National Chemical Laboratory and the National Metallurgical Laboratory. The alumni of the institute provided the backbone for our national laboratories and the CSIR.

Distinguished names in science and industry have been closely associated with the institute. The industrial genius Sir M. Visvesvaraya was closely associated with the management of the institute for three decades. Nobel Prize winner Dr C.V. Raman was director of the institute for four years and did his important work on crystals and spectroscopy at the institute where he was the head of the department of physics for many years. Professor Max Born specially came to see the work being done by Dr Raman at the institute. Dr Homi Bhabha did his pioneering work on cosmic rays during the years of World War II and Lord Wavell visited the institute as Viceroy mainly to see Dr Bhabha's work. Also at the institute was Dr Vikram Sarabhai, who succeeded Dr Bhabha as the head of India's atomic energy programme. Dr Satish Dhawan, who became director of the institute in 1961, was later selected to concurrently head the Indian Space Research Organization.

When asked what are the distinguishing characteristics of the institute, its director, Dr C.N.R. Rao,* says, 'For success in intellectual endeavour the first requisite is freedom. We are the most free in India; truly autonomous. Once a member joins a faculty nobody bothers him, be he a lecturer or professor. Rank does not come in the way of a person's work. People are able to devote themselves to their research. Any staff member can get seed money for his research.'

Professor M.N. Srinivasan of the Faculty of Mechanical Engineering observes, 'The three distinguishing characteristics of the institute are: it has created an environment for research, it promotes creativity and witnesses intense activity. At all hours of the night several students—including ladies—can be walking to their laboratory through the campus to carry out their research and get computer time. All courses are taught in the framework of research and even for a Master's degree about half the time is given for laboratory research.'

The total student strength of the institute is 1,400 inclusive of students doing research work and course work. The faculty strength of the institute is 440.** In numbers, its pool of research workers is the largest in any educational research institution and next only to the Bhabha Atomic Research Centre (BARC). Staff and students of the Indian Institute of Science produce a thousand research papers a year. About one of every ten members of the Indian Academy of Sciences is a member of the institute. India's top scientific award is the Bhatnagar

* He was succeeded by Dr G. Padmanaban, an eminent scientist in the Department of Biochemistry. The present director of the institute is Professor Goverdhan Mehta, a distinguished scientist in the Department of Organic Chemistry and former Vice-Chancellor of the Hyderabad University.
** In 2003 the student strength was 1,700, with a faculty of 450. Two thousand research papers are produced annually.

Prize and the Indian Institute of Science has by far the largest number of awardees. Its research projects and funding is the largest of any academic institute in India—Rs 15 crore recurring grant and another Rs 6 to Rs 8 crore for identified research projects.* Most of the research is in the frontier fields and in the practical application of science to industry, to rural development, to low-cost housing. For example, the institute has invented a wood burning stove made of mud with an efficiency in the range of 35/45 per cent which is being used in the whole state of Karnataka leading to a 65 per cent saving in firewood. The entire poly-silicon technology of the country has sprung from the institute. The institute has contributed to the progress of India's aeronautical and space programme and assists private industry with consultancy.

The institute has a wind tunnel and a water tunnel. The wind tunnel, for example, tested the ability of the second Howrah Bridge to withstand pressures.

The institute's Continuing Education Programme upgrades the knowledge of 3,000 scientists and technologists annually.

The reason why Jamsetji Tata did not want to give his name to the institute was spelt out by him in a letter proposing his scheme to Lord Reay in 1896. Jamsetji said:

> It is my firm belief that corporations, native chiefs, sardars and native gentry will gradually see their way to bountifully help such an institution . . . . I want no title for myself, nor do I wish my name attached to anything. The national movement ought to bear a national name and every separate benefactor might be at ease as far as I am concerned that his endowment won't bear a name subsidiary to any.

That is why he did not want his name to be lent to the institute.

---

* Recurring grant was Rs 80 crore from the central government and another Rs 68 crore in identified research projects and about Rs 15 crore towards plan grants in 2002-2003.

In the Platinum Jubilee year, the institute decided to build a modern auditorium with a seminar complex and name it the J.N. Tata Auditorium.

Tatas continue to be represented on the Court, the Council and the Finance Committee which are the decision-making bodies. According to its former registrar S.S. Prabhu, 'Tatas have provided, at crucial times, the healing touch.'

When Jamsetji Tata dreamt of the institute, he wrote:

The objects of the institute shall be to provide for advance instruction and to conduct original investigations into all branches of knowledge . . . likely to promote the material and industrial welfare of India.

His dream has been fulfilled.*

* For an update see chapter on 'Tata Philanthropy' in Section B.

4

A LAMP IS LIT

Genius is one per cent inspiration and ninety-nine per cent perspiration.

—Thomas Alva Edison

Jamsetji Tata was fond of picnics and boating trips and on one Sunday he took a trip to Salsette and to the surprise of his friends opened a book of poetry and read aloud the poem on Salsette by John Ruskin. So one day after the rains when he asked his friend Nusserwanji Guzder for a launch to go around Bombay harbour, Mr Guzder was sure he was going on a picnic. Much to his surprise Mr Guzder saw Jamsetji turn up at the pier with all his top executives. Jamsetji ordered the launch to go to the Roha creek. When the launch reached there he pointed to the rainwater gushing from the river Roha. 'All this water from the Western Ghats is wasted. We should harness it—to produce hydro-electric power.' The question was, how? At the turn of the century, every plant producing hydro-electric power in the world was located at the foot of a waterfall like the one Jamsetji had himself seen at the Niagara Falls. Jamsetji envisaged creating a reservoir on the brink of the Western Ghats and to speed the flow of water through pipelines to the foot of the hills and let the artificial 'waterfall' turn the turbines. The vision was there, some preliminary work was done, but before the company could be formed Jamsetji had passed away.

A very capable English engineer drew up a scheme. To lay such giant pipelines down the uneven and craggy rocks of the mountains was a feat of considerable skill. Even the artificial dam envisaged at Walwhan outside Lonavla was a feat at that time for it was a little smaller than the original

Penstocks at Bhira, Maharashtra

great dam at Aswan constructed by Sir William Willcock.

. The object of the scheme was to supply cheap and clean electric power for the growing needs of Bombay. Tatas were convinced of the utility of hydro-electric power but many textile millowners were wedded to working with coal and there was the risk that the capacity generated by Tata Hydro would not be lifted by Bombay's industry. Electricity had yet to be tried out in Bombay. At first, only two textile millowners guaranteed to lift the electricity. In faith, the company went ahead. The Governor of Bombay, Lord Sydenham, aware of this when laying the foundation stone of Walwhan dam, said, 'This project symbolizes the confidence of Indians in themselves.' On the same occasion, Sir Dorab Tata said that to his late father who proposed the hydro-electric scheme, 'the acquisition of wealth was only a secondary object in life; it was always subordinate to the constant desire in his heart to improve the industrial and intellectual condition of the people of this country.'

With the supply of hydro-electric power, it was hoped Bombay would become a 'smokeless city,' free from the soot and grime of coal-burning textile mills and other factories. The company also made adequate plans for exploring hydro-electric capacity further up the Ghats, a measure of remarkable confidence at a time when the initial project was itself an infant. The Tata Hydro-Electric Power Supply company was established in 1910, The Andhra Valley Power Supply Company was formed in 1916 and The Tata Power Company in 1919.

It is difficult to imagine nowadays when there is a power shortage that Tata Electric had to tempt potential customers to lift their electric power. The textile mills of Bombay—the chief potential customers—did not want to switch from coal to electric power. Huge steam engines were used to propel the entire machinery of the mills. To encourage mills to switch over, the Tata electric companies offered to buy the steam engines only to scrap them later.

Today the Tata Electric system comprises three hydro generating stations and six thermal power units at Trombay, Bombay, with a total capacity of 1,624 MW.* This system is interconnected with other hydro and thermal power stations in Maharashtra, as well as with the nuclear power plant at Tarapur. Between them these power plants keep the wheels of industry moving in the largest industrial concentration in India. Nearly 20 per cent of the nation's industrial production comes from the Bombay-Pune region. The entire monitoring and control of electric supply to Greater Bombay and Bombay city is done by the Tata Electric system from its Load Despatch Centre at Trombay.

In the early 1970s when Tatas proposed a 500 MW unit, the largest in the country was 210 MW. The introduction of 500 MW technology accrued large savings in materials and costs.

India's first 500 MW unit was a significant achievement for the Tata electric companies. Its success enabled India to establish its capability in design, engineering and erection of future plants of this size. In 1984 when this unit was commissioned, only Japan had a similar sized unit in all Asia. This multi-fuel fired unit utilizes mainly low sulphur residual refinery fuel and associated gas from the Bombay High offshore shelf. Its chimney, twice the height of the Qutb Minar, soars to a height of 152 metres. An electrostatic precipitator with a collection efficiency of 99.5 per cent and a flue gas desulphurization unit, the first of its kind for any thermal power station in India, provides Bombay with efficient electrical energy and a clean environment.

Following close on the heels of the first 500 MW unit, the Tata electric companies decided to replace the older thermal units at Trombay by a second fuel efficient large sized unit of 500 MW capacity. The second 500 MW unit was cleared by the government and funded by the World Bank. Construction

* Capacity raised to 1,797MW in 2003.

of this unit commenced in 1985 and was completed on schedule in early 1990. This unit referred to as Unit No. 6 has the tallest concrete structure (chimney) in India towering at a height of 275 metres—a silent sentinel of the latest technological advances made in the world. Unit 6 is integrated into the Tata system. This expansion was accomplished during the chairmanship of the late Mr Naval Tata who has been succeeded by the former chairman of the Atomic Energy Commission, Dr H.N. Sethna.

The Tata electric companies, noted for their efficiency, have provided Bombay with the best power supply in the country till today, whereas power cuts and interruptions are common phenomena in the rest of the country. What is probably not known is the work done by the Research and Development Division of the companies. Scientists and technicians are engaged in developing advanced electronic systems which are applied for power systems and defence needs, be it in the field of advanced radar and guidance systems or in the field of computer technology. Sophisticated electronic equipment, which would otherwise have to be imported by the defence services, is being produced in India at a modern factory in Bangalore, the electronic city of India. The Tata electric companies have been awarded contracts for development of an air traffic control system simulator and are also participating in the development and supply of an operator training simulator for the National Thermal Power Corporation.

In addition to its substantial contribution to the nation, its operations abroad have included the commissioning, operation and maintenance of thermal power stations, erection and commissioning of gas turbine and turbo generating units in Iran, Kuwait, Malaysia, Saudi Arabia as well as the training of personnel in Nigeria and Sierra Leone.

It is now involved in the task of finding ways and means of utilizing its surplus night-time thermal energy. The Bhira pump storage unit proposed to be set up by the Tata electric companies will utilize surplus night-time thermal energy to pump the water back up to the lake and will be able to provide peak capacity during the day to the Bombay consumer.

The Tata electric companies have also installed a gas-based 180 MW combined cycle power plant at Trombay to provide quick start emergency power in the event of a grid disturbance. This plant helps reduce the wasteful flaring of gas, a precious national resource.

The Tata electric companies have given Bombay two of its finest public parks. At Bhulabhai Desai road, citizens of Bombay can spend their leisure hours in a lush garden along the seafront while the children gambol in the sand pits and scale the jungle gymnasium. A fish pond with a variety of goldfish attracts the attention of both young and old. Squirrels chase one another up the banyan tree and graceful white geese preen near the cascade. It is a sight that refreshes the human spirit in the brick and concrete megapolis of Bombay. The other park is called Colaba Woods. Tata companies launched a major project to restore Bombay's Horniman Circle Gardens to their pristine glory and then add modern facilities including a study corner for students.

While these are some of the facets of environmental development visible to the public, far from the public eye in the distant catchment areas of the hydro-electric reservoirs, massive tree plantation programmes have taken place. Flora and fauna in and around their lake areas have been restored. In association with the forest department of the Government of Maharashtra, the companies have planted hundreds of thousands of saplings and have even experimented with aerial broadcasting of seeds. In the process, a large variety of wildlife such as the barking deer, sambhar, wild boar, jungle fowl and peacock have found a habitat.

The lakes also provide a suitable breeding ground for fish. The fish farm located on the downstream side of Walwhan dam has been able to rehabilitate the Deccan mahseer, a fish which was fast becoming extinct. The lakes are stocked with fish like the mahseer and other carps, some of which thrived to lengths of over three feet. The fish farm has also been able to provide fingerlings to various state government projects as far away as Kashmir and Haryana. Fingerlings from Walwhan were airlifted abroad to even Laos, which has been a beneficiary of this effort. Somewhere along the banks of the lower Mekong River, a Laotian fisherman finds his fish—and daily bread—thanks to an Indian electric company.

There are more ways than one to create wealth.

5

THE TAJ MAHAL

The old Taj is the same—like a jewelled crown.
                                        —Gregory Peck

In the world's travel circles, if you speak of just 'The Taj', they ask you, 'Which one?'

Shah Jehan's dream in marble was born out of his love for his wife. Jamsetji's handiwork was born out of a love for his city.

Bombay's *Saturday Review* wrote in 1865, 'The want of hotel accommodation was never so badly felt as at present . . . When will Bombay have a rest-house worthy of the name?' The few tolerable hotels that existed catered exclusively for the 'Burra Sahibs' and the 'Chhota Sahibs'.

There is a colourful story that Jamsetji started a grand hotel in Bombay after an incident when he was refused admission to a second rate Bombay hotel which was reserved 'for Europeans only'. Sharada Dwivedi, who has researched the history of the Taj Mahal Hotel, states that she has found no historical evidence for this report, though it is likely that there were hotels at the time that did refuse admission to Indians. Jamsetji was too proud a man, she says, to visit such a hotel. It is more likely, she says, that he gave an outstanding hotel to his city because of his deep love for Bombay, a city he was proud of. From the day it opened the Taj Mahal was recognized as one of the best in the world. Jamsetji's Taj venture is distinct from his other schemes. Unlike his other enterprises Jamsetji did not calculate what it would cost. He bought the reclaimed land at Apollo Bunder and started building. The foundations were 40 feet deep, unusual for those days. The large central dome was to be flanked by long high aisles so that the sea breezes could freely circulate and cool the place. And two smaller domes would flank the two ends.

The Gateway of India was yet to be built. There, facing the mouth of the harbour, the Taj rose in its solitary grandeur. A legend has grown that a British architect designed the Taj, and got the shock of his life when he returned to find the finished building with the entrance facing the rear. To add flavour to the drama, it is even said that the architect hurled himself from the top storey of the Taj! The legend has been disproved by the original architect's drawings discovered at the Bombay University library. The architectural plans are signed by the architect Khanderao Sitaram and D.N. Mirza who so designed the Taj that some of the rooms could be perched a few feet from the sea commanding a magnificent view—with the illusion that the guest was still on board ship—while the majority of rooms could face the garden and avail of the westerly breeze. The entrance was at the rear to face Wellington Mews from where the horse-carriages drove in. W.A. Chambers was appointed architect after Sitaram Khanderao died in 1900.

In his foreign travels, Jamsetji made most of the purchases himself, lavishing upon the Taj the finest equipment Europe could offer—a soda and ice-making factory, and silver polishing machines, a laundry, lifts and an electric generator. He wrote to his son to avoid the 'abominable yellows and reds' in the decor. Jamsetji had already spent Rs 2,500,000 on it at a time when for a mere Rs 1,00,000 one could build a mansion. Jamsetji had visited the Paris exhibition at the turn of the century. He perceived there pillars of spun iron displayed for the first time. He ordered ten to be shipped home for his hotel. Today they seem indestructible as they hold up the ballroom of the Taj. The Taj opened in 1903, in Jamsetji's lifetime, with seventeen guests.

One of the first buildings in Bombay to be lit by electricity, it attracted a number of onlookers. Between Shepherd's Hotel

in Cairo and the Raffles Hotel in Singapore, there was nothing
like the Taj. Jamsetji told Lovat Fraser, Editor of *The Times
of India*, that he built it to attract people to India. He had no
desire to own the place. None of his contemporaries wanted
to own it either. They called it 'Tata's White Elephant'.

For four generations the staff of the Taj has poured out
affection and care to make the name 'Taj' synonymous with
elegance and beauty. The Taj too had its hard days and for
several years fetched a low income. Another owner would
have been tempted to sell it. But, as is their custom, Tatas
held on. It heartened Tatas to know that travel agents round
the world informed the Taj that their clients often put Bombay
on their itinerary just to stay at the Taj. Gregory Peck, who
returned to stay at the Taj in 1980 after twenty-eight years,
said: 'The old Taj is the same—like a jewelled crown.' One
of the many who enjoyed staying at the Taj was W. Somerset
Maugham. Jamsetji's dream had again come true—the hotel
had become a magnet.

The Taj Mahal Hotel features in over ninety travelogues,
biographies and novels. Louis Bromfield's *One Night in
Bombay* revolved round the Taj. With the boom in tourism
in the 1960s, prospects brightened for the hotel industry.

In spite of the highest standards, sometimes things do go
haywire. One tale speaks of a director of the Taj, J.D. Choksi
proudly presiding at a select party. He asked a waiter for a
fork. The man delved deep into a trouser pocket, then switched
on to the other, went deeper still and finally produced with a
glow of triumph, the fork. The embarrassed director enquired
why the item should be thus stored. The waiter replied in
Hindustani: 'Sir, the orders of the general manager are that
cutlery must be warmed in advance!'

In the 1970s to the baroque features of the dome and its
spacious wings has been added, in contrast, the tall and slim
Taj Inter-Continental. Like Tata Steel and the Indian Institute
of Science, the Taj too has spawned its children. In the last
two decades, hotels have been opened carrying the standards

of the Taj from New York to Muscat. Wherever the Taj builds
it encourages local craftsmen and artisans. At Fort Aguada,
Goa, for example, it introduced local clay pots as a base for
lamps, local ashtrays and cane baskets. The display in the
hotel rooms has created a permanent market from tourists.
And so the local craftsmen find a continuity of livelihood. In
New Delhi, when the Taj Mahal Hotel was built, marble
cutters from Makrana, 'pichhwai' painters from Rajasthan,
carpet weavers from Panipat, mural artists from Pune and
block-printers from Calcutta were employed. As once the
Taj Mahal at Agra demonstrated the skill of Indian craftsmen,
new hotels like the Taj demonstrate what today's craftsmen
are capable of. Encouraging this craftsmanship enables
artisans trained from father to son to stick to their craft rather
than drift away to factories and offices.

In the early 1970s, the chairman of Indian Hotels, J.R.D.

Encouragement is given to local craftsmen

Tata (who was also chairman of Air-India), foresaw that with the advent of the Jumbo jets, tourism would boom in India. A man who shared his vision and applied himself to executing it with zest was A.B. Kerkar, the managing director, who had started his career with Lyons in London. It was initially a gamble whether or not this expansion would pay off. Fortunately it did.

The reputation of the grand old Taj became the springboard. Till 1970 the Indian Hotels Company Limited had only one historic hotel. Thereafter old palaces of maharajas in Rajasthan were taken over and restored and refurbished to their former glory. One was in the pink city of Jaipur, and the other further down in Udaipur. The Lake Palace Hotel in Udaipur is a small island set like a pearl in the tranquil waters of Lake Pichola. A complex of three hotels

Fort Aguada Beach Resort, Goa

were created in Goa including one having a typical Goan village ambience. Many major cities of India were covered in the next two decades. As India enters the 21st century the Taj group which has grown into a chain of sixty-four hotels in India and abroad shows no signs of slowing down.

All the earlier hotels were in the deluxe category. In the late 1980s the Taj group saw that another prospect was opening up of foreign and Indian tourists who could not afford expensive rooms and food but nevertheless expected pleasant hotels with clean and comfortable surroundings at affordable rates. And so were built a group of mid-tier range of hotels called Gateway Hotels and Getaway Resorts.

A hotel rejuvenated was the St. James Court in London. St. James was originally built as 'flats for aristocrats, prominent politicians, including royalty, country families and others of distinction' by a notable London architect, Charles James Chirney-Pawley. Pawley conceived eight separate but connected buildings encircling a pleasant inner quadrangle. Each of the blocks had a name as quaint as Pawley's own— Kings, Dukes, Priors, Falconers, Almoners, Queens and so on. You cannot walk past the hotel without observing its magnificent frontage of red brick, white windows, and ornate grills on the balcony. The charm of 19th century London abides there, of times when Britain ruled India. Now India runs the 'St. James Court'.

J.R.D. Tata proudly says that Indian Hotels 'had not ju~ expanded. It has exploded!' The chairmanship of I~~an Hotels was the last chairmanship of an operating ~pany that he held before handing over the charge w~ he was eighty-four to A.B. Kerkar who helped to plant~ce of the Taj in several parts of India and the world. ~ged to three The majority of holdings in Indian Hotels~the Sir Ratan major Tata trusts—the Sir Dorabji Tata ~ust. The latter Tata Trust and the Lady Tata Memor-fifths goes for uses its funds for leukaemia resear~

research abroad, about £90,000* annually. Sir Dorabji Tata Trust has founded national institutions like the Tata Memorial Hospital, the Tata Institute of Fundamental Research and the Tata Institute of Social Sciences financed partially from the proceeds of the Indian Hotels Company.

'The Taj is the only hotel of its kind in the world,' they say. It is, in more senses than one.

* Outgoing international research awards £2,34,000 in 2002–2003.

6

A BREATH OF FRAGRANCE

As dawn breaks upon the back-waters of Cochin's harbour, a tiny canoe is seen in the morning mist. When the mist starts to clear a second and a third boat come into view. Along the back-waters are lush green coconut trees that abound in Kerala and, along these banks lies Tatapuram, which was established in 1917. The first integrated copra oil crushing factory to come up in India is located here. Upon the 50-acre site a small bird with blue wings, black body and a long reddish beak is pecking at its breakfast. The bird is a kingfisher; its breakfast is a worm. An hour later the factory nearby starts humming and man, to feed himself and his family, reports to work.

Xavier Arakal, who was a member of Parliament for Cochin in 1980-84, says:

When the Tatas came to Cochin seventy years ago they were one of the first to start an industry here when the economic condition of the State was very poor. They brought a two-fold benefit to the people:
  (i) They gave the coconut owning families a ready market for their products.
  (ii) They gave employment to the local people.
  Those with a steady job were able to get a steady income and educate their children and with education came social change and even a political change through the rise of a trade union. The first cooperative movement in Kerala was started in Tata Oil Mills. Once the Tatas set the trend for the industrialization of the Cochin area, others like Burmah Shell moved in.

In Tatapuram, the Tata Oil Mills Company (Tomco) was

one of the pioneers in employing women in its laboratories and administrative offices. 'At the outset,' J.R.D. Tata recalls, 'there was considerable resistance from the men to this development and on the day the first woman employee was appointed as a clerk in the main office, the poor girl was harassed by the incessant ringing of call-bells by her fellow male clerks as a sign of protest and sabotage.'

The idea of an oil mill was born during World War I. Jamsetji Tata's close colleague B.J. Padshah, one of the directors of Tata Sons, was an inveterate traveller. On board a ship from America to Japan he met a gentleman called Edward P. Thompson who styled himself 'Consulting Engineer, Vegetable Oil Industries'. The imagination of Padshah was fired at the prospect of setting up a modern vegetable oil mill in India. Thompson suggested it should begin with the crushing of copra and claimed that he was engaged in the Philippines with doing just that and that the company had given a profit of 70 per cent on its capital investment. Padshah asked Thompson to give the Tatas a report on the prospects of this industry for India and invited him to come to India.

In a letter to the directors, Thompson recommended not only one but three mills to be located at different places. Thompson told Tatas that America was substantially dependent on Indian copra and instead of sending copra to America, India should crush the copra, export the oil to America and use the coconut cake as cattle feed.

When Tatas were considering Thompson's proposal they were not aware (though Thompson should have been) that American financiers had put in heavy investments in their colony, the Philippines, to grow coconut trees. The Philippines, which had hardly produced any copra, suddenly became a large producer of copra.

Tatas accepted Thompson's proposal in 1917 and launched the Tata Oil Mills with a capital of a crore of rupees.* Even

---

* Tatas sold their holdings in Tomco to Hindustan Lever in 1994 as soap and oils were not their 'core' business.

The Tata Oil Mills, Tatapuram, Kerala

while the machinery was being purchased in America, the coconut plantations in the Philippines came into full growth and America clamped a heavy import duty on copra or its oil coming from India. Meanwhile, Thompson was merrily making large purchases of machinery in the United States. Though Thompson's purchase of a hydraulic press, expellers and other machinery could not fairly be questioned, the purchase of a fleet of ships was another matter. He bought one motor boat, a beautiful launch for himself, a tug and six barges. He also built a house-boat for himself because he felt he should stay on the beautiful back-waters of Cochin. The fleet cost Rs 10 lakh—over Rs 4 crore at today's prices. In the first operating year the company showed a loss of over Rs 17 lakhs. The boats of Thompson were never used but he managed to take the then Tata directors for a ride! The loss continued from year to year. The Tata directors saw through Thompson and dispensed with his services.

Having sorted out the financial problems, the directors took the company into ancillary products like refined deodorized coconut oil (a first grade cooking medium) marketed under the trade name 'Cocogem' and, more important, into soap manufacture. Long before soap manufacture was known to India, she had her own cleansing agents like gram flour which served her well. The first soap manufacture took place in 1879 at Meerut by an English concern. When the Tatas went into soap manufacture they ran into tremendous competition with the international giant Lever Brothers.

The Government of India had no interest in protecting an indigenous industry as, during the Raj, it was British industry which got the protection. Fortunately Gandhiji's Swadeshi movement (1931) helped the Tatas. Tatas' quality could compete with Levers so the soap was sold on the basis of its being swadeshi. Both Tatas and Levers sold similar soaps at Rs 10 for a box of 100 cakes.

A senior Tata director, P.A. Narielwala, wrote:

Levers marketed their cube soap at Rs 6/- per box in order to kill us. It was even less than the cost of the oil that went into the manufacture of the soap. It was quite a historical event, I remember, all the sales offices in India sending telegram after telegram to Mr Jal Naoroji (in charge of Tomco) saying that they could not sell a cake of soap. But he refused to budge and encouraged them by saying that Levers could not continue on this basis for any length of time, and that ultimately *we* would win through and we did. In three months' time Levers brought back the price of their soap to Rs 10/- per 100 cakes.*

By 1955 the company showed its first profit of Rs 50,000. The first dividend was given by the company in 1940, twenty-two years after it was established. There was a soap called '500' in France. Jal Naoroji, a nationalist, said India could do one better. Tomco's 501 laundry soap and its Hamam bath soap soon became household names in India. Over the years four new Tomco factories came up in western, eastern and northern India in addition to two more in the South, making a total of seven.

Tomco developed a marketing network that reached the remote areas of India, a network that assisted at least two other major Tata enterprises in finding outlets. Tomco were appointed selling agents for Tata Chemicals and Tata Tea for some years.

Tomco was the parent company of India's first major cosmetic concern. It happened through an unusual development. M.O. Matthai, the influential secretary to Jawaharlal Nehru, relates how the Tatas, who specialized in the core sector industries, made their debut into the fancy world of cosmetics in the early fifties.

In his book entitled *My Days with Nehru* Mr Matthai says:

* *Ghar-ki-baat* (Tomco's House Journal), May 1976, Vol. 1, No. 5.

When the Union Finance Minister stopped all imports of foreign cosmetics because of foreign exchange shortage, the sophisticated women of India were up in arms. In New Delhi, groups of hysterical women came to the Prime Minister's house in the mornings looking fierce. Indira's* sympathies were understandably with them. She told me that it was not the question of a craze for foreign stuff; nothing worthwhile was manufactured in India then; 'Shringar' (beautification) had been important for Indian women from time immemorial. I asked her what was the percentage of Indian women who beautified themselves with foreign stuff? This question annoyed her. She punished me for it by not speaking to me for a week. A group of women waylaid the Prime Minister in front of the Ministry of External Affairs. Some were wailing. As he strode to the office he asked me: 'Why can't somebody manufacture the stuff in India?'

The Prime Minister's offices at the Secretariat and the house were flooded with telegrams and letters from women all over India.

Finally, M.O. Mathai sent for K.A.D. Naoroji (grandson of Dadabhai Naoroji), the local director of Tatas in New Delhi. Can't Tatas go into the cosmetic business in a big way and manufacture in India the whole range of the stuff—everything that women needed? he asked. Mr Matthai assured that the Tatas could expect all the assistance from the government for this project. Tatas agreed. The government kept its word and this was the beginning of Lakmé, a new company in the Tata Group, started with French collaboration.** Given this history, M.O. Matthai concludes that 'the Indian women are the ultimate owners of Lakmé,

* Mrs Indira Gandhi was then hostess at the residence of her father, the prime minister.
** Acquired by Hindustan Lever in 1998.

though not in the financial sense.' Mrs Simone N. Tata played a signficant role in the growth of this company.†

† Thompson started the edible oil industry but the man who introduced soap to Tomco was a man called P.T. John. For his efforts he became known as 'Soap John'.

7

THOSE MAD, MAD DAYS

The Inter-War Years

*Those were truly mad days, and perhaps the maddest
feature was the supreme confidence of the public in
Tatas, and, incidentally, the over-confidence of Tatas
in themselves.*

—Sir Nowroji Saklatvala, Chairman,
Tata Companies (1932-1938) addressing
the Bombay Rotary, 1933

In 1912 Tatas gave India its first cement manufacturing
unit—India Cements—to which was added Shahabad
Cement in 1926. Both these and other cement companies were
merged in 1936 to form the Associated Cement Companies
(ACC), which today has factories in India and Pakistan.

In 1917, during World War I, when Tatas launched the
Tata Oil Mills, it also launched the Tata Industrial Bank, the
first of its kind in the country. It was a well-conceived
institution which, in the bank crisis of 1923, was forced to
efface itself and merge with the Central Bank of India.

As World War I was coming to its conclusion it looked as
if the war boom would never end. Between 1917 and 1922
Tatas launched no less than eleven joint stock companies with
an aggregate capital of Rs 27 crore. Investors fought to get
shares in new issues.

In 1919, when the Indian insurance business was
dominated by foreign companies, Tatas, inspired by the
nationalist spirit, established the New India Assurance
Company. With an authorized capital of Rs 20 crore it was
the largest insurance company in India.

In 1921 Sir Dorab Tata, the chairman of the company, told the shareholders: 'New India constituted the commencement of a new and large commercial undertaking in India. It is not a Bombay insurance company or a company working solely in India but may claim to be a worldwide Company. It is anticipated that a very large proportion of the income in future years will be obtained outside India.'

On the eve of the nationalization of life insurance in 1956, New India had become one of the largest composite insurers in the East operating in forty-six countries outside India. In 1973, its general insurance section was also nationalized.

In the inter-war years Tatas launched a number of companies that did not survive—Tata Engineering (not to be confused with Telco started in 1945), Tata Construction, Tata Electro-Chemicals and the Sugar Corporation were amongst them. Sir Nowroji Saklatvala, chairman of all Tata companies, speaking about the inter-war period noted that these companies were not launched without forethought but 'they mainly suffered from insufficient preparation before their inception . . . A number of them were over-capitalized in anticipation of rapid expansion, which was excusable, considering the conditions prevailing at the time, while others, although sound in every respect, suffered only from the catastrophic collapse of all values.'

Sir Nowroji Saklatvala concluded that the House of Tata emerged from this boom fever, 'stronger, a little sadder and certainly wiser . . . its (Tatas) achievements outweighed its mistakes and failures . . . it has made mistakes but it has endeavoured to learn from its mistakes.'

One interesting and heartening aspect of this difficult period was the way in which the parent company, Tata Sons, and occasionally the better off units, supported and sustained those companies which otherwise would have run to the ground.

As the economic depression approached, Tata Sons in 1929 had to sell a 50 per cent share in their agency commission from the hydro-electric companies to an American syndicate for Rs 36 lakh. Thereafter, the management of the hydro companies was vested in a joint Indo-American firm, the Tata Hydro-Electric Agencies Ltd., until the control reverted to Tatas in 1951.

In 1924, Tata Steel was in grave financial difficulties. The Imperial Bank of India, the then bankers to Tata Steel, insisted on additional security being provided in respect of advances already made to Tata Steel. As Tata Steel was not in a position to comply, Sir Dorab Tata provided to the Imperial Bank the necessary additional security pledging his entire personal fortune.

Subsequently, when the company required additional finance for its working capital, the managing agents made

Synthetic detergent section at the Tata Oil Mills

an arrangement, through F.E. Dinshaw, to line up a loan for Tata Steel for Rs 1 crore from the Gwalior State. Later, with improvement in the company's position, the loan was repaid. The fight put up by Tatas in the inter-war years, though it ate severely into their wealth and income, benefited their enterprises and indirectly, the progress of India's industrialization. One cannot imagine what would have happened to India's industrial growth had Tata Steel shut down under the blows of misfortune in the 1920s. Notwithstanding the reduction of the capital of some concerns and the winding up of some others, the total investment in the enterprises under Tata management increased.

In the 1930s, the firm was toying with the idea of moving into the chemical field. A Tariff Commission report in 1929 stated: 'If India is ever to become industrialized on a considerable scale, the establishment of a chemical industry on a firm basis is clearly a matter of great importance.' India was wholly dependent on foreign supplies for requirements of soda ash, caustic soda and other soda compounds required in the manufacture of textiles, glass, paper, soap and in ordnance factories. The alkali industry was known as 'the most complex, difficult and secretive branch of the chemical industry.' The formula for soda ash was jealously guarded by an international cartel. In 1937 Tatas received a proposal from the State of Baroda to start a chemical industry at Mithapur and in 1939 Tata Chemicals was launched. Its engineers cracked the code for soda ash manufacture, giving India an important base for its industrialization, next in importance only to steel and electricity. But something startling was to take place before that. Tatas decided to give India wings.

A Puss Moth

Juhu Beach

8

WINGS FOR A NATION

Tatas represent the spirit of adventure.
— Mahatma Gandhi

It was in the first decade of the century.

Two young boys spent their summer holidays at Hardelot, a beach resort near Boulogne in Northern France. One was the son of the legendary Louis Bleriot, the first man to fly across the English Channel in 1909. The other was the son of an Indian industrialist, R.D. Tata. As they played, the boys would occasionally see Bleriot's chief pilot Adolph Pegoud land a plane on the beach. Pegoud was the first man to loop-the-loop in a plane. He was a hero, especially for Tata's young son Jehangir.

In such small beginnings lie the seed of history. The exploits of the Frenchman stirred the heart of the young Indian. At the age of fifteen, after taking a joy ride in a plane at Hardelot, Jehangir decided to become a pilot and if possible to make a career in aviation. Young Jehangir had to wait nine years. He was twenty-four before a flying club opened in his home town Bombay, India—5,000 miles away from that wind-swept beach in northern France. Though not the first to register, he was the first Indian to pass out with 'No. 1' endorsed on his flying licence. And so it came to pass that India's first pilot was to pour most of his creative genius into building an airline for his country, giving his nation wings.

Those were years of adventure. In 1930, the Aga Khan announced a prize of £500 to the first Indian who would fly solo between England and India, starting at either end. Among the competitors was a young man called Manmohan Singh. His spirit was willing but his navigation was weak. Twice he left England with a flourish to fly to India. Twice he lost his way over Europe and had to fly back to England to start all over again. C.G. Grey, editor of *The Aeroplane*, observed: 'Mr Manmohan Singh has called his aeroplane 'Miss India' and he is likely to!' Another hopeful from the England end was eighteen-year-old Aspy Engineer. Still another to enter for fun, taking off from the Karachi end, was the now twenty-six-year-old Jehangir R.D. Tata. At Aboukir, near Alexandria in Egypt, JRD ran into Aspy, who had left England a week earlier and who was stranded for want of spark plugs. JRD gave Aspy his spare spark plugs, and they took off in opposite directions. Aspy reached Karachi a few hours before JRD reached England, winning the prize. On the strength of his performance, Aspy was admitted into the Indian Air Force, which had just been created. Aspy Engineer was the second Indian to be Chief of the Air Staff. JRD, meanwhile, had another ambition and he did not have long to wait.

> On an exciting October dawn in 1932, a Puss Moth and I soared joyfully from Karachi with our first precious load of mail, on an inaugural flight to Bombay. As we hummed towards our destination at a 'dazzling' hundred miles an hour, I breathed a silent prayer for the success of our venture and for the safety of those who worked for it. We were a small team in those days. We shared successes and failures, the joys and headaches, as together we built up the enterprise which later was to blossom into Air-India and Air-India International.

When JRD landed on the Juhu mud flats that October day in 1932, India's first air service was inaugurated. He does not take the credit for it. He gives it instead to a far-seeing Englishman—a former officer of the R.A.F. called Nevill Vintcent, who a year earlier had come to India barnstorming the country, giving joy rides. Nevill Vintcent offered J.R.D. Tata a project to start an airline. Sir Dorab Tata, then chairman of Tata Sons, was not a bit enthusiastic about the proposition. But the initial investment was small—Rs 200,000—and he was persuaded by JRD's mentor and colleague John Peterson to give his approval.

'We had no aids whatsoever on the ground or in the air,' JRD recalls, 'no radio, no navigational or landing guides of any kind. In fact we did not even have an aerodrome in Bombay. We used a mud flat at Juhu (fishing village-cum-beach resort near the city). The sea was below what we called our airfield, and during the monsoon the runway was below the sea! So we had to pack up each year, lock, stock and barrel—two planes, three pilots and three mechanics, and transfer ourselves to Poona (Pune) where we were allowed to use a maidan as an aerodrome, appropriately under the shadow of the Yeravada Jail!'

The annual report of the Directorate of Civil Aviation (DCA) of India for the year 1933-34 stated:

> As an example how airmail service should be run, we commend the efficiency of Tata Services who on October 10, 1933, arriving at Karachi as usual to time, completed a year's working with 100 per cent punctuality . . . even during the most difficult monsoon months when rainstorms increased the perils of the Western Ghat portion of the route no mail from Madras or Bombay missed connection at Karachi nor was the mail delivered late on a single occasion at Madras . . . our esteemed Trans-Continental Airways, alias Imperial Airways, might send their staff on deputation to Tatas to see how it is done.

Karachi was chosen as the starting point because Imperial Airways terminated there with the mail from England and the route chosen by Tatas was Karachi-Bombay-Madras. Tatas requested the government for a small subsidy for carrying the mail as was the normal practice in other countries. The subsidy asked for was small but the government declined. Tatas reduced the figure to a bare minimum. The government still declined. So Tatas decided that they would just give the service to the country collecting the little stamp surcharge which the addresser put on the envelope to connect it with the Imperial Airways at Karachi. When asked why they did so, JRD replied, 'Vintcent and I had faith in the future of aviation and believed that if we came in at the beginning of an era we had a better chance ultimately to achieve growth and leadership in the field.'

The unfolding years were to justify that faith. In 1936 the all-up Empire Mail Service was launched by the British Government, under which all first class mail travelled by air without surcharge, and Tata Airlines' revenues soared. At the beginning the aeroplanes used were so small that the service was restricted to mail, but a single passenger was occasionally allowed to sit on top of the mail bags—usually with his heels higher than his head!

In 1936 larger aircraft, though still single-engined, were introduced. Tatas felt the need to give more sophisticated training to their pilots and hired an instructor from England to start a training centre for pilots. The Bombay-Delhi service was inaugurated in 1937. Then came the World War II and all services, including Tatas', were commandeered by the Government of India.

With their airline operations severely restricted and controlled, Nevill Vintcent and J.R.D. Tata looked for alternative avenues for their brimming enthusiasm and their growing expertise. A specially exciting opportunity, they felt, offered itself in the field of aircraft manufacture. Whereas the construction of metal aircraft would have involved an elaborately equipped factory, the De Havilland Mosquito, an outstanding twin-engined fighter-bomber made of wood, could, they felt, be put quickly into production in India. Tatas, therefore, submitted in 1942 a project to the British Government for the large-scale manufacture of Mosquito aircraft in a factory they would build for the purpose in Pune. The project was approved by the British Government and a

new company, Tata Aircraft Limited, was formed to give it life. Land was acquired and a large factory building constructed. Had this plan come off, Tatas would have gone into aircraft production.

The British Government had second thoughts and decided instead that invasion gliders should be built under the project. This change was reluctantly accepted by Tatas as the work of building the factory, recruiting staff and organizing manufacture had already gone too far to be abandoned. The project was revised accordingly.

Nevill Vintcent was a man of great physical courage and resourcefulness. More than once he flew to England for discussions with the British authorities. Usually flying by Imperial Airways long-range aircraft, he was flown by a sufficiently circuitous route to keep out of range of German fighters. Tragically, however, on one occasion Vintcent, as an ex-RAF officer, arranged to get a lift on an RAF Hudson bomber on the first leg of a flight from England to Gibraltar. The plane never reached Gibraltar and was reported to have been shot down off the coast of France. The loss of Vintcent was a grievous blow to Tatas and to JRD personally, for apart from being the able and moving spirit behind Tata Airlines and Tata Aircraft that he was, Vintcent and JRD were close friends. This tragic blow was followed by the cancellation of the project itself by the British, who in response to Tatas' own enquiries on the subject, discovered that invasion gliders made by Tata in Pune could not be used in the war because there were no aircraft to tow them! Thus came to a tragic end a project on which JRD had set his heart and which, if it had gone through, as originally planned, would probably have resulted in another invaluable addition to India's industry.

In 1946, Tata Air Lines, a division of Tata Sons, went public and became a joint stock company. It was called Air-India Ltd. The age of passenger travel had arrived and there was to be plenty of competition. Even during wartime Tatas were working on a scheme to extend their services to London. In October 1947, in the turmoil of the post-partition period, Tatas proposed to the Indian government a service to Europe. They placed an order for three Lockheed Constellations, on faith that this venture would be approved. It was a measure of their faith in the newly independent India, then in the convulsions of the partition of the subcontinent.

Tatas proposed that the Indian government take 49 per cent of the capital, Tatas 25 per cent and the rest be publicly subscribed. The government had the right to buy a further two per cent from Tatas taking their share to 51 per cent and giving them total control. This was the first ever proposal of a joint enterprise between the public and private sectors in the country. The proposal was made by J.R.D. Tata at a most inopportune time, when communal strife raged in Delhi. To his astonishment, which still lingers, JRD got acceptance to his joint sector proposal from the government within weeks. Many years later he asked a senior Cabinet Minister, Jagjivan Ram, why a decision could be made so speedily in those days when today it took the government at least two years 'not to make a decision.' Mr Ram replied, 'We did not know any better then!'

The proposal provided for a new company to be called Air-India International. It was to be managed and provided with its staff, its maintenance and its services by Tatas' domestic airline Air-India Ltd. On 8 June 1948 Air-India International with its famous Maharaja spread its wings to Europe. The fledgling airline soon established itself as one of the finest air-carriers of the world.

Meanwhile India's domestic airlines were heading for a crisis. At the end of the War, planes were disposed of by the American Tenth Air Force in India at throw-away prices. For political reasons the government sanctioned every airline applicant, and India soon found itself with eleven airlines while there was room for only two or three. As a result they all ran into rough weather for there were not enough traffic routes to allocate amongst them. Except Air-India all the airlines lost heavily. In 1953 the Government took a decision to nationalize the airlines, proposing to merge them into a single state corporation with JRD as chairman. Mr Tata advised that the domestic and the international airlines of India should be kept apart and two separate corporations be formed. The suggestion was accepted and he was invited to head the international airline, a task he accepted. For the next twenty-five years he was to be the chairman of Air-India, and a director on the board of Indian Airlines.

The international airline business is ferociously competitive and JRD, chairman of some of the largest companies in India, had to give more and more time to the running of Air-India. He carried this burden happily, for aviation was his first love. He did everything he could to make Air-India as good as the best among the world's airlines. Its planes were lavishly decorated. He insisted that even if a plane was used for twenty years, it should always look as if it had come out from its factory—new, inside and outside. And it did. With Air-India efficiently run, JRD saw no reason why all public undertakings could not also be run to the world's best standards and be profitable.

As chairman, JRD believed in personalized attention. He was dubbed a perfectionist for he called upon his staff: 'Always aim at perfection for only then will you achieve excellence.' On every flight on which he travelled he kept detailed notes of his observations and would painstakingly take action on them on return to base. He gave India pride in its national airline. His forty-six-year aviation career spanned an era from the wood and fabric of the little two-seater Puss Moth to the gleaming 400-seater giant Boeing 747. He insisted that there should be no compromise on operating and maintenance standards or on service. One of the airline's publicity chiefs recalls how he once received a midnight phone call at his home from the chairman suggesting how to improve the wording on a publicity hoarding. 'We had to give so much of ourselves because he gave so much of himself,' said this executive.

Air Marshal Nur Khan, former head of the Pakistan Air Force, and later chairman of Pakistan International Airlines, when asked by an Indian magazine what he thought of his neighbour airline, Air-India, and its then chairman J.R.D. Tata, replied: 'A great airline and JRD is an epic figure.' In recognition of this epic figure's services to air transport, JRD was made the recipient of the Tony Jannus Award in 1979, named after the founder pilot of the first scheduled airline in the world, which began in Tampa, Florida, in 1912. Amongst its recipients are the inventor of the jet engine, Sir Frank Whittle; the developers of the Concorde SST, and the founders of the Douglas Aircraft Corporation, Pan-Am, Eastern and United Airlines. Other awards followed. In 1989, the Daniel Guggenheim Medal Award, first conferred on Orville Wright, was presented to J.R.D. Tata.

9

TREASURES FROM THE SEA

*Of all the Companies with which I have been concerned,
none has had to overcome so many difficulties
compounded with bad luck, as has been the lot of Tata
Chemicals.*

—J.R.D. Tata

The evening breeze is cool at Mithapur, on the coast of
Saurashtra. As you walk along the beach the waves caress
the sands gently. It is the same sea that yields its treasures
for Tata Chemicals to extract gypsum, salt, bromine, potash,
magnesium salts, which are then upgraded into numerous
basic chemicals that we live by and, in turn, gives India the
raw materials essential for the manufacture of glass, ceramics,
textiles, pesticides, leather goods and a host of other
industries. The Tata Chemicals complex is one of the most
integrated facilities of its kind in the world.

Today Tata Chemicals is a successful outfit with a
turnover* of Rs 400 crore and rising with a very large added
value component. But it was not always so. For the first
sixteen years Tata Chemicals could declare no dividends. Its
story is one of success snatched out of repeated failures—a
tribute to the men who had faith and nerve to take the knocks
so that India could have a self-reliant, basic inorganic
chemical industry of its own.

As Jamshedpur is the mother of India's engineering
industry, Mithapur—the city of salt—is the mother of India's
heavy chemical industry.

The search for a salt plant began before Tatas came on

---

* Turnover in 2003 was Rs 1,700 crore.

From the sun and the sea a dream is born—Mithapur, Gujarat

the scene. A chemical engineer, who had studied at Manchester University, Kapilram Vakil, had a dream to raise from the ocean its wealth of marine minerals of which salt was only the beginning. Salt and salt-based products were the virtual monopoly of foreign companies. Foreign companies then imported ordinary salt from Aden for India's consumption.

After a survey of the western coast, Kapilram finally decided on a point seven miles from Okha, the westernmost tip where the Gulf of Kutch begins. Like many a pioneer he ran into trouble. The then Maharaja of Baroda, Sayaji Rao, in whose territory Mithapur was, wrote to Tatas suggesting that they might like to assist with this project of national importance. Tatas could see the potential of the industry and were ready to supplement and sustain the efforts of Kapilram with their resources and know-how. But neither Kapilram nor J.R.D. Tata quite realized the magnitude of the task they had taken on nor that they were going on a long, long journey before fortune was to smile.

J.R.D. Tata became chairman of Tata Sons in 1938 and Tata Chemicals was launched in 1939, the year the Second World War broke out. Its first consignment of turbo-generators was sunk at sea. The second was ordered from Sweden, a neutral country. The manufacturers, to avoid the war zone, shipped it to Archangel in the Soviet Union. By then Russia was at war. Tatas gave up hope and placed a fresh order with the United States. A message then came that the Swedish consignment had arrived in Moscow, at the height of the war. Another message followed that the shipment had arrived overland to the Gulf. One fine day the shipment arrived in Bombay harbour.

In spite of the best astrological forecast Kapilram could elicit, the first years of Tata Chemicals were disastrous. An international expert advised J.R.D. Tata that they were in the wrong place doing the wrong job. 'This is not the first time we have done this,' an undaunted J.R.D. Tata is said to have replied, 'when we go to a place we arouse hopes in people.' For their sake as much as for any other reason Mithapur had to succeed.

The question was: How?

The rewarding business was production of soda ash of high quality. The formula and the process were the well-guarded secret of about six companies in the world. Tata Chemicals had cracked the code. It was negotiating with a German firm to raise its capacity from 80 to 200 tonnes of soda ash per day. At that time a thirty-one-year-old chemical engineer called Darbari Seth was asked on his way back from America to visit the German firm. With his experience in America, he was not impressed by what he saw. On his return he told the management board that India did not need foreign help. 'We can do it. What is more we should aim not at 200 but at 400 tonnes which is the optimum capacity. And doing it ourselves, we shall spend much less than what has been budgeted for the 200 tonnes plant.' Of the sixteen on the management board, only one agreed with him—J.R.D. Tata. He was asked to take over the design, the engineering, fabrication and installation of the new equipment and machinery to renovate the Mithapur chemical complex.

To create the soda ash, Seth and his team had to design, engineer, fabricate and erect some twenty process and power plants and then ensure that not only each one of them worked right but all of them worked right together. The average age of the working team was then only twenty-nine. They worked early mornings and late evenings and the rest of the day too. Once the plant was ready, the team was asked to take on the operation and to demonstrate whether they could produce the 400 tonnes per day. They worked with missionary zeal and in the first fortnight the plant touched a production capacity of 545 tonnes one day. The breakthrough had come. For the previous sixteen years not only was the company unable to pay dividends but for some years was unable to even keep aside funds for depreciation. During this period Tata Sons and Tata Industries guaranteed all loans, did not take their share of the commission as managing agents, and continued to provide the managerial skills.

With the breakthrough, there was rejoicing all around. But, alas, not for long. In 1962 the rains failed. Where the average rainfall was eighteen inches, only seven fell. Mithapur was fed by two lakes. Apart from the town, it was the chemical complex that devoured large quantities of fresh water which came from the two lakes.

The grim news came that the lake water would run out by October end. Friends from other parts of India wrote letters of sympathy. The union leaders were talking of Mithapur being evacuated. 'Mithapur will shut down over my dead body,' said Seth. The company did not wait till the lakes dried up by the end of October. A dedicated team under Seth generated and implemented, on war-footing, some 200 ideas, big and small, to conserve fresh water, to substitute fresh water and to produce fresh water within the complex. The team laid five and a half miles of fresh water pipes from some wells to the Mithapur water works. Then in a defiant mood the company declared a 'Lakeless Week' for the town and factory when no water was drawn from the lakes.

The fact that 16,000 people and the works could survive without drawing lake water for a week was as much a morale booster as a material triumph. By revamping the technology of water usage, consumption was reduced from twenty-two lakh gallons per day to five lakh. There was pride in the achievement and the humblest of men felt that he had played a part in the survival of the city and of the works from which he earned his livelihood. Had they caved in at that time, Mithapur may have never restarted.

For three successive years in the 1960s the rains continued to fail but production kept rising and now stands at above 2200 tonnes per day. While insulating the operations from the vagaries of the rains, self-reliance on the water front has been achieved in a very innovative manner by substitution, conservation and re-use. Mithapur is situated between the

Port of Okha and Krishna's holy city of Dwarka. Fifty years ago it was a desolate place, with scanty rains. A martial tribe inhabited the neighbouring area. The land gave them little sustenance. Now the factory has not only given some of them employment but the company has adopted the surrounding areas to ensure they have adequate water supply and health care.

Later, for four years running from 1983 to 1987, Mithapur had its lowest rainfall in living memory—'a mere 0.4 inch.' The Tata Chemicals factory and township functioned and produced results on about one per cent of the fresh water quota that any normal inland complex would have used. In 1988 the spell of drought was broken. 'Everything came alive,' said a rejoicing chairman to his shareholders. 'In my 45 years I have not seen the area look greener and lovelier.'

Tata Chemicals today own and operate the largest and most integrated inorganic chemical complex not only in India but in this part of the world. From Tata Chemicals several streams of investment have emerged. Besides owning subsidiary investment companies and acquiring respectable equity positions in several companies like Tata Tea, ACC, Rallis, Excel Industries, etc., Tata Chemicals is now implementing a Rs 1,250-crore nitrogenous fertiliser project at Babrala in U.P.,[*] a cement plant at Mithapur and a detergent plant at Pithampur in Madhya Pradesh. The company has many other projects on the anvil. A company that suffered such travails at its start is today the third largest within the Tata Group in assets and among the first ten in India.

---

[*] Please see section on Tata Chemicals (p. 225) in 'Dramatic Turnarounds' in Section B.

10

THE CULT OF EXCELLENCE

Quality is first engineered; only then is it inspected.
—A Telco Saying

A Japanese delegation drives around the huge automobile shops of Telco in Pune. I happen to be with them. Occasionally the Japanese stop to inspect the more sophisticated machinery designed and built at the Telco plant. After the visit they lunched at the guest house overlooking a beautiful lake, perhaps reminding them of Japan where ponds play such a vital role in beautifying gardens. On the lake is one small island with saras cranes walking ever so delicately on their thin, tall grey legs. On another larger island birds flock from as far as Tibet and the Soviet Union. In the delegation there is a thoughtful gentleman whose demeanour is marked with distinction. He turns to the executive director of Telco and says that what impressed him is not just the machines Telco has built but that in the huge workshops they visited there was not a scrap of paper or cotton waste lying on the floor. To the Japanese cleanliness is the hallmark of perfect standards.

The gentleman, Yoshiteru Sumitomo, is the grandson of one of the builders of modern industrial Japan. At the end of the 19th century when Sumitomo, along with Mitsubishi and a few others, were laying the foundation of Japanese industrial might, Jamsetji Tata collaborated with Japan to start a short-lived shipping line to the Far East. It was not successful. Later JRD was keen to go into another field of transport—aviation. He succeeded. During World War II Tatas were about to go into the manufacture of aeroplanes. It didn't work out. At the end of the war, Tatas turned to land transport—the

manufacture of locomotives. Later they went into commercial vehicles.

Telco—The Tata Engineering and Locomotive Company—started operations in an old workshop of the East Indian Railway at Jamshedpur. In 1945 Tata Sons purchased for Rs 25 lakh the Singhbhum workshop to set up initially the manufacture of steam locomotive boilers and later of complete locomotives and other engineering products. The company at first was called the Tata Locomotive and Engineering Company. At its peak the company reached the target of 100 locomotives a year and was proud to produce them with 98 per cent indigenous parts. Over a period of fifteen years, 1,155 locomotives steamed out from the workshop as well as 950 road rollers, 5,000 railway wagons and several boilers. The company, however, was heavily dependent on one customer; the nationalized Indian Railways which dictated the price. So Telco looked for diversification.

The opportunity came in the form of a report that Daimler-Benz A.G. was interested in locating a partner to start an assembly and manufacturing plant for commercial vehicles in Asia. General Motors and Ford who had already set up commercial vehicle operations in India had just closed down because they had no faith in the Indian market. Tatas had the confidence to take the risk and signed an agreement with Daimler-Benz.

When J.R.D. Tata and Sumant Moolgaokar applied to the Minister for Industries, T.T. Krishnamachari (TTK) for the government's approval, they got a surprise. 'Go ahead,' said the minister immediately cutting all red tape. Only TTK could do so. The first vehicle was assembled from a 'completely knocked down' pack of Daimler-Benz aggregates. Steadily, one aggregate after another was manufactured at Jamshedpur and the plant grew. As the country did not then have an automobile ancillary base, the company had to set up large forge and foundry shops. It was decided to encourage and develop good firms to manufacture ancillary components. A fledgling design section was entrusted with the task of modifying the Daimler-Benz designs to suit India's road operating conditions. The results were beyond expectations.

Sadly, the day of the steam locomotive was coming to an end and in 1960 the puffing 'iron horse' bowed out giving place to the truck. The fruitful collaboration with Germany ended in 1969. Telco acknowledges its indebtedness to its collaborator.

Over 70 per cent of the medium and heavy commercial vehicles on Indian roads are made by Telco. Telco is able to manufacture 99.8 per cent of its parts in India. A family of 1,500 ancillary suppliers furnish all kinds of components. About 50 per cent of the parts that go into the trucks are supplied by them. Over the years each supplier has been trained by Telco engineers to provide the high quality of components required. For several years such was the demand for Telco trucks that they commanded a premium

A melting furnace in the Telco Foundry, Pune, Maharashtra

price in the market but Telco held its price line. I once questioned then chairman and managing director of Telco, Mr Moolgaokar, why he did that. He replied: 'Profits should come from productivity and not by raising prices in a favourable market. Our greatest asset is customer affection.'

In the mid-1960s the company decided to set up a second unit in western India, at Pune. The idea was not only to build more trucks there but to design and manufacture the machines that in turn manufacture parts of a truck. The idea was to make India independent of imports as far as possible. Very few vehicle companies even abroad have their own facility to manufacture the machines they require.

On a vast barren and rocky land in Pune, the first thing Telco did was to plant trees—not a few but in their thousands. It was the way Moolgaokar worked. Trees needed water. So an artificial lake was created with a circumference of four kilometres. A quarter century ago when few were environment conscious, some directors looked upon this idea of Mr Moolgaokar as a waste of money. Only as the trees

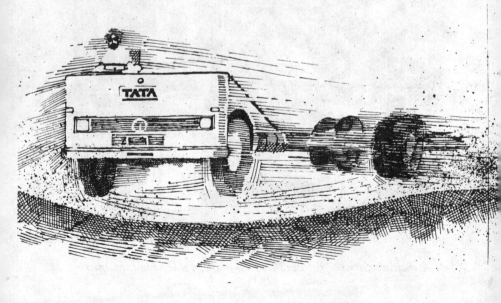

came up did the workshop rise on the land. 'We did not have to create a lake to produce a truck. But we did,' says J.R.D. Tata proudly. Telco's nursery gives two fruit trees to any villager in the surrounding areas who'll look after them.

Pune now equals Jamshedpur in its capacity to produce over thirty-five thousand vehicles per year. Telco Pune's Machine Tool Division has manufactured over 1,000 sophisticated special purpose and transferline machines. These machines help to keep Telco plants young and healthy. In the 1990s a third manufacturing unit came up near Lucknow in northern India. In 1992 it commenced production of MCV. A multi-axled vehicle, LPT 2213, was launched in 1994. Tata Sumo was launched from Pune reaching its 1,00,000 mark in three years. In 1998 the Safari, India's first sports utility vehicle, was launched.

The company's Engineering Research Centre at Pune is the pride of Telco. At first it designed a host of modifications for its heavy and medium vehicles. In the mid-eighties Japan's light commercial vehicles (LCVs) hit the market with some

of the most distinguished names in the automobile industry—Nissan, Toyota, Mazda. The public anxiously waited to see whether an Indian designed vehicle could at all compete with Japan. In 1985-86 Telco's share of the LCV market was almost nil. By 1988-89 one out of every three LCVs was a Telco product. With its inbuilt strength of research, design and manpower, Telco next launched a pick-up van called the Tatamobile. Although it was not designed to be a car its attractive frontage prompted many to mount a car body.

In 1985 Telco signed a memorandum of understanding with Honda of Japan to manufacture the Honda Accord passenger car in India. The government's permission did not come through primarily due to shortage of foreign exchange. Disappointed but unfazed Telco proceeded to produce its own vehicles with indigenous design—a sports car called Tata Sierra and the Tata Estate.

Telco vehicles, exported to fifty countries, have earned India so far over Rs 1,000 crore in foreign exchange. It is the largest exporter of engineering goods in India topping over Rs 150 crore a year. Its millionth vehicle rolled out in December 1990. Perhaps even more than machines, Telco can take credit for the skills that it has given to India.

The man who made Telco what it is today was Sumant Moolgaokar. In a country where the attitude of many is to tolerate slipshod work saying *chalta hai* (it passes), he expected and obtained standards of excellence and precision and passed it down the line to managers, supervisors and workers. 'There is a belief in our country,' he said, 'that our culture and our character cannot allow our people to attain consistently high standards and shoddiness and carelessness are our God-given ways of life. But if with faith in them, you ask our men for their best, they rise to a belief in their work and create a momentum towards improvement. Often I have seen men who were considered ordinary, rise to extraordinary heights. Do not accept second rate work; accept the best and ask for it; pursue it relentlessly and you will get it.'

Thirty-seven thousand employees of Telco are conscious

of quality. There is a quality control department but a quality inspector is like a policeman. 'What we would like is to inculcate a belief in quality in the production man himself, so as to render the policeman's role superfluous,' says Managing Director J.E. Talaulicar. 'The best quality inspector,' says a former Telco employee, 'is the conscience.' When Moolgaokar died in July 1989 he had, over four decades, shaped the character of Telco. A few months before he died the eighty-four-year-old Sumant Moolgaokar stepped down and proposed that Ratan N. Tata succeed him as the chairman.

N.A. Palkhivala, who as deputy chairman was closely associated with Moolgaokar, said that with Moolgaokar you felt that 'he was not building a factory; he was building a nation.' *The Times of India* headlined its obituary on Moolgaokar, 'Nation-Builder'.

Telco is the child of Tata Steel which is its largest shareholder after the financial institutions. J.R.D. Tata envisages that in a few years' time Telco will eclipse its formidable mother in its growth. Telco has exciting plans for the future. Chairman R.N. Tata says: 'The launch of the Tatamobile 206 pick-up truck in 1988 marked the entry of Telco into the passenger vehicle segment. While the 206 is indeed intended to be a load-carrying vehicle, it embodies the exterior and interior finishes and handling akin to that of a car. The 206 is particularly noteworthy as it is the outcome of a totally internal development programme in Telco, with no foreign collaboration. Based on the 206 platform, Telco launched two new passenger vehicles—they are the Estate station wagon and the sports vehicle Sierra. Both have car interiors and an abundance of convenience and safety features. The company is developing a new indigenous full-fledged passenger car. This task has been accomplished with the advent of Indica in 1999, Indica V2 in 2001. In 2002, a sedan, Indigo, was introduced in the market.'

Reputed to be the finest engineering company in India, Telco is equipped to go into more sophisticated fields of engineering production including aerospace.

11

CUP OF AWAKENING

In the highlands of Kerala a massive rock mountain stands against the blue sky. Its outline is the shape of an elephant's head and neck. Local tribals named it *Anei-mudi*—'anei' for elephant and 'mudi' for head. At 8,841 feet it is the highest peak in India outside the Himalayan range. Along its slope elephants and enormous bisons, prettily horned sambhars, bears, a few tigers, and leopards roam. Its prize denizen is the ibex. Threatened with extinction elsewhere, it flourishes in the Eravikulam National Park. A tea company, James Finlay, once owned this area along with about 210 square miles of forest and tea growing country. Later Tata Finlay handed over this prize forest to the nation with only two requests: to declare the area as a national park and not to construct any jeep or car tracks. Once roads are constructed the poachers have a field day.

The government has honoured the two requests. The National Park has only foot tracks. Not too many men venture into the park but elephants merrily cross the borderline. In a tea garden near the park the writer found three elephants standing still as statues—a full-grown female, a smaller cow and a calf of about three months of age. Our car halted at a distance of 150 feet on the road below. The elephants ignored us for a couple of minutes and then had the itch to exercise. No lumbering elephants these! Carefully coming on the track between the bushes the full-grown female set a brisk pace down a slope coming towards us. The best response was to ignite the Ambassador and keep moving. Five minutes later someone in the car cried out, 'Ibex.' The chocolate coloured mountain goats with brown eyes and an innocent face as lovely as a deer's were gnawing at burnt grass which contains its favourite potassium. An endangered species elsewhere, here the latest count shows the population at 800, up by 25 per cent since the last count. The local ibex is called the Nilgiri Tahr.

The sure-footed ibex is a delicacy for the tigers and leopards but when chased it often gives its powerful hunters the slip by clambering up rocks which are almost vertical. And the all-powerful tiger can only roar in his frustration.

Eravikulam National Park is perhaps the only one in the world where a private company, Tata Tea, helps the forest department in its job of looking after the park. All three roads leading to the park are on its estates and Tata Tea watchers keep guard night and day. A heritage is preserved.

On the undulating hills in the surrounding areas of Munnar one sees carpets of green tea interspersed with tall eucalyptus trees reaching for the sky. The company has planted them as a part of its energy plantation reputed to be the largest of its kind in India. In the entire High Range, where more than 22 million kilos of tea are produced, Tata Tea does not use any fossil based fuel at all. In its terrain are lakes and dams, as well as the largest tea factory in the world, at Chundavurrai, which can dry and process up to 100,000 kilos of green leaf a day. And it is not the only one either, for most Tata Tea estates have their smaller tea factories— all painted white.

The Scottish company James Finlay came to this area in 1897. Till 1957 it had only four Indians of managerial rank and over sixty British managers, mostly Scots. When the subcontinent was partitioned by the British into India and Pakistan, the Scots called Munnar 'Haggistan' after their favourite dish.

The first collaboration between Tatas and James Finlay was initially to produce instant tea for the U.S. market. In 1983, Finlays divested their holdings and the company became Tata Tea. These are only the thirty-one southern estates of Tata Tea, its other estates are in Bengal and Assam. Tata Tea is the largest tea grower in the world, with fifty-three estates and 57,000 workers. It integrates the manufacture of conventional black tea, instant tea and tea in bags, cartons and polypacks.

The Tata Tea estates in the north-east of India are dotted at various places, while in the south they are concentrated in and around Munnar in the hills of the High Range.

Munnar is unique as a plantation district because it is close-knit and self-sufficient. Roads were not well developed along the highlands in the early days and there was a remarkable network of ropeways carrying tea from various estates to the top station at 7,000 feet and from there parcels of tea rolled down the ropeway, up a hill and down again to a railway station in the plains. Today, stately horses have yielded to motorbikes, ropeways have yielded to roads and bullock-carts have bowed out to make room for tractors and trucks. As man progresses he gains in speed and loses the charm and leisure of yesteryears.

In those days, there were no televisions and videos. Planters had to make their own entertainment in areas remote from civilization. Planters played vigorous games of rugby, polo, golf, tennis. They hunted and they fished. Sport is still encouraged. TV and video have come as a boon to the wives who are almost isolated with rains varying up to 300 inches (next only to Cherapunji) down to 60 inches on the 20,000 hectares of tea and trees.

Tea belongs to the genus *Camillia,* the same tree that gives the camillia flower. There is the *Camillia Sinensis* which the Chinese discovered 3,000 years ago. It was the health drink of the aristocrats only. The Portuguese and the British traders took to it. Then one day on the banks of the Irrawady river in Burma a British soldier found a similar tree, got it tested and introduced it to Assam. *Camillia Assamica* is broad-leafed and stronger as a brew. *Camillia Sinensis* has a more gentle flavour. The Darjeeling tea is a hybrid with a flavour between the two.

James Finlay set high standards in quality, preserved the

environment and established traditions. One manager says, 'When Tatas took over we wondered what would happen. We find that they have not only kept the traditions but improved on them.' Due to uncertainty about their foreign holdings, especially fears of nationalization, Finlays hesitated to put in the investment needed. When Tatas took over with Darbari Seth as chairman they conceived and implemented a long-range plan to revive the estates and upgrade the company's technological profile. Tata Tea produces over 60 million kilos of tea, almost equally divided between southern and eastern India. In keeping with the Tata culture, they have invested equally on human assets as on the physical assets.

In the south, almost every worker of Tata Tea has his own quarters with water supply, free medical care for the family and free veterinary aid for cattle which he is encouraged to rear. In one year alone, i.e. 1984, more than 14,000 houses were electrified. Tata Tea introduced a unique social welfare system in its estates which dramatically improved the quality of life of its huge work force in the south and the North-East.

Tata Tea has launched a programme of diversification. It has embarked upon mushroom growing and made it another string to their bow. It has started a hygienic Tata Spice Centre for all spices in Cochin, its export point. Kerala is cardamom country. Tata grows 22,000 kilos of cardamom, 40,000 kilos of pepper, and extracts 7,000 kilos of eucalyptus oil.

Five kilos of fresh tea leaves contain four kilos of water. Evaporating water takes a lot of fuel. The foresight of the British planters made them plant their own fuel. Timber from *Eucalyptus Grandis* and *Eucalyptus Globulus* is estimated to save Tata Tea 35 million litres of oil. Tata Tea set up comprehensive research and development centres both in south India and in Assam.

Tata Tea is trying to develop (though they may not be the only ones) high yielding varieties of tea and its success may mean that the production of tea in Munnar may ultimately be doubled.

As you enter the High Range and approach the town of Munnar, thick mists often encircle you, and clouds float by the dew drenched, lush green mountainsides of the tea estates. In the midst of one such estate stands the polypack production unit of Tata Tea. Tata Tea introduced its first polypack in 1984. These pillow packs, which keep the tea more fresh, pioneered the concept of flexible packaging in tea. Until then, packaged tea had been sold only in carton packs. Several other firms, including multinationals, quickly followed suit by introducing their own polypacks.

Not far from the main Tata Tea office in Munnar stands the largest instant tea factory outside the USA and Tata Tea is the world's largest exporter of instant tea.* Practically unknown in India, instant tea is preferred in cold tea form consumed largely in the USA and Europe. The factory employs a high technology process for manufacture of this product, which has been developed in-house. This process is proprietary, and known to very few firms worldwide.

The instant tea factory is a 100 per cent export-oriented unit. Its product is also 100 per cent pure, with no fillers to add volume to instant tea, no additives—an approach to pure processing that has baffled competition. The very first to be introduced in the US market by Tata Finlay in 1968, it rapidly shot to the top of this segment.

Almost all the thirty southern estates have small hospitals and a well-equipped main hospital. The main hospital has become the focal point of social welfare. Liquor is the scourge of the plantation workers. On one estate alone the arrack shops have come down from nine to one. After this happened a sweet old lady came up to the Chief Medical Officer and said, in her language, a beaming 'thank you.' The CMO said:

* See Section B on major acquisition of Tetley, the second largest tea company in the world.

'This was reward enough.' Efforts are made to make smokeless *chullas* (stoves) available estate by estate. Health exhibitions and baby shows are organized to underline the importance of breast-feeding. The 2,500 regional tribals of the area looked down upon the plantation workers and had steered clear of the allopathic medical facilities of Tata Tea. To help them a few barefoot doctors from among the tribals were trained to deal with a few common ailments. Fellow tribals take their medication.

Kerala is India's top ranked state in family planning. On Tata Tea estates the birth rate has come down from 29.2 per 1000 in 1983 to 17.2 per 1000 in 1989. The less the number of mouths to feed, the better the life they can lead. Tata Tea's efforts in family planning measures taken up on a war footing in its estates won for its general hospital in Munnar a national award in 1989, and in 1990 the hospital was adjudged the best industrial hospital in the country.

The company is in the process of building a major referral hospital in Assam—a move genuinely welcomed by the people of Assam.*

---

* Please see section on Tata Tea (p. 242) in 'Some Performers' in Section B.

DREAMERS AND PERFORMERS

An industrial house that grows, needs both dreamers and men of action. The ideal industrialist is a combination of both. In his study *Jamsetji Nusserwanji Tata: A Chronicle of His Life,*[*] F.R. Harris observes that Jamsetji 'possessed a gift, which amounted to genius, for selecting the right subordinates, and throughout his life he exhibited to a notable degree the art of delegating much of his work. He kept his fingers lightly upon the pulse of a business: there was no fuss, no unnecessary worry. When he once devoted his mind to further expansion, he could call upon that reserve of time and energy which only a great organizer can keep at his disposal.'

Sir Dorab Tata, his cousin R.D. Tata, Burjorji Padshah and others shaped the growth of Tatas in the quarter century that followed Jamsetji's death. The new generation entered with JRD in 1924 and Naval Tata in 1930.

In the early 1920s and 1930s, distinguished ICS officers were to join Tatas. John Peterson, Director of Munitions, Government of India during World War I, had impressed R.D. Tata. He was appointed director-in-charge of Tata Steel. In 1931 Sir Ardeshir Dalal, the first Indian to be a Municipal Commissioner of Bombay, joined Tatas as a director.

When J.R.D. Tata became chairman in 1938 he departed from the prevailing industrial practice in Britain and in India to call upon special advisers like lawyers and other experts as and when needed. The young chairman insisted that the best talent available in the country should be accessible under one roof to Tatas on a full-time basis. A practising solicitor,

[*]   Blackies (India) Reprint 1958.

J.D. Choksi, left his firm of Wadia Ghandy and Company to join Tatas full-time. A.D. Shroff left a stockbroker's firm for Tatas. An economist, Dr John Matthai, who was then Director-General of Commercial Intelligence and Statistics to the Union Government, joined in 1940 to reinforce the elite corps Tatas were building up. For the next couple of decades these men were to steer the Tata enterprises.

Sir Ardeshir Dalal's association with Tatas began way back in 1905 when he applied for a J.N. Tata Scholarship to appear for the ICS examination. In those days the cream of the academic life of Britain and India competed for the coveted post in the 'heaven-born service.' Out of the 400 candidates who appeared, Ardeshir Dalal stood second. After a distinguished career in the Civil Service, he became the director-in-charge of Tata Steel in 1931 when the company was still going through a difficult period financially and was also suffering from unstable labour relations. It was Sir Ardeshir who introduced the profit-sharing scheme for labour in the 1930s. When he passed away, T.P. Sinha of the Tata Workers' Union said that though the union did not always see eye to eye with him, it always 'found him frank and straightforward and a perfect gentleman in his dealings with us, which greatly helped in establishing happy industrial relations.'

A signatory to the Bombay Plan, Sir Ardeshir was invited in 1944 by the Viceroy, Lord Wavell, to join the Viceroy's executive council as Member for Planning and Development. For fifteen months he applied himself to the task with vigour. The multi-purpose river valley schemes and the chain of national laboratories were first conceived during his leadership of the planning portfolio.

Sir Ardeshir was both a dreamer and a man of action. He was a precise, firm and domineering administrator. Michael Brown, later editor of the *Illustrated Weekly of India*, described him thus: 'He is rather tall and sparsely built, extremely well-groomed. His heavy lidded eyes and gentle mouth may suggest the dreamer but there is an indefinable atmosphere of preciseness about him. Even his cheroot seems trained only to scatter its ashes in the ashtray.'

When he resigned from the government he returned to his desk in Bombay House in January 1945. He became vice-chairman of Tata Steel and then started planning for the newly formed Tata Locomotive and Engineering Company.

The eminent economist Dr John Matthai began life as a barrister. One day after having successfully defended a criminal for murder and after being rewarded with a bunch of bananas for his fees, he felt he had had enough of law and went to England to pursue his real love which was different. He went to the London School of Economics and got his doctorate there for his thesis on 'Life in Ancient India'. On his return he became a professor of economics at Madras University. He came to the attention of the Government of India for his accomplishments and was appointed first a member of the Tariff Board and then Director-General of Commercial Intelligence and Statistics. He was invited in 1940 to join the house as director-in-charge of Tata Chemicals, then a fledgling enterprise. He wrote the Bombay Plan on behalf of himself and seven others. In 1946 Nehru invited Dr John Matthai to join his Interim Government. He became minister of railways and transport, then of commerce and industry and in 1948 became minister of finance. He distinguished himself in all these positions and in 1950 resigned due to differences with Nehru. Dr Matthai felt that the appointment of the Planning Commission at that stage was neither necessary nor desirable and recommended that the government should first husband the resources needed and later scheme for big things. The Prime Minister agreed there was a great deal in Dr Matthai's argument but nevertheless he said he was committed to start the Planning Commission and so Dr Matthai bowed out. Dr Matthai returned to Tatas and picked up from Sir Ardeshir Dalal the vice-chairmanship of Tata Steel. Like Sir Ardeshir he worked with precision.

'Dr Matthai does not believe in wasting his energy. That appears to be the secret of his success,' wrote a contemporary. But unlike Sir Ardeshir who was volatile in temper, Dr Matthai was a serene personality. Dr John Matthai was for some years chairman of Sir Dorabji Tata Trust and left his mark by initiating two institutes. In association with the United Nations he helped the trust to start the first Demographic Research Institute in 1956, which is today the International Institute for Population Studies in Bombay. It was during his chairmanship that the same trust in collaboration with the Royal Commonwealth Society started the Tata Agricultural and Rural Training Centre for the Blind. It was he who took Tatas into rural work at a time when integrated rural projects were a rarity way back in the early 1950s.

Dr Matthai served Tatas for another nine years. When he retired, a colleague wrote of him:

> He respected the dignity of the human personality and did not believe in violating it nor in tolerating any violation. Into the hardpressed and blasé business world he brought an air of learning and love of it too . . . His vision was without blinkers, and his mind was erudite and enlightened beyond the immediate and the present, soaring high above most things.

J.D. Choksi came to Tatas in 1938 as a legal adviser and for the next thirty years played a formative role in the post-war expansion of the company. It was he, who as the chairman of the Tata Electric Companies, struggled with foresight and tenacity getting approval for the installation of its thermal units in Bombay by anticipating Bombay's needs when the then government was confident that there was no need for additional power.

J.D. Choksi's finest hour came during the struggle to keep the Steel City of Jamshedpur functioning when the communists declared a flash strike in 1958 to test their strength against the official union. As vice-chairman of Tata Steel, J.D. Choksi rushed from Bombay to Jamshedpur and stood his ground giving confidence to those who did not want to yield. And the official union came out successful. A towering and impressive figure, J.D. Choksi was equally at home in law, finance, business and administration. He held the reins of one or another Tata company with distinction for three decades. He was also closely associated with the expansion of Air-India, from a comparatively small to one of the bigger airlines.

Just as a chance meeting of two men on a steamer cruising in the Pacific resulted in the birth of the Tata Memorial (Cancer) Hospital, a chance meeting on an aeroplane between J.D. Choksi and George Woods of the World Bank resulted in the involvement of the House of Tata with the World Bank. George Woods' first link with the House began when he was adviser to the World Bank. Later he became its president. The relationship between the World Bank and Tatas continued gainfully for almost four decades.

Soon after the news of the partition of India was announced in June 1947, J.R.D. Tata received a cable from the then finance minister, Liaquat Ali Khan, requesting immediate release of Tata Industries' director based in Delhi, Sir Ghulam Mohammed. The future Prime Minister of Pakistan said that he and M.A. Jinnah wanted Sir Ghulam to be the chief representative of the Muslim League for division of assets and liabilities of the Government of India. Sir Ghulam Mohammed was promptly released. On Partition Sir Ghulam went to Pakistan to become first the finance minister, and in 1952 the governor-general of Pakistan. M.A. Wadud Khan, director of the Tata Oil Mills, was appointed to head the Steel Authority of India (SAIL). He was later steel secretary and managing director of the giant cement combine the ACC in which Tatas have an interest.

Sir Ardeshir Dalal and Dr John Matthai were not the only ones invited by the Union Government to assist in the government of the country. Sir Homi Mody, a Tata director for twenty-five years, was also invited to join the Viceroy's Executive Council and when India became independent he was appointed governor of India's largest state, Uttar Pradesh. He will however best be remembered for his scintillating wit and irrepressible humour, which lit up many dreary hours for his Tata colleagues. He took a lively interest in the running and growth of the House of Tata and was in the front rank of its contacts with the press, the public and the government.

A comparatively young Sumant Moolgaokar joined the lunch table of Sir Homi, Dr Matthai and JRD in the mid 1940s. 'At the table', said Moolgaokar 'you felt that Tatas belonged to the nation.'

Life in Tatas was more than just business. It was a family of men who worked together, however diverse their backgrounds. Though there were understandable strains and differences between powerful personalities, they learnt to work and to laugh together. Nowhere is this better perceived than in the touching but rather unusual farewell functions before they took leave for government assignments or when they retired.

This is best illustrated in a farewell function for Sir Homi Mody in 1959. J.R.D. Tata said:

Of all the men I know, none enjoys farewell functions as much as Sir Homi. This is the third he has got from us—in 1941, 1949 and 1959. In between, he has to my knowledge extracted dozens from other groups and associations which he happened to leave either permanently or temporarily. And when there was no occasion for a farewell party, Sir Homi usually managed to get himself knighted or decorated or appointed to the Central Government or to a governorship, all of which happily called for congratulatory functions.

You may not know that Sir Homi has been, throughout his life, a prolific writer of books. In fact, he wrote two. At the tender age of twenty-seven, he wrote *The Political Future of*

India which seems to have taken a lot out of him because it was only thirteen years later at the age of forty, that he wrote his magnum opus, the *Life of Sir Phirozeshah Mehta*. There is no truth, by the way, in the libellous story that he bought all the books of both the editions. Actually, three of the first and six of the second found a ready sale. Well, exhausted by this double effort, Sir Homi has not published anything since.

This evening, talking a little more seriously, we salute in him a great human being, a great gentleman and one of the most lovable men one could ever want to meet.

Sir Homi replied: 'The very large numbers in which you have gathered here today prove to me that my impending departure has aroused a great deal of enthusiasm.' Sir Homi, who was governor of Uttar Pradesh from 1949 to 1952, spoke about the time when his assignment as governor came to an end: 'My colleagues, who never had much of an opinion of me, made up their minds that my governorship for three years must have knocked out whatever little capacity I had for serious work; and they were about to tell me so as politely as they could. But I was a little too smart for them, and before they could move in the matter, they found me on their hands. The very day I came back from U.P., I walked into Bombay House.'

He concluded his farewell with the words, 'I must thank you all very warmly for the kindness and consideration you have always extended to me, and I pray that the prestige, the influence and the power for good of the House of Tata be maintained and strengthened with the passing of the years.'

Men like Sir Homi understood that business had a higher purpose than profit. It could be 'the power for good' in the life of a nation.

Part Two

Ripple Effects

Nirmal Singh—a fourth generation worker at Tata Steel

13

ON INDUSTRY

I think that this is an exciting picture of tomorrow's world. I think that business leadership is in itself an honourable, testing, imaginative and creative job. It is not just about the creation of wealth, it is about the creation of a better world for tomorrow and the building and growing of people . . . Above everything they (opportunities of tomorrow) will call for more creativity, and just straight humanity, because business is, and always has been, about people. Management is about people, and manufacturing is about harnessing, motivating and leading people. It always has been, and I hope it will always be.

John Harvey-Jones
—*Making it Happen: Reflections on Leadership*

In December 1938, a graduate apprentice joined Tata Steel and was put to work as a 'khalasi' (unskilled manual labourer), as he puts it. Today, the same 'khalasi,' M.N. Dastur, heads one of the world's largest steel consultancy companies bidding for global tenders. He worked on a multi-million-rupee contract in connection with a steel plant in Libya. He has been a consultant to parties in Latin America, Indonesia, Oman and Egypt. The 'khalasi' has graduated to become a consultant of the company where he once worked and is now helping with the Rs 2,500-crore modernization* and expansion programme of Tata Steel.

Both Tata Steel and Telco—among the largest companies in the corporate sector—run highly concentrated

---

* Please see section on Tata Steel (p. 229) in Section B for further developments.

programmes for their staff on technical and management development. They are also in the forefront of apprentice training. The objective is not only to impart skills, but to inspire trainees to attain standards of excellence.

Long before the Apprentices Act laid down that companies should train apprentices, craftsmen and graduate engineers, Tata Steel started its technical institute. Initially in 1921, as a result of Sir Dorab Tata's proposal, an Institute of Metallurgical Technology was established. In the first year, 2,000 applied, 200 were interviewed and only twenty of the best selected. The number has now grown and the courses of training imparted have multiplied. Eight hundred students are being trained, mostly in evening classes, at Tata Steel's Technical Training School. They range from employed workers of Tata Steel (and other units) who take evening courses for two hours a day, to new recruits who have a two- or three-year full-day course. They are trained in mechanical engineering, metallurgical engineering, refractory engineering, in lathe operation and the like. Fitters, welders, mechanics, blacksmiths, moulders, pattern-makers have come out of this institute for decades. That is perhaps why, when the public sector steel plants were launched one after another at Rourkela, Bhilai, Durgapur and Bokaro, a reservoir of trained manpower was already available.

In addition to the regular training programme held by Tata Steel within Jamshedpur, 12 km from Jamshedpur there is the Management Development Centre in a beautiful setting of the Dimna Lake. In its decor and facilities it equals any five-star hotel. It is used for seminars and meetings and conferences away from the madding crowd. This centre is used for select groups of about thirty residential participants.

Telco has its own management training centre at Jamshedpur and runs about 100 courses a year. Most of the courses deal directly with managerial skills but to give the managers wider perspectives, lectures on subjects such as transcendental analysis and leadership in public life are also

The Tata Management Training Centre, Pune, Maharashtra

held. The Telco Management Centre specializes in problem-solving. A manager can come and tell the centre what problem he has to cope with and a course is built around that need of a department or a person, sometimes orienting a course to a target.

An umbrella organization for management training for Tata-promoted companies is the Tata Management Training Centre at Pune. It is housed in idyllic surroundings of rambling grounds with leafy trees and a gracious main building designed by George Wittet, architect of the Gateway of India. About forty residential courses for not more than thirty-six people at a time take place every year, mostly of a week's duration. Imparting management skills is only one part of the training. An effort is made to develop the personality of those taking part in it by attempts at inculcating an analytical spirit at the job and an understanding of human behaviour. The courses are carefully thought out and in each course seemingly outside subjects are introduced, like appreciation of arts and music, lectures on film-making or on the political environment or on defence management. A.K. Sen Gupta from Jamshedpur, one of those taking a course, was asked by this writer what he had gained from it. He promptly replied: 'Twenty new friends.' When probed whether he found it easier to make friends at this residential course than at the place of his work, he replied: 'Yes, I realize here that life is not meant to be a rat race but a relay race.' He learnt to enjoy team work. The Union Government has sent the seniormost IAS officers for training at this Tata Management Training Centre.

When the new plant of the Tata Engineering and Locomotive Company (Telco) was being set up at Pune, after the tree planting, the first buildings to be constructed were for the training and housing of apprentices. Telco, Jamshedpur, has 600 apprentices taking a three-year course, and Pune has an equal number. A World Bank report on Telco issued in 1973 stated: The company's training programmes are among the best in the world considering scope, recruitment and facilities.'

The company encourages programmes of job enrichment. For example, in Telco's spacious apprentices workshop at Jamshedpur is a working model of an 1885 three-wheeled Daimler-Benz diesel car. Four such models were made by the apprentices. Another group made a working model of a train. In encouraging their creativity Telco has given these youngsters a taste of what they are meant to do for the future advancement of this country.

Tatas have exported their skills to other nations. The Singapore government invited Tatas to run its Government Training Centre in Singapore. The two others who invited were Philips of Holland and Rollei of West Germany.

Among the internationally renowned organizations which have agreements and tie-ups with Tata Consultancy Services are IBM, Cray Research, the makers of super computers, McDonnell Douglas Information Systems, Oracle Corporation, Lotus Development Corporation and Online Systems International. For several years in succession, TCS has won prestigious awards for its outstanding performance in software exports.

In India, TCS's services have been utilized by the Government of India, state government departments and large public and private sector firms.

The Tata electric companies have qualified hundreds of power plant operators from various electricity boards, BHEL, and other industries, as well as technicians from neighbouring countries like Iran and from the Middle East.

The apprentices trained by the Tata group of companies go to other companies—as many of them do—to carry standards of excellence into their new fields of endeavour.

For Tatas' own requirements of an administrative cadre, they started in 1956 the Tata Administrative Service to which about a hundred executives belong.

Planting Men

If you want to plan for a year, plant corn; if you want to plan for thirty years, plant a tree; but if you want to plan for hundred years, plant men.

—Chinese Proverb

Beneath a banyan tree, nothing grows. Under an oak tree, life abounds.

Dattu Tukaram Wadhekar of Suresh Press Works, Chinchwad, Pune, is a supplier of truck ancillary parts to Telco. Thirty-eight people work in his shed. He supplies ancillaries to one other Pune industry also. Dattu is about fifty years old. He has wide open eyes, a cheerful grin and hair that tends to spring up vertically in spite of his efforts to press it down. He comes from the village of Umri in District Akola.

Dattu started life at a Pune factory in 1962 at Rs 3.50 per day. He relates in Hindi and Marathi the considerable hardships he underwent when he gave up his job and started on his own. He could not even afford to maintain his wife and children and sent them to his in-laws. Every rupee earned went in purchasing machinery. He started in the hope of supplying components to Telco.

He is one of Telco's most prompt suppliers, deeply attached to the company. He says his assets are worth Rs 4,50,000 all of which are invested in his workshop, his shed (which is expanding) and in raw materials of which he stocks supplies for nine months. When asked if he had difficulties in getting payments for his supplies from Telco, Dattu replied: 'Whenever I am short of funds I ask them and that very day I get my payments. I also supply parts to another factory but I feel shy of asking them, but to Telco I go freely. They have given me *izzat* (dignity) in the way they have treated me.'

The head of the ancillary department does not take the

credit. Instead, he passes it on to the Dattus of life who keep Telco's workshops humming. 'They,' he says, 'are the unsung heroes of Indian industry.'

Across the river from Jamshedpur, at Adityapur, is Arjun Singh Hanspal. Arjun Singh came as a refugee after the Partition, having lost everything in Pakistan. He started in a small way, making metal furniture for the Tata Hospital. Today he makes complicated castings and fabrication for the overhaul of the blast furnaces.

The manager of Tata Steel's Sources Development Cell says: 'We treat them not as our suppliers but as our partners.'

The small-scale sector lives because there is a large-scale sector it can supply to. They are two wheels of a chariot. One can ill-afford to operate without the other.

Technology Abreast of Time

At Trombay, across the Bombay harbour, are six operating generating units of the Tata electric companies. Nestled in the thick green trees on the hillside on the eastern side is the Bhabha Atomic Research Centre.

In a country that suffers consistently from power shortages, the Tata electric companies have a 500 MW thermal unit with a phenomenally high plant load factor of 92 per cent compared to the national average of 55 per cent.* Poor maintenance, lack of timely annual overhaul of generating units account for frequent power shut downs and load shedding. India spends thousands of crores of rupees setting up new 500 MW plants, but if the existing plants run at least at 80 per cent efficiency she may not need that level of investment.

It is estimated that nearly 30 to 40 per cent of generating capacity can be lost due to operator errors following major system disturbances. To ensure the finest technical training for their operators, Tata Electric fabricated the first power training simulator of its kind in this part of Asia. The simulator can create conditions of breakdown or faults in machinery and operators can be trained to detect and take corrective action. State electricity boards from all over India send batches of trainees for training. The circle of excellence widens.

The pride of Tata Electric is the load despatch centre with its six computers at Trombay, which assures a stable system-control for the supply of electric power in the Bombay region. There is seldom load shedding in Bombay. The on-line process computers have been inter-linked with an interactive cathode ray tube display system. This enables the operator on duty to control the continuously changing system load requirements.

---

* Please see section on Tata Power (p. 244) in 'Some Performers' in Section B.

It also ensures a higher availability of power supply to the consumer at minimum cost.

Production facilities have been established at Bangalore, designated as Tata Electronic Development Services, where various electronic equipment for applications in the power utility, industry, defence and business fields are manufactured. The research and development of Tata Electric has grown into a major development agency in the area of advanced electronic systems, ranging from digital telemetry and telecontrol to missile/rocket launching and satellite image processing. For their pioneering efforts in research and development, the companies were awarded the prestigious FICCI award and the national award from the Department of Scientific Research, Ministry of Science and Technology.

Next to oil, the most serious energy shortage is of high quality coking coal. While ordinary coal is plentiful in the world and India has its fair share of it, only Poland and Australia have exportable resources of coking coal which is an essential fuel for blast furnaces. The intense heat it generates helps to suck oxygen from the iron ore. Only three countries in the world have developed the sponge iron process of sucking oxygen from iron ore using ordinary coal in a rotary kiln. One is the US, the other West Germany, and the third India. Tata Steel's research department did it for India.

A considerable saving is the production of Tiscon bars. Tiscon bars possess high-tensile strength but consume 40 per cent less of steel. The cold twisted bars are invaluable for reinforced concrete construction.

The Tata Oil Mills developed its own process of using inedible oils for the manufacture of soaps, thus conserving edible oils for food purposes.

Pathfinding

We do not claim to be more unselfish, more generous or more philanthropic than other people. But we think we started on sound and straightforward business principles, considering the interests of the shareholders our own, and the health and welfare of the employees the sure foundation of our prosperity.

—Jamsetji Tata in 1895

The premier industrial enterprise in India, Tata Steel became the target of many forces who wanted to gain control of its labour. The management, too, learnt as it went along how to handle the largest industrial force any single Indian company had. It took some time before the company settled down to a state of happy industrial relations. Today, the relationship of the workers with their management is a model. Workers and management celebrated on 19 October 1989 sixty years of industrial harmony.

In the course of the early unsettled years many a national figure was associated with the labour front in Tata Steel. Gandhiji came to Jamshedpur with C.R. Das and C.F. Andrews. The company recognized the Jamshedpur Labour Association and C.F. Andrews became its first president. Gandhiji was later to refer to R.D. Tata as a humane and considerate employer who had granted certain requests of his employees. In the years to follow, Subhas Chandra Bose, Dr Rajendra Prasad, Jawaharlal Nehru and V.V. Giri were associated with the industrial relations of the company. At one time Jayaprakash Narayan tried unsuccessfully to gain support of the workers for a socialist trade union. In 1958, the communist leader S.A. Dange made a bid to capture the loyalty of the workers and in spite of a strike caused by inter-union rivalry, he failed to succeed in his objective.

Tatas' tradition of dealing with labour began with the

founder whose attitude was humane though, in keeping with his times, somewhat paternalistic. Even in the late 19th century Jamsetji showed fatherly care for his workers as related earlier.*

When the steel plant came up Sir Dorab Tata wanted labour welfare to be 'one of the first cares' of the employers. The well-known social scientists like Sydney and Beatrice Webb were invited in 1917 to write a memorandum on 'Medical Services in the Welfare Work at Sakchi'.

Although decent housing, sanitation and clean water supply were available at Jamshedpur, there was restlessness and trouble. There were strikes in the steel plant in 1920 and 1922. The most serious of the strikes took place in 1928 lasting from February to September and was led by one called Manek Homi. The strike came at the start of the worldwide economic depression just as Tata Steel was recovering from a serious financial crisis. Subhas Chandra Bose, who had succeeded C.F. Andrews, came on the scene and after a careful study of all aspects of the question, strove for an immediate settlement, honourable both to the company and to labour.

The fighter that he was, Subhas Chandra Bose battled for the workers' rights vigorously. His attitude to management was always one of respect as revealed in his correspondence with them. He comprehended the company's struggle for survival as part of a national struggle. In February 1929 when disruptive activities were afoot, in a public statement on the Jamshedpur situation he thundered forth:

Mr Homi's object as far as I can gather is to stir up the workers to go on strike again. This will no doubt hurt the company and everyone knows that if the company lands itself in losses once again, it may ultimately pass out of Indian hands. But the point is whether labour should be used as an instrument for hurting the company. Jamshedpur as an industrial centre has a special importance because it is an epitome of India and

* See chapter 'The Man and His Vision' in Part One.

people from all the provinces congregate there. It should be the object of every well-wisher of labour to build up an ideal labour organization there. The Company is helping labour not only by recognizing their association but also by collecting monthly subscriptions on pay day on behalf of the Labour Association. The workers undoubtedly have got standing genuine grievances—but we can hope to remove them only by having a strong united Labour Association. By dividing labour, Mr Homi is serving neither labour nor capital. It will be an evil day for India if the whims and manoeuvres of one individual are allowed to undermine a public cause. Jamshedpur labour has to be saved and in order to save labour, the Indian Steel Industry there has to be saved from bankruptcy.

Thanks to Bose's exertions a settlement was brought about and the agitators broke away and started a rival Jamshedpur Labour Federation. During the depression years the unemployment rate in Britain was 2.5 million and in America 6 million. The US Steel Corporation effected a cut of 10 per cent in salary. There was retrenchment of steel workers in the West. Tatas, however, refused to retrench a single person and in 1934 as the world was emerging from the depression, Tatas introduced a profit-sharing bonus scheme.

In 1932 V.V. Giri, later to be the President of India, started a Metals Workers' Union. Though it did useful work, it failed to unite the rival factions. In 1937, Professor Abdul Bari, a man with a volatile temper, was sent by the Congress to organize labour at Jamshedpur. He revelled in rousing labour in a language which he felt they could understand. But when it came to responsible negotiations he made life very difficult for the management. The company invited Dr Rajendra Prasad (later first President of India) and Jawaharlal Nehru (later the first Prime Minister) to arbitrate between the company and the Tata Workers' Union. Their report gently chided the fire-brand union leader, Professor Abdul Bari, whose choice of words for the management was not always the most elegant, although Bari claimed he used it for effect. After Professor Bari's death, Michael John took over and under his responsible leadership labour received many benefits and the company enjoyed an era of industrial peace.

In the 1940s at one of the first post-war meetings of the ILO's Iron and Steel Committee held at Cleveland, USA, a crusading American delegate charged that workers in the Indian steel industry were working under conditions of slavery. K.A.D. Naoroji, who happened to be a delegate to the committee, got up and described how Tata Steel had introduced an eight-hour day in 1912, long before it was accepted in America or Europe. (Under Britain's Factory Bill of 1911 the legal limit was a twelve-hour working day.) Naoroji noted that leave with pay was introduced by Tata Steel in 1920 when it was unknown in either England or the USA. In the same year a provident fund scheme, then little known in British industry, was also introduced, as also was accident compensation.* Naoroji, in addition, observed that free medical and educational facilities were provided to all the workers plus a general bonus and a profit-sharing bonus were introduced more than a decade ago. The American crusader was crestfallen.

The Tata Workers' Union as it is today is the result of the effort of many figures in national life but special credit goes to Michael John, who passed away in 1976. For more than three decades he moulded the union into a powerful constructive force. He was succeeded by V.G. Gopal, who was the general secretary of the union since 1943. Gopal, a former member of Parliament, is a soft-spoken man. He articulates his thoughts with clarity.

Tata Steel pioneered at Jamshedpur a system of joint consultation between management and employees way back in 1956. This is a three-tier system comprising forty-seven Joint Departmental Councils at the base, the Joint Works

* See Appendix D.

Council and the Joint Consultative Council of Management at the apex. In each council, there are an equal number of representatives of management and employees. Only about half a dozen other industries have successfully followed the lead of Tata Steel and established joint departmental councils. The joint councils decide on the entire spectrum of labour and industrial problems except collective bargaining. Wages are in any case settled on a national scale as there are other steel plants.

Industrial relations, working conditions, environment, safety, medical facilities, all these are resolved jointly by labour and management. V.G. Gopal is particularly proud that 'our facilities system has flowed into the public sector.' In 1979 Tata Steel instituted a new practice; a worker is deemed to be 'at work' from the moment he leaves home for work till he returns home from work. The company is financially liable to the worker if any mishap takes place on the way to work or from work to his home.

Management is not the only section that goes in for charitable trusts. Tata Steel workers have their own charitable trust from which employees' families are given assistance for higher education and in the event of personal tragedies in the families. Speaking of all that the workers have achieved, Gopal concludes: 'We are very proud, that is why we are not for nationalization.' When nationalization proposals were aired by a couple of ministers of the Janata government, the Tata Workers' Union passed a resolution in January 1979 to say that 'the company (Tata Steel) has been maintaining a very high level of production, cordial industrial relations over the past several decades, which is the envy of the rest of the country . . . Any disruption in the present system of the working of this company would lead to considerable discontent among the workers leading to a loss of production in the country . . .' In fact, the workers were just ahead of the management in their protest against nationalization.

Such loyalty cannot be purchased at any price.

Every employee realizes that he is not producing for a steel company but for a group that looks after his wife when she is in hospital and looks out for his child at school. The aim is to create a sense of belonging. Thomas Abraham, former secretary to Jayaprakash Narayan, says that once when JP failed in an undertaking in Bihar, he wrote in a letter: 'In Bihar, except the Tatas nobody has ever succeeded, not even the gods.' Maybe it is a blend of various factors, not the least of it the human touch, that has enabled Tatas to succeed. Even so Tata Steel cannot rest on its oars.

From Webb to Schumacher

When Jamsetji Tata was looking for a consultant for his steel works, he searched out the best the world had available at the time—Julian Kennedy in Pittsburgh. Once Jamshedpur came up, his successors enlisted the foremost welfare consultant to plan the social services of the Steel City. As stated earlier, Sydney and Beatrice Webb, pioneer socialists of England, were invited with a team from the London University to give their recommendations on the establishment of social, medical and co-operative services in Jamshedpur. Mr Webb headed a committee of London University professors to plan the welfare services and the execution was taken up by such dedicated Indian social workers as A.V. Thakkar, popularly known as Thakkar Bapa.

In 1918 Tata Steel requested the Servants of India Society for the services of an able labour welfare organizer and they chose Thakkar Bapa. He moved decisively from the start. World War I had resulted in a spurt in prices. With a scheme to eliminate the middleman, he got the company to purchase essential commodities in bulk and ensured that the workers got them at a cheap rate. Next he decided to tackle the Pathan money-lenders who were charging the poor labourers an interest between 75 and 150 per cent. Thakkar Bapa organized a dozen co-operative credit societies for different categories of workers in order to stop this exploitation. 'These societies paid off the Pathans and took upon themselves the entire money-lending business for the benefit of the workers. Within a few months, there was an improvement in the economic condition of the workers. . . The next seven months saw a number of primary schools, sports clubs, children's parks and canteens coming up in Jamshedpur. He also drew up a scheme for airy and open quarters for the entire labour force working for the company and initiated action for its implementation.'*

As the years went by the concept of social services advanced and the steel company realized that the worker's family needed attention, too. Today the company gives prenatal care where the mother's health is checked and deficiencies rectified. At the same time, the ground is prepared for family planning. Jamshedpur repeatedly rates top position for family planning in the state.

Two years before it was officially undertaken by the government, the first urban community development programme was launched by Tata Steel in Jamshedpur in 1958. Now there are twelve community centres. In the morning, the centre helps to look after the little children while the mothers themselves come to learn sewing, stitching and other handicrafts. In the same centre there is a section for the youth. Those who need extra help in physics, chemistry and mathematics are given special coaching free. For women there are adult literacy classes. When evening comes sports are organized, from *kabaddi* and *kho-kho* to basketball, volleyball to football. These games are supervised by referees and some of the coaches are highly trained by the National Sports Institute in Patiala. All these facilities are available to any person in Jamshedpur—not only to families of Tata employees. The company purchases its dusters, gloves, uniforms from these family welfare centres. Perhaps the most moving sight is to see widows and less fortunate among the women learning a trade or earning from a trade. The welfare centres come in touch with a wide cross-section of the people and help to deal with such social evils as the dowry system, and put in touch those families who are against the dowry system. Money-lenders are a scourge who often appear at the time of marriages. The company helps with their

* From *Thakkar Bapa* by Viyogi Hari, Builders of Modern India, Publications Division (1977).

settlement and sometimes uses its authority to deal with those money-lenders who may be unduly exploiting the workers.

The needs of the retired are not neglected. They are invited to assist in teaching trades to the younger ones of *bustees* who otherwise would be wasting their time. Trades like machining, plumbing, air-conditioning, car maintenance and so on are taught. Some are absorbed ultimately in Jamshedpur and others elsewhere in the industrial belt of eastern India which is rich in coal and iron ore.

Special care is given to the mentally retarded children. There are seventy such children in Jamshedpur's School of Hope. The ratio of teachers to pupils is very high—one for every five. Teachers are sent for advanced training by Tata Steel to special institutions in Bombay and Bangalore. The latent skills of these children could also contribute to the wealth of the nation, if they are trained.

In 1970 major Tata companies incorporated into their Memorandum and Articles of Association a clause on their social obligations to consumers, employees, shareholders, society and the local community. In furtherance of that, various Tata companies have launched plans for assistance to their neighbouring areas. Tata Steel assists a total of 276 villages in the neighbourhood of Jamshedpur and of its far-flung mines of coal and iron ore. The village projects include agriculture, dairy and poultry farming, piggery, cottage industries, horticulture and forestry. Tata Steel is the first Indian company to have a social audit of its activities by a small group of personalities whose judgement and views command nationwide respect and confidence. The committee consisted of the former Chief Justice of Bombay, S.P. Kotwal, as chairman and professors P.G. Mavalankar and Rajni Kothari as members.

Tata Steel's Rural Development Society has a training school near Dimna to give training in craft and agriculture to the villagers. The society has found that tribal women are more responsible than tribal men in the operation of co-

operative societies for their village products which the company helps to market.

On the fringe of Jamshedpur is a settlement of the Kalindi tribe who live in a village called 'Bhalubasa'. 'Bhalu' means bear and 'basa' means home. Sixty years ago wild bears roamed there. Now the bears have retreated to a respectable distance in the Dalma Hills. The social service wing of Tata Steel found that this tribe was traditionally good at cane-weaving. The company established a small building and co-operative society. It brought one of the best known weavers of Patna, Bhupendra Mahatre, to develop the skills of the weavers. Individuals in the village produce exquisite and useful cane items and sell them through the co-operative. An investment of Rs 50,000 in a lathe can give employment to only one man. Tatas' investment in this enterprise was a negligible Rs 18,000 which has resulted in 250 individuals finding employment and an outlet for their skills. The late E.F. Schumacher, author of *Small is Beautiful*, would have rejoiced to see so many people so gainfully employed, with such little investment. A large house had helped the small man.

14

BEYOND BUSINESS*

The Tata Trusts

The concept of trusteeship fostered by Mahatma Gandhi received a much needed fillip in Tata enterprises. After all what is this concept of trusteeship? Under it all wealth is a social trust and every individual—the employer, the engineer or even the ordinary mistry—is a trustee entitled to its proper utilization for the common good. True to the ideals of its founder, the House of Tata has always promoted this concept of trusteeship and today more than 85 per cent of its profits go to trusts.

—Jayaprakash Narayan

'Trusteeship' was a by-product of the desire Jamsetji Tata and his sons had to tackle the needs of the nation. Their wider concern made them look beyond their business interests. For example, when Swami Vivekananda spoke of the rise of the ascetic spirit in the country, Jamsetji Tata (who had met him aboard a ship) wrote him in 1898 suggesting 'the establishment of monasteries for men dominated by this spirit, where they could devote their lives to the cultivation of sciences—natural and humanistic.' He offered to 'cheerfully defray all the expenses of publication' for a pamphlet by Vivekananda and doubtless would have financed a monastery or two.

Jamsetji Tata had a burning zeal to pitchfork his country among the great industrial nations of the world. His schemes

---

* It is advisable to read this chapter along with the chapter 'Tata Philanthropy' in Section B.

for steel, hydro-electric power and the institute of science were geared to this one aim. So was his passion to train young Indians. In 1892 he started giving scholarships to deserving students for higher studies abroad. Jamsetji said: 'Though I can afford to give, I prefer to lend.' Thereby students, after they qualified, could return the loans and thus help others to go in for higher studies with the same funds.

Once the ranks of the Indian Civil Service were opened to Indians, Jamsetji was eager that enough Indians reached the highest ranks of administration. And a fair number of scholarships were awarded to ICS aspirants who had to travel to England. In 1924 it was calculated that out of every five Indian ICS officials, one was a Tata scholar.

It is the measure of a man who lived ahead of his times that he pioneered higher education among women. The first name in his register for scholarships in 1892 was that of a lady medical doctor, Miss Freny K.R. Cama. She was loaned in those days Rs 10,000 which in terms of today's money is worth thirty times the amount. She returned as one of India's pioneer gynaecologists. In 1902 an agreement was signed with Krishnabai Kelavkar, who went on to become FRCS, Dublin. On a single page of the register of the J.N. Tata Endowment Fund for the period 1905 to 1909 appear the names of the following scholars: A.R. Dalal, who became director of Tata Sons and a member of the Viceroy's Executive Council; J.C. Coyaji, later Chief Justice of the Bombay High Court; B.N. Rao, ICS who rose to be a judge of the International High Court at The Hague; Dr Jivraj N. Mehta, eminent physician and chief minister of Gujarat. Later scholars included nuclear scientist Dr Raja Ramanna, economist Dr V.K.R.V. Rao and the future President of India, K.R. Narayanan. The last three were also ministers in the Union Government.

The register bears brief interesting remarks on the candidates, occasionally on their travails and their performance. In 1915-16, S. Ranganathan stood third in the

ICS examination. In the remarks column, alongside his name, the trust authorities solemnly note: 'All clothes stolen from his trunk at Marseilles. Fresh sum sanctioned by the Trustees for new clothes.' A host of distinguished civil servants to be given study loans by the trust includes C.M. Trivedi, S. Bhoothalingam and V.T. Dehejia.

In one case both father and son have been Tata scholars. In 1928 V.V. Narlikar was given a scholarship to study applied mathematics at Fitzwilliam House, Cambridge. In 1957 his son, J.V. Narlikar, was given a scholarship for the mathematical tripos at the same Fitzwilliam House. The Hoyle-Narlikar theory expounded at Cambridge was a product of this scholarship.

From 1977, as a tribute to the founder, some major companies of the Tata group have made annual contributions to enable J.N. Tata Endownment to select a larger number of Tata Scholars and to augment the amount of the awards. For brilliant students it is not just a question of obtaining the finance needed for study abroad. There is a prestige attached to being 'a Tata Scholar' and on the strength of it many a scholar has gained admission in universities abroad. Currently about 2,000 apply. About 300 are called for the interview with a panel of experts in their course of study. They must qualify with conspicuous distinction throughout their career and be under twenty-seven years of age to be J.N. Tata Scholars. About 100 are selected each year. A decade later the numbers of those applying are 3,000, called for interview 600 and selected are upto 150.

Jamsetji was fortunate in his sons. His younger son, Sir Ratan Tata, sensed the importance of the work of Gopal Krishna Gokhale in India, and of the then little-known Mohandas Karamchand Gandhi in South Africa.

For a number of years Sir Ratan supported Gokhale with generous contributions. Able men renounced their ambitions to serve in Gokhale's Servants of India Society. On 19 October 1909, referring to Sir Ratan Tata's help to the society,

Gokhale wrote of 'the deep gratitude I feel for your overwhelming generosity to my Society. There is no parallel to it anywhere in the country. I can only say that members of the Society will ever cherish your name as that of their greatest benefactor.'

Sir Ratan contributed to Gandhiji's campaign for racial equality in South Africa, a sum of Rs 1,25,000—not a negligible amount for those days. Sir Ratan wanted the best institution in the world to do research into the causes of poverty and its alleviation. In the last six years of his life he gave each year £1,400 to the London School of Economics for this purpose. The trustees continued the donation some years after his death. It led to the establishment of the Sir Ratan Tata Department in 1912, now called the Department of Social Sciences at the school.*

In 1913, the London School of Economics advertised for applicants for a lecturer for the Ratan Tata Department. Only two applied. One was a young man called Clement Attlee and the other was called Hugh Dalton. The authorities 'after very careful consideration' selected C.R. Attlee for the post. Thirty-two years later Attlee became the Prime Minister of Britain, and Dr Hugh Dalton was to be a Chancellor of the Exchequer in the Attlee Cabinet. In 1947, as chance would have it, it was under Attlee's government that India was granted independence.

In *100 Great Modern Lives* edited by John Canning (Souvenir Press, London), in the galaxy of personalities only two Indians feature—Mohandas Karamchand Gandhi and Jamsetji Tata. The chapter on Jamsetji Tata concludes with the paragraph: 'Probably no other family has ever contributed

---

* Listed in the library of the London School of Economics are publications of the Ratan Tata Foundation, and they include some early surveys on the 'Feeding of School Children' and 'Casual Labour in the Docks'. Among the researchers were R.H. Tawney and Arthur Greenwood. These were pioneer studies of their kind.

as much in the way of wise guidance, industrial development and advancing philanthropy to any country as the Tatas have to India, both before and since independence.'

Sir Ratan and Sir Dorab Tata established pioneering trusts geared to building the educational, social and scientific infrastructure of this nation. At a time when most charities were only communal in nature, the Sir Ratan Tata Trust (1918) and the Sir Dorabji Tata Trust (1932) established a precedent of being universal in their generosity. The Anjuman-i-Islam or a Hindu institution could lay as much claim on its resources as any Parsi charity could—and they did.

Sir Dorab was particularly clear on this point, mentioning in his deed of trust that 'without any distinction of place, nationality or creed', the trust should institute, maintain and support schools, educational institutes, hospitals and offer relief in cases of distress caused by natural disasters. He also stressed 'the advancement of learning in all its branches especially research work in connection with medical and industrial problems.'

The trustees of Sir Dorabji Tata Trust followed the example set by the founder of Tatas, Jamsetji Tata, who had planned the Indian Institute of Science in Bangalore as a pioneering institution to provide the country with the trained personnel needed to man its future factories and laboratories. In addition to giving grants liberally each year for the advancement of learning and the relief of distress caused by natural disasters such as floods or drought, the trustees established some major institutions of a pioneering character, like the Tata Institute of Social Sciences (1936), the Tata Memorial Centre for Cancer Research and Treatment (1941), and the Tata Institute of Fundamental Research (1945), conceived by Dr Homi Bhabha, which became the cradle of India's atomic energy programme.

After an interval of twenty years, one of the trustees, Jamshed Bhabha, proposed that the resources of the trust which had hitherto been reserved for the fields of medicine,

The Tata Theatre, National Centre for the Performing Arts, Bombay

science and technology, should also be channelled into the area of the arts and humanities where there was a pressing need for a pioneering institution. Although music has for centuries been an indispensable part of the culture and civilization of India, it has no form of notation such as makes possible the preservation of western music in the form of printed music scores. Its survival has depended entirely on oral tradition and master-pupil links. This has been jeopardized in the last fifty years by the disappearance of old sources of patronage which had assured a source of livelihood for the great masters and teachers, and since the independence of India by the creation of new job opportunities in business and industry which tended to draw the brighter children of artistes away from traditional family vocations.

In 1966, by virtue of the support of J.R.D. Tata, the Trustees adopted Jamshed Bhabha's project for a National Centre for the Performing Arts. In addition to a programme of large-scale archival recording of classical and folk music and the sustenance of the *Gurukula* (master-pupil) system through the medium of master-classes, the centre has constructed India's first national theatre—the Tata Theatre. Since then the Jamshed Bhabha Theatre has opened.

In the decade of the 1980s Sir Dorabji Tata Trust has played a leading role in establishing the Centre for the Advancement of Philanthropy in Bombay, to assist the formation of new trusts and the functioning of the existing ones. The centre publishes its own journal, *Philanthropy*, the only one of its kind in India. The trust also conceived India's first helpline for drug addicts and assisted Kripa Foundation to launch it in Bombay. At the initiative of the trust the first directory of facilities available in an Indian city for the treatment and rehabilitation of drug addicts was compiled and published by the Tata Institute of Social Sciences.

Every few years Sir Dorabji Tata Trust has a tradition of setting up a major innovative project. Professor Rustom Choksi who had handled with distinction Sir Dorabji Tata

Trust for four decades noted that:

> What distinguishes a Trust is not its ability to give or the extent or range of its giving but the character of its giving. It is important for a Trust to maintain its 'pioneering' character and this can only be done adequately where from time to time a Trust initiates and fosters new institutions and new types of service to society. For a great Trust the large project, carefully designed and executed, must always be a major objective. Even in the routine giving of grants and donations the Trust must constantly bear in mind the 'pioneering' factor.

In pursuance of this policy Sir Dorabji Tata Trust started in 1989 the National Institute of Advanced Studies with Dr Raja Ramanna, former chairman, Atomic Energy Commission, as its director.

Very often the two trusts of Sir Dorab and Sir Ratan move hand in hand. The Sir Ratan Tata Trust took the primary responsibility for erecting the J.N. Tata Memorial Centre at Navsari, giving the birthplace of Jamsetji a civic centre, an auditorium and a library. To the Sir Ratan Tata Trust's initial donation of Rs 25 lakh, the Sir Dorabji Tata Trust and a number of Tata companies happily joined in taking the figure to Rs 55 lakh. The industrial house of Mafatlal made a contribution of Rs 5 lakh for the gardens.

Sir Dorab Tata gave his trustees considerable latitude to take up new projects to meet changing situations.* Many of these earlier contributions were made in the 1930s and 1940s when the value of the rupee was ten to twenty-five times that of today.

---

* This includes establishment of the Tata Memorial Centre; the Tata Institute of Social Sciences; the National Centre for the Performing Arts; the Rural Welfare Board; the Tata Institute of Fundamental Research and the National Institute for Advanced Studies.

The two trusts and their outreach reflect the different personalities of the two brothers. Sir Dorab, the elder brother, was a domineering, efficient, industrial magnate. It was he who pioneered in bullock-carts the search for iron ore and built up the steel plant and other industrial ventures.

Sir Ratan Tata, as his photograph shows, was a sensitive and artistic personality, interested in paintings, sculpture, archaeology and the like. In his will he noted:

Sir Ratan Tata

If I leave no children, I give the rest or the residue of my property . . . for the advancement of education, learning and industry in all its branches including education in economy, sanitary science and art or for the relief of human suffering or for other works of public utility . . . Such work is not (to be) undertaken from a stereotyped point of view but from the point of view of fresh light that is thrown from day to day by the advance of science and philosophy on problems of human well-being.

Sir Ratan died in 1918 at the age of forty-eight, leaving behind his widow, Lady Navajbai Tata, who was to outlive him by forty-four years. The residue of his property amounted to Rs 81 lakh. Although the Sir Ratan Tata Trust has contributed significantly to the great institutes launched by the Sir Dorabji Tata Trust, Sir Ratan had a very distinct personality of his own that reflects his sensitivity to the suffering of mankind. The Ratan Tata Industrial Institute is well known for providing women from lower income groups a framework for a decent livelihood.

The trust has spread itself out contributing generously to homes for the homeless, hospitals, outpatient dispensaries, village schools, blind schools and the like. The National Metallurgical Laboratory received the major grant of Rs 12 lakh from the Sir Ratan Tata Trust while the National Centre for the Performing Arts and the Tata Institute of Social Sciences have each received about Rs 10 lakh from it. Other beneficiaries have been the Indian Institute of Science at Bangalore, the Delhi School of Economics and the Bombay University. Incidentally, Sir Ratan's art collection which included works by European masters, worth a fortune now, was donated to the Prince of Wales Museum, Bombay, where it is housed in a special wing along with the art collection of Sir Dorab Tata. The Tata collection was one of the first major gifts which enabled the museum to be launched and Tatas have a representation on its board.

A distinctive aspect of these Tata trusts is that in recent years the Tata enterprises have undergirded the initiative of the Tata trusts as has happened with the National Centre for the Performing Arts.

There are other Tata trusts that have made their own contribution. Among them are:

The Lady Tata Memorial Trust was started in 1932 by Sir Dorab Tata in memory of his wife, Lady Meherbai Tata, who died of leukaemia. In those days very few were engaged in leukaemia research and the Lady Tata Memorial Trust made its impact as an early comer on the world stage. The trust promotes research principally by means of international awards in addition to a fifth of its income being allotted for Indian awards. Its advisory committee in London has eminent European experts on its board. At a symposium on leukaemia held by Ciba in London in 1953, it was found that of the world experts who had assembled, more than a third had secured support from the trust at one stage or another in their career. It may be mentioned that this trust's funds for leukaemia research rose to £90,000 annually for foreign scholars alone in the 1980s.

Lady Meherbai D. Tata Education Trust (1932) also established by Sir Dorab Tata in memory of his wife, has so far disbursed Rs 11 lakh to enable women graduates to proceed abroad to study social work.

The J.R.D. Tata Trust, established in 1944, is a multipurpose trust for the advancement of learning and the relief of human suffering. It has disbursed over a crore of rupees.

The Jamsetji Tata Trust (1974) was designed to assist innovative projects and has expended considerable sums for the rehabilitation of the blind and for helping the aged. Recently it has started giving grants to J.N. Tata Scholars who receive loans from the J.N. Tata Endowment. These grants have been made possible by generous donations to the corpus of the trust by the leading Tata companies from their operating profits.

The Homi Bhabha Fellowships Council (established in 1966) is sponsored jointly by the Tata trusts and the Ford Foundation.

The last of these was launched in 1966 in memory of Dr Homi Bhabha. The programme was not for higher formal studies but for the promotion of excellence in any field of endeavour, be it research in arts, literature, social sciences, economics or technology. A handsome scholarship—and where required travelling allowance plus equipment—is also provided. Amongst its fifty recipients to date are Girish Karnad, a well-known name in the field of drama and films; Arun Shourie, the eminent journalist who is a Cabinet Minister now and the well-known journalist Prem Shankar Jha.

When the crunch of the energy crisis hit the world in 1974, Tatas, spearheaded by Tata Chemicals, founded the Tata Energy Research Institute (TERI).

In order to ensure a quick take-off, TERI identified and sponsored numerous energy research projects in various national institutions. In addition, it has set up a very large documentation centre and is supporting projects of energy scientists in the country.

The trusts have also been pioneers of rural uplift, having launched the major programme at Maan Taluka in Maharashtra in 1953 at about the same time when the government launched its Five Year Plans. Tatas' programmes of relief of distress started in 1934 with the Bihar earthquake and relief programmes have been continuous in a vast land afflicted frequently by ravages of nature plus the cruelty and indifference of man to his fellowman.

Between themselves the Tata trusts have created an infrastructure for the balanced development of the nation in science, technology and the social sciences. They have launched pace-setting institutions that have given India its first institute for social sciences, its first cancer hospital and research centre, and its first institute for fundamental research in physics and mathematics that gave India a head-on start in its atomic energy programme.*

---

* See chapter 'Tata Philanthropy' in Section B.

The Tata Institute of Fundamental Research, Bombay

Cradle of Atomic Energy

It is not an exaggeration to say that this institute was the cradle of our atomic energy programme, and if an atomic energy establishment at Trombay has been able to develop so fast, it is due to the assisted take-off which was given to it by the institute in the early stages of its development. It is equally true to say that the institute could not have developed to its present size and importance, but for the support it has received from the Government of India.

—Dr Homi Bhabha

In Colaba, south Bombay, stands the Tata Institute of Fundamental Research, an island of beauty near a concrete jungle of skyscrapers. Its spacious green lawns, its majestic trees, its spotless main building adorned with one of the finest collections of modern Indian art, seems a world in itself, a peaceful haven. In this setting four hundred highly qualified scientists work on the frontier regions of science. They research in pure mathematics, in pure and applied physics and related fields. Conceived as a 'Centre of Excellence', it still is one.

The institute was born due to the vision of Dr Homi Bhabha who had returned to India at the outbreak of World War II, after a distinguished career at Cambridge. At thirty-one, Dr Bhabha was elected a Fellow of the Royal Society, the second youngest scientist ever to be so honoured. He was then in charge of cosmic ray research at the Indian Institute of Science, Bangalore.

On 19 August 1943, Homi Bhabha wrote to J.R.D. Tata that 'lack of proper conditions and intelligent financial support hampers the development of science in India at the pace which the talent in the country would warrant.' He mentioned that he himself had the idea of accepting at the end of the World War II a job at Cambridge or Princeton but had come to the view that provided proper facilities were available, 'it is one's duty to stay in one's own country' and build up schools comparable to those of other countries. In an encouraging reply J.R.D. Tata wrote: '. . . if you and/or some of your colleagues in the scientific world will put up concrete proposals backed by a sound case, I think there is a very good chance that the Tata trusts would respond.' Spurred by Mr Tata's reply Dr Bhabha sent a formal letter to the chairman of the Sir Dorabji Tata Trust on 12 March 1944.

Sitting in Bangalore with only the knowledge that nuclear fission had been discovered, he wrote to the trustees of his proposal for an Institute of Fundamental Research in Bombay, so that 'when nuclear energy has been successfully applied for power production, in say a couple of decades from now, India will not have to look abroad for its experts but will find them ready at hand.' This letter was written eighteen months before the first atomic bomb exploded and the world awakened to the power of nuclear energy.

The Sir Dorabji Tata Trust cleared Dr Bhabha's request after interviewing him. Very wisely the trust included from the beginning the Central and state governments in the venture. In June 1945 the institute opened at Bangalore and soon shifted to Bombay. It was first housed in a modest bungalow with only 6,000 sq. ft. It grew rapidly and moved to the Yacht Club with its 35,000 sq. ft. of space and in 1962 to its present magnificent premises with 3,25,900 sq. ft. The Union Government was quick to realize the importance of the institute and each year came in with a larger proportion of the expense till it took full responsibility for the institute with Tatas on its governing council. J.R.D. Tata has been the chairman.

When the Atomic Energy establishment was started at Trombay, the Tata Institute of Fundamental Research (TIFR) had already prepared a pool of highly qualified scientists and techniques ready for service. One of the first tasks the TIFR undertook for the Atomic Energy Commission was the setting up of a small group to design and build electronic instruments without which work in atomic science is not possible. 'The control system of "Apsara", the first reactor in Asia, was built under the auspices of this institute in a wartime hutment, and many parts of the reactor in the institute's workshop,' Dr Bhabha noted.

Laying the foundation stone of the new buildings of the TIFR in late 1953, the Prime Minister Jawaharlal Nehru paid a tribute to Tatas for the advancement of science in India:

'They have a vision to look ahead without the profit motive. I might add a word of appreciation of the tradition of Tatas for their pioneering spirit in formulating such beneficial schemes.' With the support of Jawaharlal Nehru, the TIFR grew to gigantic proportions. The Union Government, which finances it, has retained the institute as an autonomous body, which still bears the stamp of the man who started it.

The contribution of the institute goes far beyond the field of atomic energy. It has done pioneering work in cosmic rays. In 1954, only three isotopes produced by cosmic rays in the atmosphere were known. In the following five years, eight other isotopes were detected. Out of them five were discovered as a result of investigations carried out by members of the institute, especially Professor Lal.

For research in frontier areas of x-ray, gamma ray, infra-red astronomy and study of atomic sciences, the USA developed the technology of manufacturing plastic balloons which it tracked optically and by radio, thousands of feet in the air. Quite independently, for purposes of cosmic ray research the TIFR developed its own balloon technology in the late fifties and early sixties, when information in this technology was still classified by the western countries. TIFR polyethylene balloons were capable of carrying scientific payloads of 100 kgs over 1,00,000 ft. Today TIFR's balloon facility at Hyderabad carries ten times that payload up to an altitude of 38 kilometres. The facility is used not only by

A Polyethylene Balloon

national laboratories and universities in India for their research but also by foreign countries like Japan.

With no other country has the TIFR such a prolonged collaboration as with Japan over the last three decades. It has come about as a result of the collaboration of two distinguished scientists, one from Japan and another from India meeting in the 1950s at the MIT. They were working with Professor Bruno Rossi who was researching in cosmic rays. The Indian, B.V. Sreekantan, who later rose to be director of the TIFR, says:

> Minoru Oda and I got to know each other well. We had a lot to discuss and on return to Japan, Oda started the Air Shower Project at the Institute of Nuclear Studies in Tokyo and I started the Air Shower Project at Ooty (Ootacamund).

The collaboration started with Professor Sabura Miyake of Osaka City University in 1960s. He was the first in the world to record spectacular pictures of central parts of cosmic ray air showers going through his large cloud chamber. The TIFR was engaged in a deep underground expedition in the Kolar gold fields with the deepest mine in the world. Miyake came to the Kolar mine to work at 9,000 ft below sea level. Miyake then helped TIFR to design the world's largest multiplate cloud chamber still operating at Ootacamund.

Another major project of Proton Decay was taken up as an Indo-Japanese collaboration in 1979. Collaboration in other fields like higher mathematics have proved extremely rewarding to both. 'Though the language,' says Dr Sreekantan 'was a problem in the early years, it is no longer so since English is now spoken and understood by a majority of (Japanese) scientists.'

If cosmic rays is a frontier area in physics, cancer is in the field of medicine. While western countries have a higher incidence of colon cancer, Indians have a higher incidence of mouth cancer.

The TIFR's dental unit has undertaken a major programme for the eventual control of mouth cancer. It has made a detailed study of 1,50,000 cases in five states undertaking a laboratory examination of the lesions and has kept records with pictures. A twenty-year follow-up of 66,000 individuals has been completed. This study has shown that it is feasible to educate villagers to stop their tobacco chewing and smoking and this would have significant impact on the risk of oral cancer. Seldom has such a long term study been undertaken in any part of the world. This study was financed by the National Institute of Health in Washington for thirty years and led by the late Dr Fali Mehta. His deputy, Dr Dinesh Daftary, says the findings of this study have resulted in a number of papers in journals. 'Oral cancer is the only cancer that is preventable for pre-cancer lesions can be easily detected and are in a reversible condition and targetable. Alas, India has no national programme that works on it.'

At Ootacamund, set in the picturesque Nilgiri Hills, TIFR has its large cylindrical parabolic radio telescope. Its gathering power is four times that of the 250 ft 'dish' telescope at Jodrell Bank in England. Placed near the geographical equator, its observations are of interest to astronomers all over the world. It is so poised that its axis of rotation coincides with that of the earth. It is built with indigenous know-how by Tata consulting engineers.

A Giant Metrewave Radio Telescope (GMRT) is being set up by TIFR as a national facility at Khodad, 80 km north of Pune. The academic headquarters of the GMRT is to be located in the University of Pune campus.

When completed in 1992, GMRT will become the most powerful facility in the world for astronomical research in the metre and decimetre wave-bands.* It is being designed to investigate a wide variety of celestial objects, reaching from

* It has come up since. For further information please see chapter 'Tata Philanthropy' in Section B.

our solar system to the very edge of the observable universe. An important scientific goal will be to verify the prediction of the Big Bang model for the origin of the universe. This telescope will search for massive neutral hydrogen clouds which are expected to have existed some 15 billion years ago, prior to the formation of galaxies, according to the Big Bang model of the origin of the universe.

A seed sown by a Tata trust and a man with a vision has put India in the front rank of scientific advance.

A Chance to Live

This hospital will become a spearhead of the attack on cancer in this country, providing not only a centre where specialized treatment can be given, but also one from which the knowledge of new methods of treatment and diagnosis will go out to doctors and hospitals throughout the country.
—Sir Roger Lumley, Governor of Bombay, inaugurating the Tata Memorial Hospital in 1941

The idea of India's first cancer hospital was born on a ship sailing in the Pacific Ocean. Two passengers were chatting on board. One was Dr John Spies, head of the cancer service of the Union Medical College in Peking, China. The other was Sir Nowroji Saklatvala, who had succeeded Sir Dorab as chairman of Tata Sons and of Sir Dorabji Tata's Trust. Dr Spies was one of the first resident doctors of New York's Memorial Sloan-Kettering Cancer Centre, a pioneer institute in the United States. He had the know-how. Tatas had the vision backed by resources.

Sir Nowroji mentioned to Dr Spies the late Sir Dorab Tata's thought to establish a radium institute in Bombay. Sir Dorab's wife Meherbai had died of cancer. Sir Dorab had left his wealth in a substantial trust. Dr Spies was invited to India. The American doctor felt that the idea of a radium institute or an additional wing to a Bombay hospital was too modest and would in the long run prove ineffective. In his report he stated to the trustees: 'The best interests of the cancer patient demand that all effective methods of treatment be made available at one place, so that a judicious choice of a well-considered combination of methods may give to such a patient his best chance of a cure, or failing that, his best chance of life and the relief of pain.'

The trustees accepted the findings and began preparations

for building and equipping India's first cancer hospital—the Tata Memorial. They sent the best young doctors and nurses they could find for training abroad. Entire facilities for surgery, x-ray, radium, research and education were made available under the one roof of a seven-storeyed building at Parel, Bombay.

For nine years it was the only hospital of its kind in this part of the world, till another was opened at Calcutta with the help of a patient cured at the Tata Memorial Hospital in Bombay. Then, as now, patients flocked to the Tata Memorial from Afghanistan, Pakistan, Burma, Sri Lanka, the Arabian peninsula and the entire sea-board of eastern Africa.

The Bombay government contributed after some time Rs 1 lakh per year, but Tatas bore the brunt of the expenses with 75 per cent of the beds being free of any charge. Eighty thousand patients from India and abroad were treated in the fifteen years that Tatas ran the hospital. By 1957 Sir Dorabji Tata Trust had poured Rs 1 crore into the hospital which on a modest estimate is about fifteen times in terms of modern

Tata Memorial Hospital

value. The cost can be estimated but not the value of the investment. For who can measure the joy in the heart of a wife or a mother to see her loved one and the breadwinner recover and return home?

By 1957, Tatas realized that the demands on the hospital were enormous. They had to choose between holding down the growth of the hospital or to invite expansion. And the one source that could expand it beyond Tatas, was the government.

In May 1957, Tatas handed over the hospital to the nation. At first the Union Ministry of Health ran it but found it impractical to continue its support. With all its commitments, the Ministry of Health could not put behind an institution of a special character like the Tata Memorial the weight needed for its sustained growth. Fortunately, Dr Homi Bhabha was apprised of the matter. Taking as a precedent the US Atomic Energy Commission, which ran four cancer research hospitals in the US, he approached the Prime Minister, Jawaharlal Nehru, and persuaded him that the Atomic Energy Department should take over the running of the hospital. The

Prime Minister gave his assent and since then a more orderly development has been ensured. Today its budget is Rs 16 crore a year and annually 18,000 patients are actually treated for cancer.* The initiative of Dr D.J. Jussawalla and his colleagues at the Tata Memorial resulted in the Indian Cancer Society being formed in 1951. It conducts its own programmes of detection, chemotherapy, cytology and rehabilitation. The society also runs India's journal on cancer research.

Significant laboratory research takes place at the Cancer Research Institute of Tata Memorial.

To relieve the pressure on the hospital the Dr Borges Memorial Home was developed at Bandra, a suburb of Bombay, to house up-country patients who have to visit the hospital for radiotherapy and chemotherapy. Free transport is provided for the patients.

Tata Memorial's greatest problem is over-crowding. For its golden jubilee (1991) the Atomic Energy Commission financed a huge annexe at the rear of the existing two buildings. Apart from enabling better patient care the new building houses facilities for services like cancer prevention, education and screening of high-risk population.

On the occasion of the golden jubilee, seventy outstanding cancer specialists of the world participated in seminars and workshops at the Tata Memorial Hospital providing a stimulus not only to the staff of the centre but to young professionals from all over the country.

In 1994 India will play host to the 16th International Cancer Congress, an invitation for which was extended by Tata Memorial on behalf of India. At Vashi, New Bombay, on 60 acres of land provided by CIDCO will rise a complex for cancer treatment, education and research, the like of which can be compared with the best anywhere in the world. Perhaps a decade from now when the complex is completed it may become a university for cancer research, education and treatment.

---

* Covered in the chapter 'Tata Philanthropy' in Section B.

Most of the significant advances of the 1980's have come about under the leadership of Tata Memorial's chief surgeon and director, Dr Praful Desai.*

Dr Desai says: 'Cancer is very much a disease of our habits, attitudes and lifestyle. Nearly 50 per cent of cancers are a direct result of our lifestyle. A third of all cancers occur in the mouth, throat, tongue and food pipe, owing to tobacco-chewing and smoking . . . Over a period of the last ten years the Tata Memorial has tried to act as a catalyst for efforts to cope with cancer in the country. My colleagues and I will strive our utmost to pass on this legacy to the future.'

On a personal note Dr Praful Desai says that thirty years of cancer surgery 'has changed my attitude to life, because now I understand how beautiful life is as I have seen death at very close quarters. I have also learnt to live life very intensely.'

Perhaps other doctors at Tata Memorial have also sensed how beautiful life is—not only for themselves but for their patients too. That may explain why most of them work way beyond their office hours, struggling to save lives.

* Dr K.A. Dinshaw is director of Tata Memorial Hospital since 1997. She was president of the International Society of Radiation Oncology.

The Tata Institute of Social Sciences, Bombay

Putting People Before Things

The importance of social workers was felt when India was witnessing the birth pangs of Independence. So major was the upheaval of the partition of the subcontinent in 1947 that frantic appeals came for help to re-settle, and soothe the hurts of the refugees. A trained band of twenty social workers left the Tata Institute of Social Sciences for the Kurukshetra refugee camp. Prime Minister Nehru appreciated the help. 'We found,' he said, 'the difference in their work and the work of many others who were earnest and had done their best but who did not have the training to do it well.' In place of mere sentiment, a scientific approach was introduced to social problems in India. As with atomic energy, so also with social work, Tatas had anticipated the demands of the country and established a pioneering institution now known as the Tata Institute of Social Sciences. Till Independence it was the only one of its kind on the Indian subcontinent.

The institute was the first project of the Sir Dorabji Tata Trust. In 1936, the Sir Dorabji Tata Graduate School of Social Work was established as a result of a recommendation to the trustees by an American social worker, Dr Clifford Manshardt, then director of the Nagpada Neighbourhood House, a social service centre in Bombay. He felt the urgency of training social workers, making then competent enough to deal with the complex problems that confronted one in the field. Though envisaged as 'an outstanding scholastic institution,' Dr Manshardt, who was appointed the first director of the school said, 'it will place men above books. It will seek to make men who are at present willing to do social work, actually competent to do social work.'

Establishing the institute was an uphill task. The first labour welfare officers were trained there. Employers in those days looked upon labour welfare as a matter of charity. Some far-sighted units like the Khatau Mills opened their doors for this service. It was in 1948 that legislation made it compulsory for all units with 500 and more workers to have a welfare officer. Thus, the concept of labour welfare in India directly evolved from the work of the Sir Dorabji Tata Graduate School.

The first Child Guidance Clinic in the country was established by the institute. The institute also offers a degree in personnel management and industrial relations and this is one of the most popular programmes offered by the institute. It has extended its activities in various fields of social work like criminology and correctional administration (including juvenile delinquency), family and child welfare, medical and psychiatric social work, social welfare administration, urban and rural community development. Some of the programmes, such as those for tribal welfare and rural community development, were organized to meet the anticipated needs of new governmental activities in these fields.

At any one time about eighty urban and rural research projects are being processed under contract for various U.N. Organizations such as UNICEF, WHO and ILO, the World Bank, and the Union and state governments of India. In fifty-four years the institute has completed 310 research projects. As the first and the premier institute of social sciences, it has the finest library in the field with 80,000 volumes. It subscribes to 500 journals. It has been publishing the *Indian Journal of Social Work* for the last five decades and its publication department has published over sixty books.

To ensure that the institute is in touch with the latest techniques, it has recently set up its own audio-visual and electronic data processing units.

The original name of the institute, the Sir Dorabji Tata Graduate School of Social Work, was changed to the Tata Institute of Social Sciences in 1944. From the 1960s greater emphasis was put on social science by its then director, Dr M.S. Gore. Eight research units were formed over the next several decades including one on urban and rural studies.

More recently, the government of Maharashtra has gifted the institute 100 acres for a rural campus to extend the thrust of the institute in rural training, field work and research. It has acquired ten acres near its present location in Chembur as a gift from the late Mrs Malati Jal A.D. Naoroji to extend the present campus.

The institute's contribution extends way beyond the training of its own students. It organizes scores of special courses for training of officials of the IAS, the Indian Police Service, the Indian Prison Service and other services and organizations. The staff of the institute works on policy-making bodies like the National Police Commission, the Jail Reforms Committee, and commissions for women, and helps to provide the inputs the policy-makers need.

The present director, Dr Armaity S. Desai, inherited from her predecessor Dr Gore a solid foundation of social research. In turn she has given the institute a thrust at the field level concentrating on the poor and the disadvantaged to develop strategies for their well-being. The field action projects include:

(1) Children: child labour; street children; co-ordination among agencies providing child welfare services and day-care.
(2) Women: marital conflict, desertion, divorce and family violence. The institution runs two cells in Bombay, including one at the police commissioner's headquarters, to help women who are battered, maltreated or thrown out of their homes.
(3) Tribal development.
(4) Rural development.
(5) The growing malaise of drug addiction.

In some ways an institute of this nature has to provide not only a training ground but also has to function as the social conscience of a nation.

An Oasis

*At the best of times it (Maan) is barren and desolate,
sparsely wooded even near the river . . . The ordinary
sources of water supply are wretchedly precarious even
for drinking . . . The rains consist chiefly of periodical
thunderstorms with intervals of incessant wind and dust
tempered with an occasional drizzle . . . The area of
black soil is small and owing to the scanty rain and
want of water works, what black soil there is yields
but little . . . Maan is subject to constant droughts.*
—The Gazetteer of Bombay Presidency (Vol. XIX)

In 1952 Professor D.R. Gadgil, heading an advisory
committee for the Sir Dorab Tata Trust, recommended this
inhospitable area referred to above as the focal point of its
rural development. The 'Devapur Project', as it came to be
known after a village, covered nine villages and was later
extended to thirteen.

In this area of incessant wind and dust, only *bajri* and
jawar grew. The farmers tried to eke out a precarious
existence from the land. They were devoid of medical aid
and schools. There were no roads and even clean drinking
water was not available. For over thirty-five years the Dorab
Tata Trust, through its Rural Welfare Board, contributed Rs
76 lakh of which about Rs 10 lakh has gone to medical relief.
The Rural Welfare Board also served as a liaison and
supervisory agency and managed to obtain support and co-
operation from government agencies, loans from the Bank of
Maharashtra and funds for the 'Food for Work' programme
through the Catholic Relief Services.

What could one do in an area of scanty rain? The first
major step was a crash programme of contour bunding to
prevent soil erosion. This measure increased the area under
cultivation and raised the subsoil water level. In a few years

there was not only an adequate supply of drinking water for the villagers but enough for cattle and irrigation even during the worst period of the 1972 drought. The board was instrumental in bringing to the villages medical aid, a school in every village and 65 km of roads plus electricity. The roads and electric power are the result of its relentless pressure on the zilla parishad.

A spectacular change has taken place in the cropping pattern of the villages. Cotton has been successfully grown on a wide scale and a ginning mill has been set up in the area. Double cropping has raised the standard of living of the people. Between 1958 and 1972 the total income of the first nine villages shot up by 235 per cent. The growing prosperity is reflected in the life-style of the people as evidenced by the use of consumer articles such as bicycles, watches and torches. The percentage of bicycle owners, for example, has grown from five in a hundred to seventeen in a hundred within fourteen years. The number of bicycles is a barometer of rural prosperity. The Rural Welfare Board was fortunate in having the services of S.R. Suratwala, TISS alumnus, who for three decades settled in these villages. Another gentleman called Persai, a Colombo Plan scholar trained in cattle care and

dairy management in New Zealand, concentrated on upgrading cattle and goats for over two decades. Today few highly qualified people are patient enough to settle in the villages long enough for results to be attained.

Based on his thirty-four years of experience at the grassroot level in rural development work, S.R. Suratwala says that with economic improvement and material progress, the finer qualities of man often disappear. 'With prosperity,' he says, 'people tend to become selfish and care less for their neighbours. But when people live under difficult conditions and are under stress there is more concern for each other, a desire to help and share with the community.' There is more 'prosperity' but less 'happiness' in the villages today! Mr Suratwala tried to discuss this problem with some others who have also worked in the field. They say that this is all 'a part of the game of development.'

The Sir Dorabji Tata Trust appointed a noted economist, Y. S. Pandit, to do two critical evaluations of this programme. Pandit recorded both the successes and the failures of this experiment. There is often more to learn from failures than from successes. These two evaluations were possible because of the foresight of the founders who, before embarking on

the project, had a socio-economic survey done by the Gokhale
Institute of Politics and Economics in Pune of the villages
concerned.

The government went into community development in
1952; the Sir Dorabji Tata Trust decided to embark on its
community development programme in the same year.

In his report, Y.S. Pandit says that while the project has
been successful in supplying the felt needs of the people like
drinking water, medical provision, contour bunding and
schools, 'there has not been much noticeable change in the
attitude and the outlook of the villagers. The desire to be
self-reliant and to do hard work is weak.'

Y.S. Pandit observes that the board has met with little
success in tackling the traditions and customs of the villagers—
namely borrowing for marriages—and it has not succeeded
in instilling in them a concern for public health and sanitation.
The village leaders have not shown the requisite 'aptitude
for constructive rural work.' Many of the economic gains
have been diluted by the enormous growth of population and
family planning activities should have been taken more
seriously at the outset, says the report.

This candid assessment does not take away the fact that
much has been achieved and learnt. The report concludes:
'Notwithstanding the few qualitative deficiencies that might
exist, the Devapur Project is an oasis in the famine tract of
Maharashtra.'

The Sir Dorabji Tata Trust was one of the first to go into
the field almost forty years ago. Today hundreds of voluntary
agencies and industries are engaged in this endeavour
including several Tata companies. The trust now has a role
to advise those who are engaged in rural work.

15

ON PEOPLE

'Make Sure the Tree Survives'

When the first steel plant opened, men came to learn and to work from north and south Bihar, from far away Punjab and the Gulf of Kutch, from nearby Orissa and Bengal, from distant Madras. Sometimes men had to be enticed, for in the early years of this century movement of people was not so common. In Jamshedpur, they were welded into a nation. They learnt the skills of steel-making and became a part of the industrial growth of India. Some worked for two generations, some for three, and a few for even four. Father handed over to the son, the son to the grandson and the grandson to his children in turn. They have all contributed to the Jamshedpur of today, a city of 7,00,000.

Nirmal Singh is a fourth generation worker. So is his brother, Amarjeet. Nirmal is a millwright (fitter) in Tata Steel. His father, Kartar Singh, tells Nirmal, 'Whenever we go to the highest official in the company, we are listened to; whenever we go for any donation for our gurudwara we are never turned back with empty hands.'

When Kartar Singh retired, the great problem facing him was accommodation. He personally met J.R.D. Tata and got it sanctioned. 'He stops his car and talks to us,' says Nirmal Singh. Kartar Singh tells his sons: 'Keep our good name. Lift it higher, don't let it down.'

Kartar Singh's father Jhanda Singh was general foreman of Steel Melting Shop No. 3. Jhanda Singh told his grandsons:

'Your great-grandfather, Asha Singh, put up the first column in the machine shop. He planted a tree. You make sure that the tree he planted survives.'

Thirty-nine-year-old Shah Nawaz is a fourth generation worker. In 1918 his great-grandfather, Noor Mohammed, joined the coke oven section of the steel company. His grandfather worked as a fitter; his father, Abdul Gaffar, still works in Tata Steel's employment section. Shah Nawaz, a science graduate, works for the company's internal audit. When asked why they prefer to work in Tata Steel as a family, Shah Nawaz replies: 'It is because of the facilities we are given, medical and educational, and the goodwill that is there for us and around us.'

When questioned, 'The company has given you so much, what are you giving to the company?' Shah Nawaz replies: 'Service, loyalty, honesty.' After a very long pause, Shah Nawaz, discloses: 'I am in the internal audit section. I have helped to uncover irregularities, some serious ones. All this benefits the company.' Proudly he adds: 'My boss has given me letters of appreciation for the work I have done.' Shah Nawaz says he would like his fifteen-year-old son, Shamsh Nawaz, also to join Tata Steel when he finishes his studies. He will be the fifth generation from his family.

A Framework for Reconciliation

One morning when I was researching on Tata Steel in the head office of the company at Jamshedpur, there was a knock on the door. A man and a lady from the employees' welfare services walked in. As I had expressed an interest in observing how they worked they invited me to join them soon at their counselling centre. I readily agreed.

At the counselling centre I found a couple, the husband's father and two relatives. As I entered the room, there was a pall of gloom. Sensitively, a lady social worker tried to draw them out one by one to speak their minds freely. They did, often accusing each other. The daughter-in-law, who spoke the least, wore a red sari, had sharp features, and a dark complexion. Her face was a study in unhappiness. She sat stone-faced through the discussion.

It seemed that this daughter-in-law walked out of the house in a huff and lodged a complaint for harassment and maltreatment against the father-in-law and the husband. The father-in-law, in turn, had lodged a police complaint accusing the daughter-in-law of carrying away her marriage jewellery without permission. It was suggested that each looked inwards to see if he or she was perhaps 10 per cent wrong even if the other may be 90 per cent wrong. After a brief time of quiet they spoke in turn what they were beginning to discover about themselves.

After about one and a half hours, I left. The session continued for another four hours! Some days later, the social worker saw me again and said: 'You will be happy to learn that the Jamshedpur couple has agreed to reconcile and to withdraw their police complaints. They want to make a go of their marriage and to celebrate it with a tea party at which they want you to be present.' I went to the family tea party in a small crowded room in the workers' colony. There was an air of relaxation. The dark lady with sharp features holding her two-year-old son was unrecognizable. 'What has happened to you?' I asked her. She answered with a charming shy smile. Her countenance was radiant.

Response to Distress

The *Indian Express* of Monday, 13 August 1979 carried an eight-column banner headline, '5,000 Die in Morvi Floods'. The floods were a sequel to breaches in the Machchu Dam on the upper reaches of Morvi.

The evening papers the same day carried a news item that Tatas had donated Rs 2.5 lakh to the Gujarat Chief Minister's Relief Fund. 'In a message to the Chief Minister,' said the report, 'Mr Tata assured that Tata Chemicals was standing by to assist in the relief operations and that a relief team from Mithapur would go into action as soon as communications were restored.'

A week later, a compact relief team of thirty-five from Mithapur, 300 kilometres away, moved in with its own generator, medical unit, public address system and other facilities. A thousand people were fed and housed at the Tata transit camp which was a model of cleanliness and efficiency.

The official relief authorities were so impressed by the camp that they requested Tata Chemicals to send its engineering team to restore the drainage and water supply system of the town. Bulldozers, which had cleared the thick mud left behind by the floods, had in the process damaged the pipelines. No map of the water connections of the town could be located. 'You need an astrologer, not an engineer,' said a Tata Chemicals director to the relief officials. Even so Tata Chemicals acceded to the request. In three weeks the water supply and drainage were restored including 65 kilometres of water piping.

After a visit to Morvi, this writer went to Mithapur, the home of Tata Chemicals. He noticed the damage caused by incessant rains to the chemicals complex where large areas of the salt works had been washed away. The small railway tracks were submerged or broken as also the mud earthing. The loss to Tata Chemicals was estimated at Rs 2 crore. To gather a team of thirty-five experts at such a time within a span of thirty-six hours was a heroic effort. When complimented on their willingness to assist when they were themselves in need, an official replied: 'It is the Tata tradition.'

The 'Tata tradition' goes back to 1934 when a devastating earthquake struck Monghyr (Munger) in north Bihar. Tata Steel sent the first relief train from Jamshedpur packed with food, medical supplies and other assistance. Within a day of arrival they erected a temporary hospital for 400 patients, and each day inoculated thousands against cholera, smallpox and tetanus. The Viceroy, Lord Willingdon, arrived in Monghyr just as the Tata relief staff was getting underway. The town lay in ruins but there was a functioning hospital on one side and sheltered enclosure for the thousands of homeless on the other side. Stirred by what he saw, the Viceroy cabled the general manager of Tata Steel at Jamshedpur: 'TATAS HAVE DONE SPLENDIDLY—WILLINGDON.'

When World War II broke out the trustees of the Sir Dorab Tata Trust made generous contributions to the Lord Mayor's Fund in London for the relief of the victims of German bombing. Throughout World War II Tatas made funds available for those from Europe displaced by the war and to refugee organizations.

Both Sir Ratan and Sir Dorab Tata made a special note in their trust deeds about helping those in distress.

This help to the distressed comes not only from the charity trusts but from the various Tata companies. In addition the employees on their own collect and add their mite to what the company offers.

At the time of the Koyna earthquake in December 1967, the Tata Relief Committee had received donations from some Tata companies, trusts and employees totalling about Rs 7,00,000 and of this about 30 per cent was contributed by individual employees. At the height of winter, bed rolls, woollen blankets, aluminium utensils, two sets of clothes and other assistance was given to 870 families. The Tata Relief

Committee built seventy houses in two different districts which were specially designed to absorb the stress of earth tremors.

In 1975 Patna lay prostrate under two metres of water. All communications by road, rail, air, telephone and telex were severed. On receiving the news of the tragedy a Tata Steel plane with relief essentials landed at Patna airport outside the town, the first civilian aircraft to land. Of the 118 medical teams sent by various organizations to assist, Tata Steel's was the first. Its workers had voluntarily donated one day's salary.

Be it the Panshet Dam disaster, the Gujarat floods or the Maharashtra drought of 1972, Tata relief teams have been among the first on the scene. Jayaprakash Narayan, chairman of the Bihar Relief Committee, said in 1967, 'Tatas have provided a ray of hope in the dark clouds of dejection and despair. If others emulate their example, the picture of India will be different.'

At the time of the Bangladesh crisis, Tatas looked after 10,000 refugees for seven months in specially erected camps. All facilities were supplied and the stipend provided to the refugees by the government for their food and fuel was untouched by Tatas and so the stipend came in handy to the refugees for their other needs. But this created one problem for Tatas. The Tata camps became too inviting for refugees from other camps and the population kept swelling with uninvited guests.

In 1977 a devastating cyclone hit the coast of Andhra Pradesh. It was accompanied by huge tidal waves that struck huts and buildings over a vast area. The receding waters carried away thousands of helpless men, women, children and cattle into the Bay of Bengal. The Tata Relief Committee chose the hardest hit area and built 600 houses and eleven community centres. New octagonal houses of cement were built to withstand future flood fury. Tata engineers and architects, on the basis of experience of other cyclone-prone areas of the world, erected the community centres on stilts to secure the community in case of another cyclone fury. These community centres served as schools or dispensaries in normal

Andhra cyclone relief—the aftermath

times but were designed to provide shelter for 1,200 persons in an emergency.

In May 1979 the dreaded event took place again. The same areas were struck by a second cyclone. Thanks to earlier warnings the villagers in the area of Repalle and Avanigadda rushed to the Tata-built community centres. They shook as they witnessed, through the windows of the centre, telephone and telegraph poles torn apart and houses built by other agencies being razed. A cyclone of high intensity hit the same district of coastal Andhra Pradesh again in 1990 sweeping aside entire villages. Tata relief officials awaited news of whether their community centres had withstood the fury. The *Indian Express* reported on 10 May 1990 'the cyclone shelters built after the 1977 cyclone have come in handy to house the evacuated people from low lying areas of the coastal districts.' They had withstood the test of the cyclone fury.

End of A Menace

To rejoice at a success is not the same as taking the credit for it. To deny oneself the first is to become a hypocrite and a denier of life; to permit oneself the second is a childish indulgence which will prevent one from ever growing up.

—Dag Hammarskjöld

The Chotanagpur division of Bihar* is a vast area of 65,000 square kilometres, larger in size than either Punjab or Kerala. The area is an undulating plateau between 1,500 ft and 2,500 ft. The region consists of forests, ravines, valleys and wooded hills. Underneath them lie the richest resources of coal and iron ore in India. Above this area are studded thousands of villages and some major towns like Ranchi with its heavy engineering complex; Dhanbad, the coal centre of India; and Jamshedpur, the city of steel. Over eleven million people reside in this area of whom one-third are adivasis (tribals).

In 1974 this division of Chotanagpur became the epicentre of a smallpox epidemic. The World Health Organization (WHO) and the government estimated that between January and June 1974, 6,000 lives were lost through smallpox, apart from many thousands crippled by the disease. A couple of foreigners in Japan were found to have had smallpox and it was traced back to Tatanagar station. Dr Nicole Grasset, head of WHO, New Delhi, rushed Dr Larry Brilliant, an expert from the USA, to Tatanagar for personal investigations. WHO had, a few years earlier, launched its campaign to eradicate smallpox and this outbreak came as a great disappointment to the world organization.

If the epidemic could be controlled and eradicated from this division, WHO estimated the other states would pose no problem and only Ethiopia would then remain. If tackled

* Now in Jharkhand.

vigorously at this stage WHO believed that smallpox could be eradicated by 1976.

Dr Larry Brilliant called on the managing director of Tata Steel, Russi Mody. Dr Brilliant had a tall order. He requested Tatas' help to have fifty doctors, 200 para-medical supervisors, 600 to 900 vaccinators-cum-searchers of the dreaded disease, fifty vehicles and innumerable other facilities. Asked as to when he would like to have this arrangement from, he replied, 'From yesterday.'

Tatas responded instantly. Doctors were drawn from the main hospital in Jamshedpur, some of its officers were put in charge with Sujit Gupta as chief co-ordinator (Administration) and Dr Pesi Bharucha, chief co-ordinator (Medical). Fresh staff were recruited as accountants, stenographers and drivers. Tatas put thirty-two jeeps and other vehicles at the disposal of WHO and OXFAM and WHO produced another thirty-six. The staff recruited had to be trained within seventy-two hours in vaccination and the essentials of smallpox control and containment. It was a round-the-clock operation. Come the seventy-two hours the teams were on the road.

In a fortnight 400 outbreaks were discovered within the 45-mile radius of Jamshedpur and lakhs were treated with vaccination as part of the containment strategy. It was not smooth sailing either. The adivasis preferred to worship the goddess Sithala and visit the medicine man when they were ill rather than permit the approach of outsiders. One tribe of Santhals refused to permit the doctors and vaccinators to touch their people until they had the green light from their great leader. The problem was that the great leader happened to be in hiding with a price on his head! A small team of Tata officers had to go blind-folded, transferred from one jeep to another and then taken by road to the hideout of the chief. The chief gave his permission orally and Tatas had to tape-record him, return to the villagers in the area and play back the tape to convince the tribals that the great man had given his permission.

Evenings were preferred by vaccinators because the menfolk were home from their fields. One day an innocent vaccinator had knocked on the door of a tribal hut. When the door opened, two tribal ladies equipped with darts and arrows charged at the poor vaccinator, who ran for his life. It was only the undergrowth that allowed him to emerge unscathed though shaken—his vaccination scalpel perhaps lost in the excitement. Within six weeks the area was declared by WHO to be under control. Phase 1 of the operation was over.

Though Tatas' immediate responsibility was completed, Dr Brilliant appealed to the chairman, J.R.D. Tata, for help of the field organization that had been built up through Tatas in order to tackle smallpox in the entire division of Chotanagpur which included eighty-two towns and 20,500 villages. The time-scale of the operation was six months. The Tata Steel Board met and sanctioned the project, the total cost of which was Rs 43 lakh. Telco and some other companies of Tatas joined hands to make up the total.

The second phase of containment was launched with fifty-six teams fanning the entire area. This operation stretched the resources of Tatas to the limit, some of its finest officers went at some risk to remote areas in forests where hygiene was unheard of. Dr Pesi Bharucha, the superintendent of the hospital, recalls that in these far away places they could often take only three items of food. The first was a dish of tea, where tea, milk and water were boiled on a stove but nothing was strained for fear of infection. The second was chapatties which were picked up and eaten fresh from the fire. The third dish available was boiled potatoes. There were 'flies, flies, flies everywhere.' Often in the late evenings, as the sun set upon the wild forest Dr Larry Brilliant would turn to Bharucha and say: 'Now Doctor, where shall we go for dinner tonight? To the Sheraton or to the Hilton? You name it and I'll come with you.' Invariably the two tired doctors and their small team would settle down at a village tea shop on packing cases to their three-course meal. There were instances when entire teams got lost in the jungles and once the Tata Steel plane had to search for a team that had not reported back for two days. The team, including lady supervisors, was at last found in a remote village where they had taken shelter when their vehicle had broken down. Their only comment on being discovered was: 'We did not waste our time, we have found the cases, contained the contacts and searched this area thoroughly. We have made numerous friends.'

Phase II of the operation was declared highly successful. The success was all the sweeter because Rs 10 lakh were saved from the original allotment estimated by WHO, thanks to the strict control on the money handled by Tatas.

WHO wanted Tatas to go the extra mile and join Phase III, namely, of consolidation. If this phase was successful the cherished dream of WHO of eradicating the menace from the world could be achieved. In Phase III the operation was on a low key. The surplus of Rs 10 lakh was spread out over another six months ending June 1975. When that period was completed a message came from WHO, New Delhi, that India was free for the first time in history from indigenous smallpox. J.R.D. Tata congratulating WHO on its successful efforts said: 'It is for me and for all of us in Tatas a matter of deep satisfaction that we played a useful part in assisting you and the Government in this task.' In May 1980 WHO declared that smallpox was eradicated from the world.

Russi Mody, who first geared up Tata Steel, on hearing the appeal of Dr Brilliant, wrote: 'Those who have been involved in the campaign from the beginning have had the rich experience of sharing the sorrows of the downtrodden and poor, of the neglected and forgotten segment of society. Perhaps by their efforts a line in the history of mankind has been written . . . .'

16

CREATING A NEW INDUSTRIAL CULTURE

'Behind every civilization lies a vision,' says Christopher Dawson.

Over a hundred years ago Jamsetji Tata had the vision of an India that could hold its head high in the community of nations. To that task he addressed himself by introducing to India the industrial revolution. But he believed in something more. At a time when captains of industry in Europe and America were exploiters of their workers, he thought for his workers. He cared to give them filtered water, sanitary hutments, cheap foodgrains, medical facilities, provident fund and accident insurance. While most captains of industry believed—and many still do—that man is meant to serve industry, Jamsetji believed that industry was meant to serve man. In 1895 when an extension of Empress Mills was being opened, Jamsetji Tata said the words, noted earlier: 'We do not claim to be more unselfish, more generous and more philanthropic than other people. But we think we started on sound and straightforward business principles, considering the interests of the shareholders our own, and the health and welfare of the employees the sure foundation of our prosperity.'

It is this policy of Jamsetji which resulted in the steel company beginning in 1911 with an eight-hour day for labour when factories in the western countries worked a minimum of ten and even twelve hours a day. Tatas were years and sometimes decades ahead of government legislation on labour (See Appendix F). As noted earlier Sir Dorab asked Sydney and Beatrice Webb to organize the social services of Tata Steel. J.R.D. Tata asked for a social audit by an impartial outside committee on whether the company had fulfilled its social responsibilities. In Jamsetji's tradition Tata Steel introduced a profit-sharing scheme in the 1930s. J.R.D. Tata planned in the early 1940s the personnel department of Tata Steel and in the 1950s encouraged negotiations with the union for joint councils of management and workers, a system of day-to-day management by consensus in the factory. This agreement signed in 1956 opened a new chapter in industrial relations and has underpinned the happy labour-management understanding for the last decades. Though copied by many companies it has succeeded in very few.

In the 1890s Jamsetji was thinking of the health and welfare of the workers. Eighty years later J.R.D. Tata was thinking of a company's responsibility beyond obligations to its own workers. He saw his companies and townships as islands of prosperity in an ocean of poverty. He searched for what his companies could do for the surrounding areas of darkness. In a speech,[*] Mr Tata said that the companies should contribute to public (not just employee's) welfare. He said:

Every company has a special continuing responsibility towards the people of the area in which it is located and in which its employees and their families live. In every city, town or village, large or small, there is always need for improvement, for help, for relief, for leadership and for guidance. I suggest that the most significant contribution organized industry can make is by identifying itself with the life and problems of the people of the community to which it belongs, and by applying its resources, skills and talents, to the extent that it can reasonably spare them to serve and help them.

[*] Anantharamakrishnan Memorial Lecture, 'Business and Industry in the Seventies—Tasks and Obligations', Madras, 15 December 1969. From *Keynote* by J.R.D. Tata (Tata Press), pages 43 and 44.

Let industry established in the countryside 'adopt' the villages in its neighbourhood; let some of the time of its managers, its engineers, doctors and skilled specialists be spared to help and advise the people of the villages and to supervise new developments undertaken by co-operative effort between them and the company. Assistance in family planning in the villages would be a particularly valuable form of service.

None or little of this need be considered as charity. While no doubt some free services and financial relief may at times be required, most of such activities could and should be in the form of co-operative self-help ventures between the company and the people of the villages. The benefits of such a joint venture will no doubt initially flow chiefly to the village, but it is also clearly in the interests of industry that surrounding areas should be healthy, prosperous and peaceful.

To put JRD's ideas into action, the Articles of Association of leading Tata companies were amended and social obligations beyond welfare of employees was accepted as part of the objectives of the group. For example, the Articles of Association of Tata Chemicals were altered after confirmation to state that the company could 'subscribe or continue or otherwise to assist or to guarantee money to charitable, benevolent, religious, scientific, national, public, political or any other useful institutions, objects or purposes.'

In the 19th century Baron Edward Thurlow, the poet, asked 'Did you ever expect a corporation to have a conscience when it had no soul to be damned and no body to be kicked?' The answer from Tatas was 'YES'.

Older Tata companies first began to implement this objective with the result that newer Tata companies began with social responsibility as a part of their way of life. Titan Watches in south India was established in a remote backward area of Hosur, Tamil Nadu. It was expected that they would train young local talent for use in their watch-making plant—which they did. But they went beyond it and within three years of establishment awarded scholarships for higher studies to students in this poverty-stricken area. Titan established a record by employing the highest percentage of handicapped people in any factory of India—eighty out of 1,800 employees, higher than the recommended percentage of 3.5 per 100, when most companies have not reached even 1 per cent. What is more, they started housing for their staff and workers. They took these steps in social responsibility in the first three years before they could declare their first dividend to their shareholders in 1990!

What is heartening is that the concern shown by the management has become a part of the culture of several of the staff and the workers of companies. They feel it is their company and the surrounding area is part of theirs as well as the nation's responsibility. Often when a national disaster strikes—such as a cyclone—workers of Tata Steel and Telco offer to contribute a day's wages. The amount of salary per day of a big company can be up to several lakh. The board of directors of the company either match the staff and workers' donation or give more.

The Tata Relief Committee in Bombay managed by the Sir Dorabji Tata Trust primarily looks after the western and the southern regions while the Tata Relief Committee in Jamshedpur started by the various Tata companies manufacturing in the region take responsibility mainly for their part of India, though they have handsomely contributed to relief for the Andhra cyclone of 1977 and elsewhere too.

In the beginning there was the paternalism and care of Jamsetji; then the concern of Sir Dorab for the workers' welfare; then JRD's vision for companies to assist the surrounding areas. More recently the circle has widened and workers and staff at their own initiative go out to assist in the surrounding areas of need. Abdul Kadir is a bespectacled, earnest man with curly hair. He is a chargeman of Telco, Jamshedpur. He went to a nearby village and found that health was a big issue. So he organized two health camps.

After winning the adivasis' confidence, he made bold to organize a blood donation camp. Twenty-six tribals donated blood—two of them women. This was his reward and delight.

Kadir says that he was inspired to take this initiative by a lecture on Jamsetji Tata. He said to himself: 'Jamsetji Tata was a great man whose dreams were converted into reality but what could an ordinary man like me do?' He felt that in return for what Jamsetji's life and vision had done to create Jamshedpur he could give back something, however small, to the city of Jamshedpur and the surrounding areas. 'We often go to the surrounding villages on our own on Sundays and off days,' says S.N. Singh of Telco, Jamshedpur. 'We do not take the company vehicle. The village chief knows we have not come with money on our backs. On the contrary he has to give *us* a cup of tea. If we think beyond industry we find a purpose for industry and our industries can become more effective.'

Football is the sport of eastern India and they are indeed good at it, but there was no proper training for the young people and talent could seldom flower. Russi Mody, chairman of Tata Steel, decided that the company should have a sports foundation of which the Tata Football Academy would be a division. The academy was designed to 'provide a perennial pool of champions for the mainstream of national football.' The academy takes thirty youngsters in the age group twelve to fifteen years and trains them for three to four years. The academy has got the facilities of a gymnasium, swimming pool and a library and is staffed by trained coaches, physiotherapists, nutritionists and other personnel. Each youngster gets a handsome stipend. This is perhaps the first attempt to encourage sporting talent in such a concerted way. One of the first ventures of the Tata Steel sports foundation was to invite a Brazilian football team to give demonstration matches.

Some multi-crore giants announce with pride that they look after one or two villages. Tata Steel looks after 276 villages in the vicinity of Jamshedpur and the far-flung mines of Tata Steel. The annual philanthropy and social uplift budget of Tata Steel is probably larger than that of any single Indian charitable foundation or company.

'There will be only one Jamsetji,' says a Tata officer, 'but many others can take on the responsibility for our nation.' The circle of those in industry concerned about the lives of their fellowmen is widening. Concern brings joy. Its visible expression is in quality. Its mainspring is 'love for one's fellowmen' for which the original Greek word is *fil-anthra-pi.*

The Tata trusts are only tangible expressions of philanthropy. The intangible expression of it is in countless little acts and decisions of men from the chairman and managing director to the man who sweats in the heat of the blast furnace, who works in the din of the machine shop or on his desk at the office. It is in the hearts of these people that a new industrial culture has already dawned.

Part Three

The Facts

17

HOW DO TATAS FUNCTION?

It is not getting to the top of the Everest that matters in life. It is how and why you get there.
—Lord Hunt, leader of the first
successful expedition to Mount Everest.

There is a mystique about Tatas that needed to be unravelled, and to unravel it the best person to meet is J.R.D. Tata himself. Shy and self-effacing as a person, he was exacting and meticulous as a chairman. Jehangir Ratanji Dadabhoy Tata was born in Paris of a French mother and a Parsi father in 1904, the year Jamsetji died. Jamsetji had spoken at the wedding reception of his parents in Paris. JRD's father, R.D. Tata, and Jamsetji had a common ancestor in Ervard Jamsheed Tata, a priest of Navsari. Ervard Jamsheed, great-great-grandfather of Jamsetji, was also the great-great-great-grandfather of R.D. Tata. Jamsetji's father Nusserwanji had married the sister of JRD's grandfather, Dadabhoy.

JRD's education was constantly interrupted and before he was twenty he had studied in Paris, Bombay, Yokohama and in England. At twenty-one when he came to settle in India, his father, a director of Tatas, took his son to the room of John Peterson, a former ICS official, who was then director-in-charge of Tata Steel. R.D. Tata requested Peterson to take on his son and train him. Peterson promptly allotted the young man a desk in his own room.

'From that day I was at every interview. Every letter going to the desk of Peterson went through me and was sent out through me so I could study his comments.' And it is from this Scotsman that JRD picked up the ways of business, including making notes of important interviews. He learnt a

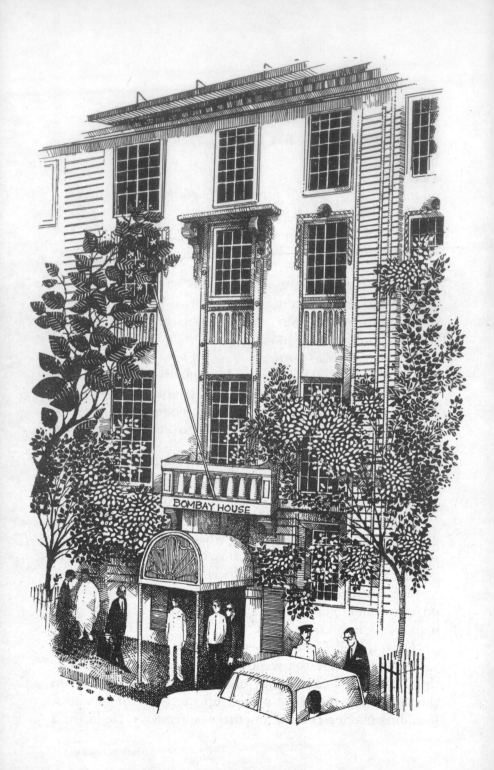

great deal by observation and by listening at all the interviews.

Unfortunately, within a year of JRD's return to India his father, R.D. Tata, died. Six years later in 1932 the chairman of Tata Sons, Sir Dorab died and Sir Nowroji Saklatvala became chairman. JRD, then only twenty-eight, moved into a cabin next to Sir Nowroji's and became his right-hand man on matters relating to Tata Steel in addition to the aviation side for which he was responsible.

In 1938 Sir Nowroji suddenly died of a heart attack. All the other directors, senior to him, elected the thirty-four-year-old JRD as the chairman of Tata Sons making him the head of the largest industrial group of India. He is rather reticent to answer why he was chosen at such a young age but finally concedes that perhaps it was because of his experience with Tata Steel and 'because I was hard working.'

From the beginning the young man stamped his style of working on the organization. He quickly shed the chairmanship of the electric and textile companies; he started a process of devolution of power. He democratized the working of Tatas. For example, a self-opinionated director had ordered that only directors could use a special lift. He reversed that order. He brought to bear the precision of an aviator on *terra firma*. In the days when he started flying single-engined planes, he operated without runways or proper airports. He had to be a mechanic as well as a navigator. If anything went wrong there was no second engine. Therefore details and perfection were important considerations. Even at eighty-six every little detail interests JRD. For the exact meaning of a word he will refer to more than one dictionary. Though he is meticulous about the use of money and the shareholders' funds, of himself he says, 'I never had any interest in making money. None of my decisions were influenced by whether it would bring me money or wealth.' His interest is people. One day, when he was seriously ill in July 1943, he wrote from his sick bed a thoughtful 2500-word note on human relations in Tata Steel.

'If we have 50,000 machines,' he noted, 'we would undoubtedly have a special staff or a department to look after them . . . but when employing 30,000 human beings, each with a mind of his own, we seem to have assumed that they would look after themselves and that there was no need for a separate organization to deal with human problems involved.' He wanted the workers to have a say in their welfare and safety, and he wanted their suggestions on the running of the company. The note resulted in the founding of a personnel department. As a further consequence of that note two pioneering strokes of Tata Steel came about, namely, a profit-sharing bonus and a joint consultative council. These measures pre-empted any labour trouble and Tata Steel has enjoyed peace between management and labour since then.

For over half a century he was the chairman of Tata Sons, which holds a financial interest in companies promoted by Tatas. At the start of the 1980s J.R.D. Tata was chairman of Tata Sons, Tata Steel, Tata Industries, Tata Chemicals, Tata Oil Mills, Indian Hotels, Tata Burroughs and three Tata offices abroad in London, Zug (Switzerland) and New York. By 1990 he had shed all these except Tata Sons and the following year he retired as chairman of Tata Sons.

J.R.D. Tata defined the role of the chairman of the parent company in the 1980s:

My being chairman (of Tata Sons) today is very different from what it was before 1970, when the Managing Agency System* operated and I was the head of Tata Industries. As the chairman of the Managing Agency, the executive authority of Tata Industries was part of the contract of management of each company. So I was in fact in a position of authority. Today the companies are free to operate independently and in fact they do. Today, except in Tata Sons I do not wield any kind of

* The Managing Agency System originated during the times of the East India Company in 1833. It enabled British investors who would have found it difficult to supervise operations abroad, to invest their funds in India. The managing agents took managerial responsibility and were promoters of companies. They acted as agents for sales and purchases of the company. The managing

executive authority. But because I am senior in age, I operate more on the basis of influence and confidence.

He went on to say: 'There is something absurd about Tatas, in so far as we have no more interest than any other shareholder in most of the companies. We get nothing extra for managing them. For example, till 1978, 90 per cent of my time went between Air-India and Tata Steel as the chairman of both, and what did Tata get out of it? In Tata Steel we are only shareholders like any other and after the managing agency system was abolished, we get nothing.'

Then why do you run Tata Steel?'

'Partly because of Jamsetji's tradition. Profit was not the sole aim. Partly, to save it from being taken over and ruined. That is why I fought for Tata Steel against nationalization. The spirit of goodwill and co-operation we have built up between management and labour will be no more if Tata Steel is nationalized.'

Mr Tata was requested to explain how the Tata companies functioned before and after the managing agency system was abolished.

'Till 1938 when I became chairman of Tata Sons it was the tradition for all Tata companies to have a common chairman. I changed that. I kept the chairmanship of Tata Sons and Tata Steel and some others. But I shed the

---

agents took a commission on sales—irrespective of the profitability of the companies. The first person to change this system was Jamsetji Tata, who in 1886 changed over from a commission on sales to commission on profit only so that loss-making companies did not go further into the red.

Though there were some outstanding Managing Agents there were others who abused the system and drained away public funds. The Monopolies Inquiry Commission in its report (1965), while agreeing that the managing agency system played an important part in quickening industrial development, observed that it produced a high degree of concentration of economic power in the hands of a few family groups. The system was abolished from 2 April 1970.

chairmanship of Tata Textiles, and not long after that of the Tata Hydro-Electric companies. Later on (in 1972) I did the same with Telco. Otherwise one can spend all the time going to board meetings rather than doing creative work.'

In a nation where families controlled businesses J.R.D. Tata was the first to professionalize Indian management. In 1938 Tata Sons was more of a family affair. Four out of its six directors belonged to the Tata family compared to two out of seventeen in 1990.

In 1945 at JRD's instance a wholly owned subsidiary of Tata Sons called Tata Industries was set up.

'Why did you do that?'

JRD replied:

I created Tata Industries because as more and more companies came in including Tata Chemicals and a few others I said we can't go on increasing the number of directors of Tata Sons.* Tata Sons were the managing agents under the law in which all executive power of every company was centred. I could be the chairman of all companies but I couldn't be the managing director. So I said we must have a system where we can invite anybody who was in charge of the operations (to confer as a group). By the end of the World War II, I foresaw the need in the coming decade for increasing professionalism in the management of Tata companies.

Tata Industries became his instrument for doing that.

To give Tata Industries financial muscle the managing agencies held by Tata Sons were transferred to Tata Industries.

Professional management did very well in the decades to come. From 1945-1970 Tata Industries started new enterprises and became the 'think tank' of the house. It could have done more had the government's policy in the 1960s been more liberal. As stated earlier unlike many other managing agency companies that charged a commission on sales irrespective of whether profits were made, the policy of Tatas was not to

* Later in the 1980s the numbers were gradually stepped up till they reached seventeen on 1 June 1990.

Chairmen of Tata Sons

Jamsetji Tata
1887-1904

Sir Dorab Tata
1904-1932

Sir Nowroji Saklatvala
1932-1938

J.R.D. Tata
1938-1991

Ratan N. Tata
1991-

charge a commission if a company made losses. In its early years a company such as Tata Chemicals could not break even for sixteen years. It was nursed by Tata Sons and then Tata Industries till it became successful. However the managing agency system was abused by others and mismanaged. On 2 April 1970 the government abolished the managing agency system. Overnight the New Delhi representative of Tatas who used to visit government offices with one visiting card stating 'Tata Industries' was advised to carry eighteen visiting cards— one for each major company. JRD was no longer the sovereign whose writ ran legally over every Tata company as he was not chairman of all the Tata companies but only of some. Thereafter he had to move with powers of persuasion and influence. Tata Industries became a discussion forum.

Between 1970-1981 Tata Industries had a great name from its former days but no function. No fresh funds came in. In October 1981 JRD decided it was time for a younger man to take over the chairmanship of Tata Industries from him. Though he did not believe in a hereditary or a family raj, he was conscious that there was a magic in the name 'Tata' and in Ratan Tata there was a well-educated person, then in his early forties, imbued with modern ideas of management. Ratan Tata had spent two decades working for the house and was a director of both Tata Sons and Tata Industries. JRD proposed Ratan's name as chairman of Tata Industries.

'The chairmanship,' says Ratan Tata, 'was a titular one. Tata Industries had a great aura about it but it was only a Rs 60-lakh company. I had no plan at the start. It was a soul-searching time to begin with. Tata Industries was a 100 per cent subsidiary of Tata Sons. The first decision was to reduce the ownership of Tata Sons and to sell 70 per cent of it to the rich operating companies, and then to have a rights issue and raise the holdings. Nine major companies came in and a capital of Rs 6 crore was raised. Before that came the exercise of strategic planning.'

Within a year of his appointment as chairman of Tata Industries Ratan Tata's mother was seriously ill, receiving treatment at the Sloan-Kettering Hospital, New York. He was in a difficult position to decide whether to be with his mother in New York or to attend to his official duties in India. He thought to himself, 'After all I have only one mother.' He left India to be with his mother. Days stretched into weeks. There were long periods when there was nothing he could do. It was in that hospital that he started drafting a strategic plan. It was submitted to the group in 1983. It predicted India's industrial trend in the coming years. The accent was to be on electronics and biotechnology. The plan looked at each of the areas Tatas were engaged in and outlined possible directions. Tata Industries is in a rather unusual position. It does not have a core business of its own. As an official puts it: 'Its business is to create core businesses.' Moreover, it must not conflict with other Tata companies' activities.

Ratan Tata believes it is good to define and re-define a business as you go along. For Tata Industries the seven hi-tech industries started in the 1980s with an initial investment from Tata Industries were:

1) Tata Honeywell
2) Tata Telecommunications
3) Hitech Drilling System
4) Keltron Telephones
5) Tata Finance
6) Matrix Materials
7) Tata Elxsi India

Tata Industries had a small holding of only 10-20 per cent in each, the rest came from other Tata companies and public funds. Between 1982 and 1989 Tata Industries had increased its capital and profits by ten times.

As the decade of the nineties begins Tatas are poised for considerable expansion denied to them under the restrictive policies of the 1960s and 1970s. The beginning of the liberalization of policy took place in the mid 1980s and it seems this trend will continue in the 1990s, the difficult foreign exchange situation being the only inhibiting factor. Tata's flagship Tata Steel has already modernized and is expanding its capacity by 30 per cent. It is diversifying into cement, using the mountains of slag it has collected over decades which encircle the steel works like a fortification. In addition to more than Rs 2,500 crore investment on steel, it is planning on a further Rs 250 crore investment in the cement plant and a major thermal power unit for the steel works.

Indian Hotels is moving from 5-star comfort into the 4-star category of hotels under its subsidiary Gateway Hotels and Getaway Resorts. It is now offering its technical know-how and constructing hotels at Tashkent and Moscow.

Ratan Tata, chairman of Telco, thinks any diversification of that company will have to be in more advanced fields of engineering like aerospace and not in consumer goods.

Tata Chemicals has taken on a major fertilizer project of Rs 1,250 crore at Babrala. As stated earlier, the largest single joint-sector project of Rs 3,000 crore to be undertaken by the private sector partner is the Haldia Petrochemicals Project which came to Tatas amid tough competition because, said the Chief Secretary of West Bengal, 'Tatas as a group are considered best by all.'

What has been the style of JRD's operation as chairman all these years?

A close colleague for fifty years, proudly says of JRD, 'He is a democratic chairman.'

'Sometimes too democratic,' says another and elaborates: 'JRD has inspired ideas. Over a weekend he rings and tells me about them. And I am thrilled. At one sitting he can beautifully draft out his ideas. Then he does the fatal thing. He circulates it to eight or ten of his colleagues. They all put their mark upon it. Then he sits down and painfully tries to incorporate their suggestions in a final draft and in the process the grandness of his vision is at times lost.'

Some of the more impatient directors feel JRD is too much of a 'consensus man.' What is JRD's reply?:

When a number of persons are involved I am definitely a consensus man. But that does not mean that I do not express my views. But basically it is a question of having to deal with individual men heading different enterprises. And with each man I have my own way. I am one who will make full allowance for a man's character and idiosyncrasies. You have to adapt yourself to their ways and deal accordingly and draw out the best in each man.

He then spelt out the strength and style and weaknesses of the four top Tata chairmen, all able men. Returning to himself he added, 'It may be, that because all others were older than me when I became the chairman (at thirty-four) I became a consensus man.'

He went on to reveal the secret of his teamwork, 'If I have any merit, it is getting on with individuals according to their ways and characteristics. At times it involves suppressing yourself. It is painful but necessary . . . To be a leader you have got to lead human beings with affection.'

'Consensus,' says JRD, 'is weak in some respects but strong in the long run. Consensus never works 100 per cent but by and large I think I have succeeded.'

JRD thinks the future of Tatas will be very much linked to the future of its two biggest companies, Tata Steel and Telco.

'How would you define the house of Tatas? And what, would you say, links the companies together?'

Slowly and deliberately JRD framed the definition:

I would call it a group of individually managed companies united by two factors. First, a feeling that they are part of a larger group which carries the name and prestige of Tatas, and public recognition of honesty and reliability—trust-worthiness. Each company enjoys its share of the privilege. They use the Tata emblem. The reason is, you might say, enlightened self-interest. The other reason is more metaphysical. There is an innate loyalty, a sharing of certain beliefs. We all feel a certain pride that we are somewhat different from others. This factor has also worked against our growth. What would have happened if our philosophy was like that of some other companies which do not stop at any means to attain their ends. I have often thought of that and I have come to the conclusion that if we were like other groups, we would be twice as big as they are today. What we have sacrificed is a 100 per cent growth, but we wouldn't want it any other way.

JRD and his wife Thelma have no children. The Tata family is not blessed in its offspring. Neither of Jamsetji's two sons had any issue. When Lady Ratan Tata became a widow at about forty, a family council met and suggested she might like to adopt the son of one of Sir Ratan's cousins. She selected thirteen-year old Naval Hormusji Tata as her heir.

At that time, in 1917, Naval Tata was studying in an orphanage. Naval's grandmother Cooverbai and Jamsetji's wife Hirabai were sisters. His grandfather and Jamsetji Tata were also related. Owing to the premature death of Naval's father his part of the family was not well-to-do. Naval had known poverty. When he was adopted he found himself catapulted to one of the most affluent homes in India. Naval said that for him in his early teens, it seemed as if a magic wand was waved and a fairy godmother had appeared. Naval graduated from Bombay University with economics and after a short course in accountancy in England joined Tatas in 1930. Thirty-two days younger than JRD, Naval was an active director of Tata Sons for forty-eight years and deputy chairman from 1962 till his death in May 1989. He began as secretary of Tata Aviation and ended his long career as chairman of the three Tata electric companies.

Naval Tata held a record for being elected as employers' representative to ILO's governing body (of eighteen members) at every election from 1951 for thirty-eight years. Wilfred Jenks, director-general of the ILO, speaking in New Delhi in January 1971 evaluated Naval Tata's contribution to the International Labour Organization. Mr Jenks said: 'He was among the first to urge us to embark on an active programme of management development. Indulgent towards human frailty, he has been tolerant of diversity of outlook and divergences of view and interest always, tolerant of cant, evil or meanness never . . . These are the qualities which have left their impress on Indian industry and which have given him his distinctive stature in the ILO.'

Naval Tata was also associated with the International Chamber of Commerce and was a vice-president of the International Organization of Employers, Geneva, for over two decades. When India established the All-India Council of Sports to administer and financially assist all branches of sports organizations in India, Prime Minister Jawaharlal Nehru nominated him the first president of the All-India Council for Sports.

In the eleven years he was president of the Indian Hockey Federation, India won the world hockey title at the Olympics.*

Though affluence, authority and honours came his way Naval never forgot that he was once poor. This recognition perhaps accounted for his wide sympathies and his common touch with people.

His elder son Ratan Tata, born 1937, studied architecture and structural engineering at Cornell University. He was well settled in the USA. It was the urging of his grandmother Lady Ratan Tata that made him decide to return to India in 1962. He was trained the hard way on the shop floor of Tata Steel and Telco. Later as director he looked after Tata enterprises in electronics and textiles before moving into the hi-tech field after 1981, when he became chairman of Tata Industries. He became chairman of Telco in December 1988, chairman of the Sir Ratan Tata Trust after his father's death in 1989.

Minocher Kaekobad Tata was born in 1930.** He is the grandson of Jamsetji's sister Virbaiji, and the nearest male descendant of Jamsetji's father. In that capacity he inherited the two settlements of Jamsetji Tata. He is a trustee of Sir Dorabji Tata Trust and a director of some Tata companies like Tata Oil Mills and the Investment Corporation of India.

In his lifetime JRD has widened the base of Tata Sons. In 1980 there were only eleven directors. In 1991 there are

* See Appendix F, 'Tatas and Sports'.
** He passed away in 1994. His wife Pilloo now manages the M.K. Tata Trust.

eighteen.* Many of those who have played a part in the growth of Tatas are now made directors of the parent firm.

On 25 March 1991, J.R.D. Tata stepped down as chairman of Tata Sons and proposed the name of Ratan N. Tata to succeed him. Newspapers were generous in their tributes to a man who had upheld values for more than half a century in the rugged world of big business. *The Economic Times* (26 March 1991) wrote:

> Under Mr Tata's leadership, the group has earned a special place in India's corporate life in two important ways. First, it has professionalized management to a degree that few other indigenous business houses have done, and done it to a point where professionals have emerged as corporate stars in their own right. Second, it has consistently stayed in tune with national priorities, and ventured into the fields which urgently required private investment . . . In JRD's own time, the group has diversified into automobiles, chemicals, exports and power. Throughout, the emphasis has been on building solid businesses, and not on seeking quick returns, capitalizing on shortages, or manipulating government policy to personal advantage. This group culture should hold it in good stead in the future as well.

Then looking into the future *The Economic Times* added:

> Mr J.R.D. Tata has ensured that a shared business vision and strong ethical traditions provide the bonds of partnership in a clutch of companies which see a mutual strength in staying together. Mr Ratan Tata can foster these bonds because he personifies the Tata traditions. With age on his side, he has used his position in recent years to spearhead the group's entry into hi-tech areas like electronics, computers and oil drilling, and played a key role in strategic planning for the group . . . Mr Ratan Tata can be expected to handle his new role with finesse and maturity, in the same manner that he has since he was marked out as JRD's successor a decade ago.

* On 1 January 2004 there are again eleven Tata Sons directors.

Some months prior to his stepping down as chairman, JRD foresaw that a change in style would be inevitable when he ceased to be the chairman of Tata Sons. He said: 'I have an influence outside (of Tatas) which is not really justified and apparently have a reputation of my own . . . The style of the group today is somewhat an odd style. In some big companies there are powerful individuals who stamp their character.' He talked of a few of his close colleagues. Some, he said, were authoritarian in style, unlike himself. 'I think Ratan will be more like me,' he noted and continued, 'Some industrial houses like Birlas have split up when the head of the family passed away. Others have split up even before that event. I have seen so many other groups break up because of their sons and cousins. I said to myself this must not happen in Tatas. So the only way I could guide the group—I cannot run it—is through consensus. It could break up if there was no strong kind of cohesive centre which happens to be me. I had the name which helped. Secondly, I had a reputation for being reasonably intelligent, patriotic and honest and in that sense I provided a protective aura to the group. We have got a higher name and reputation today than ever. I had to find out some way of maintaining my influence and being able to control policy. The only way I could find was to be firm in principle and easy going on details so long as the principles of honesty and integrity were not affected. And that is consensus operating.'

The nearest organization one can compare Tatas to is the Commonwealth. Like the Commonwealth Tatas is a club of men who have had links and associations in the past and many share an *esprit de corps*. Though independent now, they come together to discuss larger issues and to consider broad lines of policy. Of course, they have their differences of opinion and the pulls of their own ambitions. The group chairman has to keep the team as one. The tapestry of Tatas is woven by the hand of history. For its own sake and for the sake of the nation it is important it holds together.

Section B

1992 to 2003

18

LIBERALIZATION: CHALLENGE & RESPONSE

A company or business that remains static is a business that will die. A company that constantly changes and accepts that there are better ways to do things than the way they are done today is the company that will survive in the global market that we face.

—Ratan N. Tata

At the age of forty in 1978, Ratan N. Tata was a director but was still at the periphery of the Tata group. While powerful satraps ran major companies he was assigned NELCO, the electrical and electronic arm of Tatas then functioning at a low key. Nevertheless the young man was one of the few who was looking beyond the interests of one company to the interests of the Tatas as a whole.

In May 1978 he sent a confidential note to J.R.D. Tata, entitled, 'Strategic Plan for Tatas'. The note was significant and reveals a depth of thought and concern. The note, which called for the initiation of a 'Tata Plan', read as follows:

For the past few years there has been an increasing tendency for the development and growth of our business activity being restricted to the framework of individual operating companies. There has been, in my view, inadequate strategic planning at a group level to determine the business areas into which Tatas should go, or develop further. I therefore, propose that the chairman should undertake to initiate a 'Tata Plan' which would seek to:

1. Provide a long-term direction for existing and future activities, product areas, and international operations for the group.

2. Define objectives for growth, earnings, technology utilization, R&D, industrial relations and employee benefits, which could all become operating guidelines for companies within the group.

3. Project the necessary group structure to best meet the stated objectives. (This could cover issues like the amalgamation of companies in related businesses, separation and/or shedding of unrelated or unprofitable business activities, and the creation of new corporate entities to undertake new lines of business.)

I am strongly advocating the initiation of such a document by the chairman as I personally see signs of our disintegration as a group. The first issue which needs to be addressed is whether we, as Tatas, see ourselves operating in the next 5 to 10 years as a single unified group, or a loosely-connected agglomeration of independent companies . . . If at all it is decided that Tatas should operate as a group, then several strategic decisions would need to be taken relating to the projected organizational and operational structure of Tatas.

He attached to his note eleven points Tatas needed to consider for the future. Significant among them was point six where he pleaded for a presence in petrochemicals:

'Tatas have been absent from the petro-chemical and chemical areas, apart from basic chemicals. Although efforts have been made in the past to enter these fields, have these efforts been adequate or forceful enough? Have we been persevering enough to enter these areas?' he asked.

On 29 July 1981—the 77th birthday of JRD—he addressed another note to him titled 'Strategic Plan for Tatas'. It was shorter than the previous one and attached were a list of issues to be addressed in the making of such a plan.

There is a growing feeling amongst some of us that Tatas are no longer operating as a unified organization, but instead as diverse fragments under a common name. There is therefore in my view an urgent need to arrest and reverse this trend . . . I honestly believe we are losing the strength and synergy inherent in a group of our size and diversity.

Ratan Tata felt that certain individual companies had made their plans so that 'they are not sought to be integrated.'

Three months later, on 7 September 1981, possibly expecting the young man to execute some of his own plans, J.R.D. appointed him chairman of Tata Industries. From that day on the business world woke up to his presence. As he says, Tata Industries was actually a shell company, a 100 per cent subsidiary of Tata Sons that in years bygone had been the vehicle for launching some great Tata companies. He set about transforming it.

The following year Ratan Tata's mother was seriously ill with cancer and was being treated at a New York hospital. He had been appointed to his distinctive position in Tata Industries less than a year earlier. In spite of business demands, he decided that his place was with his mother and the next three months he was with her.

He spent endless hours outside the hospital room of his mother in New York and it was there that he wrote out his fuller strategic plan for the Tatas. But the plan was stymied because of resistance from the powerful chief executives of some individual Tata companies, who saw the younger Tata's effort as an intrusion into their own turf.

In the 1980s there were also other seasoned contenders who could have assumed office of chairman of Tata Sons. In the mid 1980s Ratan Tata spoke to me of his ideas like levying a charge for using the Tata brand name and about co-ordination between companies then going their own way. When he became chairman of Tata Sons he made it all happen albeit up to ten years later. Before he took over as chairman of Tata Sons, he had already thought out what he wanted to do and pursued it with tenacity.

When Ratan Tata took over the 104-year-old house in 1991, for half its lifetime J.R.D. Tata had been its chairman. JRD brought lustre to the house and stamped his personal style on it. In the evening of JRD's life some other powerful chairmen and managing directors sought to put their own stamp on the individual companies, depending on their personal equation with JRD. JRD's style was prompted both by his charismatic personality and more so by the MRTP (Monopolies Restrictive Practices Act) which had come into effect in 1970 making it mandatory for the group to enforce a loose, federal style of management. Tata Sons/Industries 'directors-in-charge' of various companies were withdrawn. Autonomous boards ruled each company. S.A. Sabavala who was Tata's representative in New Delhi had one visiting card earlier. Overnight he had eighteen visiting cards for different companies!

In July 1991 many provisions of the MRTP Act were scrapped by Dr Manmohan Singh and India was on the high road to liberalization. Ratan Tata was fortunate in taking over just three months earlier.

In March 1991 when he took over as chairman of Tata Sons one of the first challenges he had to deal with was to consolidate a disparate group of individual companies which, under powerful chairmen or managing directors, were going their own way. He set a retirement age for chairmen at seventy-five and for managing and executive directors at sixty-five. He streamlined existing companies, decided to exit from others, started new companies and later acquired some. In the 1990s he accomplished what he wrote in 1978. In his first decade at the helm, Tatas have exited from sixteen companies and started thirty-two new businesses.

Over the years, the growth of Tatas shows:

1874-1900	1900-1920	1920-1940	1940-1960
Textiles	Hotel	Tata Airlines (domestic)	Air-India International*
	Electric Power	Chemicals	Heavy Trucks
	Steel		Air-conditioners
	Cement		
	Soaps		
	Insurance* (New India)		

1960-1990	1990-2002
Software	Cars
Watches	Telecom
Light Commercial Vehicles	Insurance
	Fertilizers

* Nationalized   : Aviation (1953)
                : Life Insurance (1956), General Insurance (1972).
                 Tatas exited from textiles in the 1980s and 1990s.

The accent today is on the growth points of I.T., software, automation and telecommunication where they are present at all levels—land, internet, cellular—and internationally through VSNL.

Broadly Tatas has seven core groups as it enters the 21st century* :

Materials	Steel, Advanced Plastics
Energy	Power
Chemicals	Inorganic fertilizer, Pesticides
Engineering	Automobiles, Auto Components, Air-conditioning

* For a complete list of Tata Companies as on 31 March 2003 see Appendix D.

Information Systems and Telecommunications	Software, Industrial Automation and Telecommunications
Consumer Products	Tea, Coffee, Watches
Services	Hotels, Retailing, Financial Services, Insurance, International Trade

In the last decade Tatas have sold their interests in soap and edible oils (TOMCO), cosmetics (Lakmé), paints (Goodlass Nerolac) and pharmaceuticals (Rallis and Merind). They also sold their holdings in cement (ACC and Tata Steel); computer and telecommunication hardware and oil. They withdrew from their joint ventures with IBM, Lucent and Timex. Between 1992 and 1997 the Indian economy boomed, demand surged, savings and investments peaked, customer choice expanded, and assets appreciated. The next four years witnessed a slowdown in the economy, with sharp fluctuations in agricultural growth, lack of growth in jobs, deflation in assets, and demand slowdown.

Tatas made a concerted bid to return to aviation in partnership with Singapore Airlines. They finally withdrew. *India Today*, 24 February 2003, questioned Ratan Tata in that context: 'You couldn't handle the politics?'

He answered: 'In the case of the domestic airlines, three governments changed the law to keep us out. They changed the percentage of equity partnership and finally when all else failed they said a foreign airline could not be a partner.'

Next question: 'You couldn't handle the political manipulation?'

Ratan Tata: 'I am proud I cannot handle that kind of political manipulation.'

In that context, talking to the same magazine Ratan Tata said: 'Nobody stood in our way in the case of passenger cars. In none of the businesses that we are in did the government really block us. But in some of the major projects in which we were involved, there were vested interests who didn't want to hand over control.'

He observed: 'Earlier, very often you would find government agencies concerned with constricting growth. Now, in many areas, business units want to pre-empt competition and restrict the entry of new players. It is contradictory to the national ambition of becoming an open-market economy.'

Their bid to recover their lost creation of 1948, Air-India, also was not successful.

*

Jamsetji Tata spoke about 'considering the interest of shareholders as our own.' That, and the interest of the depositors with a Tata company, came under a severe test with Tata Finance. Tata Sons alleged that poor governance and dubious dealings by top management of the company accompanied by suppression of information and misinformation resulted in a Rs 350-crore loss.

Unlike with other business scandals in India, the Tata Group itself blew the whistle. It dismissed the top management and filed criminal cases against those responsible, made provisions to neutralize the excessive exposure to some shares and the siphoning out of money, and initiated a business restructuring and cost-reduction exercise. Tata Sons and Tata Industries pumped in an estimated Rs 350-crore (apart from guarantees) into the company and its subsidiaries to ensure that depositors and lenders were not hurt.

There is scarcely an instance when any other industrial group has acted so honourably on such a large scale.

Another blow was the Rs 500-crore operating loss of Telco in the fiscal year 2001. The heavy investment in the new car project coincided with the collapse of the commercial vehicles market. With a tremendous effort the company reduced the loss to Rs 100 crore next year and in fiscal year 2002-03 it posted a profit before tax of Rs 500 crore. (Details in the next chapter.)

Laying Foundations for the Future

When Ratan Tata became chairman of Tata Sons, the old order changed not only for the house of Tata but also for the nation. Far reaching liberalization of the Indian economy coupled with globalization heralded an era of new opportunities and challenges. To meet these challenges he took a number of measures, among them:

Increasing Tatas holdings in companies it managed. In the old days Tatas had such support and trust of the shareholders (including financial institutions) that they could manage a major company (Tata Electric) with a holding of only 2 per cent. Holdings of Tatas in some companies, in 1992 and in 2002 are noted hereunder:

	1992	2002 (in per cent)
Tata Steel	8	26
Telco	17	32
Tata Chemicals	30	30
Tata Tea	30	30
Voltas	22	25
Indian Hotels	41	37

In some of the newer companies the Tata stakes are:

	(in per cent)
Tata Infotech	74
Trent Ltd.	26
Tata Infomedia	50

To consolidate and direct group policies the following steps were taken:

A Group Executive Office was established in 1998 comprising the group chairman and five members involved in group companies, group finance, group HR and new group projects. Later on, in 2002, a Tata Group Corporate Centre (GCC) was established which included the GEO members and comprised Mr R.N. Tata, Mr N.A. Soonawala, Dr J.J. Irani, Mr R.K. Krishna Kumar, Mr R. Gopalakrishnan, Mr Ishaat Hussain and Mr K.A. Chaukar.

A code of ethics was formulated to warrant the use of the name Tatas. If any company flagrantly defied it, the name of Tatas is to be withdrawn from it. While Tatas do not claim to be perfect, JRD often told me: 'But Tatas are different.' In official, as in personal life, people have their moments of frailty and may cross the ethical fence. Then they at least know that they have done so and can always return. When all the moral fences are down, there is no point of return.

The Tata Business Excellence Model was initiated in 1994. The Tata brand is immensely valuable. Recognizing this, the group leadership also realized that while many Tata companies take positive steps to enhance the brand there were also several companies which were not performing very well, and which were eroding the brand. In the mid 1990s a decision was taken to have a more formal relationship between Tata Sons and each Tata company. This saw the birth of the Brand Equity and Business Promotion (BEBP) agreement.

The philosophy is that every Tata company is an independent entity, but is also a member of the Tata family, for a number of reasons that include stake-holding, directorships, value systems, etc. It is essential for good corporate governance that before signing the BEBP agreement, the board of each company must independently decide to sign the agreement. The Tata Sons board takes its own view on this. Once both agree to proceed, the agreement is signed and the benefits of the use of the Tata group composite mark and the attendant brand promotion schemes flow to the company. A company that signs the agreement commits to two things:

It commits to adopting the Tata Business Excellence Model (TBEM) as a 'way of life'. The TBEM, which is a near clone of the Malcolm Baldrige Model used by the U.S. government to recognize high performing companies, is essentially a set of criteria distilled from high performing companies in the U.S. and converted into generic 'What do you do?' and 'How do you do it?' questions.

Companies that achieve a score of 500 are emerging industry leaders in the international context. Of the companies that signed the agreement Tata Steel was the first to surpass the 500 mark which is a recognition that they are amongst the best in the field by international standard. Tata Consultancy Services, Tata Engineering's Commercial Vehicle Business Unit, Titan Industries and the tube business of Tata Steel have all crossed the 500 mark level. They will cross 600 within a short time, as they continue to improve.

Now, nine years after the programme was initiated, forty companies have signed the BEBP agreement. Most (but not all) are progressing well. Of the companies twenty-eight meet the eligibility criteria (400 points) and are entering the External Assessment Programme.

A decade ago when some in the industry were still lobbying for protection for their industry, Tatas set about to make Tata companies—that so chose—to be globally competitive and to meet strict international criteria for their operations.

- The Tata name carries a high brand equity and the companies subscribing have to pay a small percentage of 0.10 to 0.25 per cent of their net profits for the use of the Tata name in the company and/or the product. A new Tata logo was also designed.
- Efficiency rather than the size of the group became the criteria. Unless the group had a leadership position or

could attain it in the first three ranks, exit could be considered. The growth potential had also to be considered.
- A new look was taken at its portfolios.

The new specific entries of the decade 1992-2002 are in:

Automobile
- Passenger Cars   -   Tata Engineering
- Auto Components   -   Tata Auto Components

Telecommunication
- Service-Basic   -   Tata Teleservices
- Cellular   -   Birla-Tata-AT&T, now Idea
- International Long   VSNL (through acquisition)
           Distance

Fertilizers   -   Tata Chemicals
Global Tea   -   Tetley Plc (through
                                 acquisition)
Insurance   -   Tata AIG

The exit from companies brought into Tatas a sum of Rs 2,500 crore ($0.50 billion). Entries cost over Rs 10,000 crore ($2.2 billion).

The major acquisitions of Tatas since 1992 have been: Tetley, VSNL and CMC—Computer Maintenance Corporation—the latter two divested by the Government of India. Hindustan Lever Chemicals was acquired from HLL.

- Portfolio restructuring means rationalization. There seemed no point in Tata Steel running its own captive power plant. It was sold to Tata Power. The three Tata electric companies were merged into one and called 'Tata Power'.

Voltas, an engineering company, was also in agrochemicals which was hived off to Rallis India. In addition to Tata International (formerly Tata Exports), Tata Steel was also trading internationally. That function was handed over to Tata International.

When Ratan Tata came to to the top position, his first challenge was to put the companies in a framework where they would move in one direction. He got a firmer hold of the companies. 'We have endeavoured to leave much of the autonomy of the company to the company. If a company wants to enter a particular business—say, the armaments business—and the group feels that it should not, it will object to the move as a shareholder. If the company persists in pursuing that line we will sell our stake in the company.' (*India Today*, 24 February 2003)

Manufacturing accounts for about 65 per cent of Tatas turnover and services for 35 per cent.* However, services constitute a much larger percentage of the group's profits.

Tatas are a global player in I.T. and in tea, and to a lesser extent in hotels. Tata Consultancy Services is the largest I.T. company in Asia. The Tata Tea-Tetley combination makes it the world's second largest in tea company. Tata Tea has the largest acreage of any tea company in the world.

When Ratan Tata stepped down as executive chairman in December 2002, he could claim that Tatas were no more a loose confederation of companies but a tightly knit group streamlined to meet the challenges of the future. Some well-known names in Indian business who did not undertake this task in time have disintegrated. JRD with his stature and charisma had a personalized style of working. To hold the group together for the future the system of working needed to be institutionalized. Ratan Tata has accomplished this.

---

* *Source*: Tata's Department of Economics and Statistics.

19

DRAMATIC TURNAROUNDS

Telco (now Tata Motors)

In the early 1980s Tata Chemicals and Telco were two of the largest companies of India.

What can a large concern do if the market for its product plummets overnight by 45 per cent and it registers a loss of Rs 500 crore? This happened with Telco in 2000-01. What would you have felt—and done—if you were called by the chairman and asked to assist him actively in the revival of the company?

This happened with Mr R. Gopalakrishnan, director of Tata Sons.

'What was your first reaction?' I asked him.

'I was overwhelmed, and felt privileged too.'

When he regained his composure two thoughts came to his mind. One was a quotation: 'When you work, work as if everything depends on you; when you pray, pray as if everything depends on God.'

The second thought was: 'The only one who can solve this problem are the guys in the company and not you. The reality is that the guys who know the problem will know how to solve it.'

He observed that the entire staff of Telco were seething with anger that the company they were so proud of had suddenly fallen in esteem—however unfavourable the external circumstances.

Anger can have one of two effects. It can either destroy or resuscitate. It is the Telco workers and staff that set about to re-energize the company. And they did. 'The credit goes to them,' says Mr Gopalakrishnan.

Between 1993 and 1997 Telco sales had shot up from Rs 2,500 crore to Rs 10,000 crore. The sales plummeted in 2000-2001 just when the Indica car project had absorbed Rs 1,700 crore. That year the sales sank to Rs 6,637 crore and the loss was a stunning Rs 500 crore.

When such a crisis happens, the in-built strength of a company and the spirit of its people counts. Dr V. Sumantran, (formerly with General Motors) now with Telco, says: 'The loss rattled the pride of the company's officials and workers. Out of that awakening of the spirit came the determination, "We can show everybody what we can do." And they did it. In an industry of global giants on Indian soil it needed a conviction to say: "We'll take them on."' And they did.

The infrastructure of the company was sound and though its trained staff were often poached upon by newer competitors, its in-built talent and human resources were considerable.

'The crisis unified the company as never before,' says Prakash Telang, Senior Vice-President. 'It is not just one person; the whole organization was part of the revival.'

They set about drastically cutting the costs by Rs 600 crore in two years. They worked feverishly on improving the quality of the Indica.

A major component of the quality upgrading was the Six Sigma methodology of near flawless products and services.

The chairman, Ratan Tata, had realized the need much earlier and asked the leadership to change, shed the arrogance that 'we are the best'. The company had embarked upon a change management initiative—business process reengineering in 1997 to bring in process improvement resulting in customer focus, quality and cost improvement.

The implementation of the recommendations involved a time frame of maximum three to five years. To convey to the organization the importance of the task in hand, the team came out with a name—Top Gear (Telco's Operations and People towards Global Excellence and Resurgence). It was envisaged that the project should have a distinctive identity, a unique and easy name to remember and signify the change management agenda. The Top Gear team identified the scope of the project though an internal brainstorming process. The Top Gear team was assigned the task of improving the supply chain, reviewing the work practices and analysing the organizational systems and HR policies.

In a short span of time, forty action teams consisting of 230 operating managers were working on the assigned tasks. These action teams were cross-functional teams. All the cross-functional teams (CFTs) were drawn from Tata Motors and consultant resources.

Teams worked day and night and converted data into useful form for further analysis. These analyses were then presented to the concerned areas for validation. Validated data was then compared with the operational vision statements and gaps were drawn out. The gaps were glaring. These gaps were then converted into action initiatives.

The senior management team, right from the chairman, met many youngsters and high performers in the company and tried to feel the pulse of the organization and noise in the wheels. They also threw open the problems to these selected employees and sought their opinions. These interactions also helped in finding out the main issues and prioritizing them. Leadership found that the employees were eager to help the company regain its position as a high performer in the corporate world. Leadership supported team work. In most of the cases where the issues were clearly identified, 'cross functional teams' were formed to tackle the problems and to implement the solutions. The other important step taken by the company was deployment of special training programmes such as 'winning ways at work' (www) and finance for non-finance staff. In addition, during the period 2000 to 2002, fourteen sessions were conducted to impart the learnings from Nissan's turnaround story. An essential requirement for taking part in the programme was that the employee must be a good performer and these were arranged in such a way that every batch comprised a mixed group drawn from all locations and across all grades and levels of management. The leadership was focused on creating a seamless and result-oriented work culture.

It was a great turnaround story. The result was there for every one to see in that a loss of Rs 500 crore in 2000-01 was turned into a profit before tax of Rs 500 crore in the year 2002-03.

Indica was Ratan Tata's dream in 1993. Telco officers went round the world and paid experts not to buy a licence or a technology but to develop the car they wanted. They wanted a car with the space of an Ambassador and the external dimensions of a Zen. The styling was from Italy; the engine design from France; instrumentation from Japan. Masterminding all the processes and manufacturing were Indian engineers.

'This project is attributed to me emotionally,' says Ratan Tata and adds: 'Not so. It is just that I had a strong conviction that our engineers, who could put a rocket into space, could produce our own car. And when we took up the challenge, we went out and got expertise wherever it was necessary. Everything we had in it was ours. So to me it was a great feeling of national achievement.'

Indica, when it came out in 1999, had over 1,15,000 orders registered with full payment. The pressure of production resulted in some cars being below par in quality. The new model, Indica V2, had rectified the earlier lapses and in 2002-2003 Indica was at the top of that segment in sales. In 2002 Indigo, Indica's first sedan, rolled out.

Rovers of England were looking for a world-class car in that segment and signed an agreement with Telco to sell Indica V2 in Britain and the continent of Europe—1,00,000 over five years under the name City Rover. The first batch was dispatched in 2003.

Tata Motors signed an MOU in 2003 to acquire Daewoo's

commercial vehicle company in South Korea.

When asked what was the major factor in Telco's turn-around, Dr Sumantran, in charge of passenger cars, replied: 'To me the most compelling factor is the spirit of the people of this company.'

In 2003 Tata Motors crossed the three million production milestone.

Ratan Tata now speaks of building a 'people's car' for Rs 1 lakh and notes that India needs to believe in itself, in its abilities, in its courage and in its people.

The heavy commercial vehicles division that accounts for most of the profit and has over 60 per cent of the Indian market is set on a major programme of producing a world-class truck. Graeme Maxton, managing director of the leading auto industry portal Autopolis, believes that the Tata group has made enormous progress and their low-cost approach to manufacturing will pay off in the long run. Unlike five years ago, the Tatas are now actually very close to European standards. It is coming from behind but accelerating at a much faster pace. In charge of this operation is Ravi Kant who joined Telco from Philips in 1999. He says: 'Telco grew up with the belief that it made the best trucks. That had to be entirely demolished first.' It was back to basics. Kant and his team vigorously attacked costs, cleaned up the supply chain, forced the hierarchy-conscious organization to push forward its bright, young managers to positions of responsibility, galvanized the product development processes and heightened quality.

Tata Chemicals

Tata Chemicals was a pioneer in inorganic chemicals in India and reigned supreme till liberalization. Soda ash and urea were its main business. However, it found it difficult to change gear in time once liberalization came in. In the early 1990s it had three attainments to its credit. The commissioning of the

'Babrala fertilizer (urea) plant in U.P.; the setting up of Tata Kisan Kendras to meet several requirements of farmers; and the launch of branded edible salt—Tata Salt.

Tata Chemicals Limited's fertilizer division at Babrala, commissioned in December 1994 manufactures urea, a widely used chemical fertilizer, and has an installed capacity of 8,64,000 tonnes per year, which constitutes nearly 12 per cent of the total urea produced by the country's private sector. The complex also houses an ammonia plant with a capacity of 1,350 tonnes per day.

Considered to be one of the best industrial facilities in India and comparable to the best in the world, the Babrala complex has set new standards in technology, energy conservation, productivity and safety.

The Babrala project was the first step towards the fulfilment of a long-standing commitment—to provide the Indian farmer with an optimal package of agricultural inputs and services. This is the largest single greenfield project that the Tatas have undertaken and its gestation period has been exceptionally short; it began making profits almost immediately after going into commercial production.

Reflecting its commitment to the environment, Tata Chemicals has invested over Rs 200 crore in its cement plant that was set up solely to make productive use of the solid waste from the soda ash process.

In spite of these efforts in 1999, with heavy dumping of soda ash from China coupled with a reduction in the fixed retention price of urea, it headed for a serious crisis. For the first time in its history, in the June quarter 2000, the company declared a loss. The company's assets were far greater than the market value of the shares quoted but investors look for quick profits, not assets gathered in the flowering years.

A new management under Prasad Menon was put into place and they started to re-focus and revamp the company.

Its manufacturing strength was still there but strategic planning was needed to get its advertising and marketing act in order. It took six significant steps:

1. Development of its human resources—workshops were held on skill development and customer-awareness.
2. Specialized training in marketing, and progressively taking over the marketing function into the company from third party agents.
3. Adoption of the Tata Business Excellence Model.
4. Exiting from detergents, which would cost a lot and require a new set of skills.
5. Linking its distribution processes to Information Technology.
6. The marketing department estimated the demand to tell production what to produce and of what quality rather than setting marketing targets on the basis of production capacity.

In early 2003 it acquired Hindustan Lever Chemicals which had synergy with its existing business. Fertilizers and bulk chemicals is the core business of Tata Chemicals Limited, with inherent technological strengths. Also, its product portfolio and geographical spread are complementary to that of Hindustan Lever Chemicals Limited. While Hindustan Lever Chemicals is a leading player in the phosphatic segment, commanding over two-thirds of the market in West Bengal, Bihar, and Jharkhand, Tata Chemicals is strong in urea in the northern region, with a complementary dealer network. Both companies have built up very strong brands over the years through intensive farmer extension programmes. Hindustan Lever Chemicals' factory is in Haldia, while Tata Chemicals' factories are in Mithapur in Gujarat and Babrala in Uttar Pradesh. The merged company will be able to offer a comprehensive portfolio of phosphatic and nitrogenous fertilizers in the east and in the north.

Tata Chemicals profit which had dropped to Rs 30 crore in 2000-01 climbed sharply to Rs 200 crore in 2001-02 and

Rs 268 crore in 2002-03. Its turnover is Rs 1,700 crore.

Tata Kisan Kendras brought to farmers not only fertilizers, pesticides and equipment on loan but also the benefits of imagery and remote-sensing technology. The kendras help to analyse soil, track crop health and pest attacks, and map the quality of soil. This helps farmers adapt quickly to changing conditions. The result: healthier crops, higher yields and enhanced incomes for farmers. The command area of the kendras covers the states of Uttar Pradesh, Haryana and Punjab.

Prasad Menon, who joined as managing director in 2001, was asked what would happen to the company if dumping was resumed in future by foreign companies. He replied that the government now (unlike earlier) responded to dumping in four or five months. The competition could come from the USA. The cost of soda ash is very low in America because they have natural soda ash. Fortunately for India, the cost of transporting soda ash from the centre of America to India is quite substantial. Even so, the only answer is to keep costs competitive in a globalized economy. A good test of competitiveness is to constantly export a proportion of production. Rather than complain about imports, Tata Chemicals now exports 10-15 per cent of its production. The challenge before Tata Chemicals is now to consolidate and grow.

20

PLANNING AHEAD FOR SUCCESS

*May God grant that in serving the Tatas you will also
serve India and will always realize that you are here
for a much higher mission than merely working for an
industrial enterprise.*
                    —Mahatma Gandhi visiting Tata Steel,
                              Jamshedpur, 8 August 1925.

Tata Steel

As the 21st century dawned there was an excess of 25 per cent in steel capacity across the world. Tata Steel had planned way ahead. Till 1982 it got the best out of its old machinery, some of which went back to World War II. Various plans that were put before the board in bits and pieces were not accepted because in those days money was hard to come by. In the early 1980s the then general manager, Dr J.J. Irani, told J.R.D. Tata: 'If we do not modernize the steel plant, in a few years time you and I will be standing outside the steel plant selling tickets to visit a steel museum.' Mr Tata laughed heartily but he and the whole board took it seriously and acted. Meanwhile, Prime Minister Rajiv Gandhi had also shown signs that India would have to enter into the emerging globalization. While Telco needed a loss to awaken, Tata Steel had a man with foresight who planned ahead.

The modernization was implemented from 1988 till 2001, old machinery was replaced by new and production enhanced. They gradually phased out ordinary steel manufacturing to make only special steels.

When asked whether it was the cold rolling mill that ushered Tata Steel into the new steel age, Dr Irani (who became managing director in 1992) replied:

'Making steel may be compared to making a chappati. To make a good chappati even a golden rolling pin will not work unless the dough is good. The mistake many people make is to first introduce new finishing facilities and expect the product to be good. We did it the other way round. We first started with the coke oven, making better use of the raw material. We ensured that the blast furnaces were more productive and the five mills in the cold rolling complex came as the icing on the cake.'

When plans for the cold rolling mills with a capacity of 3 million tonnes were to be put up, Ratan Tata questioned Dr Irani whether India had the capacity to absorb so much more special steel than it was absorbing at that time. He got an affirmative reply. In 2003 Tata Steel has the capacity to supply special steel to the whole of India and at a price that is near to the cheapest in the world.

An advantage Tata Steel has are its captive mines, thanks to the vision of Jamsetji Tata who in 1902, on getting the go ahead from the Secretary of State for a steel plant, sent a cable to his company from London to get licences for iron ore, coking coal and fluxes. The disadvantage Tata Steel had to cope with was its enormous work force. Between the plant and the mines it had 78,000 employees which, with the voluntary retirement scheme, has been reduced to 43,000.

It was not easy to reduce the work force. There was a tradition—and it was once written into the agreement with the union—that every retiring worker would nominate a person to take his job (usually his son) when he retired. The management finally convinced the union that for the sake of survival this clause would have to be changed. Dr J.J. Irani addressed meeting after meeting with the workers and the staff. At one of these meetings an agitated worker shouted: 'But what about a job for my son?' Dr Irani replied: 'I am not worried about a job for your son, I am worried about your job and mine. If we don't change, this company will shut down and neither you nor I will have a job.'

The point went home.

Tata Steel exited from all activities which were not directly connected with steel, for example, a cement plan and a captive power plant it owned were sold. The former to a French company and the latter to Tata Power. These companies had the competence to do the job as well as or better than Tata Steel.

Tata Steel got external consultants to create new operational skills. They moved up the value chain in their product mix.

B. Muthuraman, managing director of Tata Steel, recalls: 'In the last ten years we have done major re-engineering, fanatical cost-cutting, manpower reduction, market-expansion exercises and made use of information technology. All these have helped us enhance our profits and put us in a position to plan our growth for the next ten years.'

While some steel plants around the world were closing down and others were struggling, Tata Steel, whose profit had dipped to Rs 282 crore in 1999 rose to Rs 422 crore next year, Rs 533 crore the following year to over Rs 1,000 crore in 2002-2003.

The main architect who spearheaded this turnaround with advance planning, Dr J.J. Irani, passed out with a gold medal in metallurgy at the Sheffield University in 1962. He was a J.N. Tata Scholar. The director of the J.N. Tata Endowment sent a letter to J.R.D. Tata giving him the news of this young man's achievement. J.R.D. Tata sent back the letter with the remark: 'If ever this young man wants to return to India ask him to first knock on the door of the Tata Iron and Steel Company.' After passing out, for five years Irani worked in Sheffield. The managing director of Tata Iron and Steel Company, Savak Nanavatty, took the unusual step of going to Irani's office to interview him in Sheffield and ask him to return to India. Irani did.

J.R.D. Tata and Sumant Moolgaokar, then vice-chairman, invited him to join the research team. Irani agreed but told them that after six months he would decide whether he wanted to stay or go back to his job in England. At the end of six months JRD and Moolgaokar asked him his decision. Irani said he wanted to go back. Overnight they shifted him to the works as superintendent, then works manager, general manager and finally, managing director from 1992-2001.

After being appointed managing director by the board in Bombay he was flying back to Jamshedpur. On the plane he jotted down his guidelines:

What I (as CEO) must do:

- Develop a personal vision—what do I want to accomplish in life.
- Tell the truth about current reality.
- Do the tough things no one else wants to do.
- Restructure the TOP TEAM, if necessary.
- Build a powerful guiding coalition—management and board.
- Guide the creation of a shared VISION.
- Take the responsibility of being the main change agent.
- Create endless opportunities for two-way communications.
- Create opportunities for innovations in the rank and file.
- Maintain Focus.
- Realign HR systems, overcome obstacles.
- Model the desired managerial behaviour—above all maintain CREDIBILITY.
- Preserve the core values of TATAS (and my own).

It is people who build companies, not just ideas. For a company to survive for a 100 years (the centenary is in 2007) the organization should have at its head the right man at the right time.

21

GROWTH POINTS FOR THE FUTURE

In 1968, planning for the impending introduction of the Monopolies Restrictive Trade Practices (MRTP) Bill Tata Sons diversified in four consultation units of its own, leveraging its skills:

1. Tata Consultancy Services
2. Tata Consulting Engineers
3. Tata Economic Consultancy Services
4. Tata Financial Services

In that year, P.M. Agarwal, managing director of Tata Electric Companies, felt the computer industry, then in its infancy, had a future. A full scale computer in those days could occupy a whole room. Initially, it made smaller computers as aids to calculation.

The Tata Consultancy Services

After a few faltering steps in a field unknown to India, Faqir Chand Kohli, one of Tata's brilliant electrical engineers, was put on the job. Soon Kohli's research papers were winning international acceptance. He won recognition when he installed the digital based load despatch and system management network for electric power at Trombay, Bombay, when only four to five utilities in USA had digital systems. Even UK, France, Germany and Japan were on analog systems.

He was elected to the thirty-member governing board of the 3,00,000 strong Institute of Electric Engineers, USA, for a two-year term, 1973-1974. There he had among twenty-nine colleagues, the top research university heads and other experts to work with. He visited some of them in the universities where the fledgling technology was being researched and developed. When the term 'Information Technology' was not familiar to India, he noted in a speech in 1975 to the Computer Society of India, as its president: 'Many years ago, there was an industrial revolution; we missed it for reasons beyond our control. Today there is a new revolution—a revolution in information technology, which requires neither mechanical bias nor mechanical temperament. Primarily, it requires the capability to think clearly. This we have in abundance. We have the opportunity to participate in this revolution on an equal basis; we have the opportunity, even, to assume leadership in this revolution. If we miss this opportunity, those who follow us will not forgive us for our tardiness and negligence.'

He realized India's strength lay in its brain power, second to none in the world, and made the Tata Consultancy Services (TCS) a first-rate software engineering and service provider. Today it has 20,000 software engineers and has been the stable for providing software engineers to India and abroad. 'We,' said F.C. Kohli, 'are in the business of building people.'

The road in India was bumpy for the new technology and any man with vision. There were many hurdles in those early years, especially the negative mindset of the government, politicians, bureaucrats and labour unions, which considered computers to be a cause of unemployment. TCS developed PAN number for the income tax payees in 1977 for the Income Tax Department. Thereafter, TCS was given an assignment to computerize the entire processing of income tax (which incidentally would have put India ahead of many other countries). However, Mr Charan Singh on becoming the finance minister, decreed that there would be no computerization in departments under the finance ministry. He feared that computerization would create unemployment! People did not understand. It was Rajiv Gandhi and his dreams of taking India into the 21st century that first eased the path for India to build herself as a significant player in software on the international scene.

By 1984 Tatas had links with Burroughs Corp. and other big U.S. companies. A proposal came to merge TCS with Tata Burroughs—a company jointly owned by Tatas and Burroughs. Wiser counsel prevailed and TCS remained an independent division of Tata Sons. It was only after 1992 and liberalization of the economy that Information Technology got a boost in this country and sales of TCS more than doubled over two to two and a half years, making it the most profitable Tata company with the minimum of investment. For years it maintained a low profile. In 2003 it was the largest of its kind in Asia with a revenue of over $1 billion. It is expected to go public soon though Tatas is expected to keep a very substantial holding for a long time to come.

Retired at seventy-five, F.C. Kohli is unstoppable. Under the umbrella of TCS he has developed a system to use the computer to speed up the spread of literacy all over India. There are almost 200 million adults who cannot read and write. Currently, illiteracy is reducing at the rate of 1.5 per cent per annum. At this rate, we will need twenty years to attain a literacy level of 95 per cent. The Central and state literacy missions have done a remarkable job over the years. The constraints have been the availability of trained teachers, and the use of conventional methods of learning from alphabets to words, which requires 200 hours of instruction. After thirty hours of computerized instruction without the aid of a trained teacher, the women started reading the newspaper in Telugu in 8 to 10 weeks. They learn by words rather than alphabet. Andhra Pradesh has encouraged it and will probably be the first state to take on the programme. Now, the social benefits of Kohli's work under the TCS umbrella will benefit millions.

Kohli gives credit to the late Nani Palkhivala who was his chairman for thirty years. Palkhivala's understanding and support were a tremendous help, especially during the early years when the field was uncharted and so few could grasp the vision Kohli had.

Apart from the fortuitous circumstances that greeted Kohli what are the other factors that have created a world-class company like TCS?

- Its investment in people, processes and technology: TCS was the first Indian software company on the scene by 1970 and ploughed a lonely furrow. R. Ramadorai, who succeeded Kohli as managing director, says: 'When TCS pioneered the industry, we started with several handicaps. We needed to learn everything from scratch. But, today we are positioned to be a global systems consulting firm, with an array of offerings in several domains and technologies, the processes to deliver complex solutions, and the competencies to sell and support these in all parts of the world. We have developed a global face.'

- Its links with the academia: It began with Kohli's links with U.S. universities but TCS soon turned to paying attention to India's academia culminating in a well thought out proposal to upgrade India's top fifty to sixty engineering colleges to the level of the IITs. The Union government has officially accepted the proposal. TCS is giving to India many times what it has received from it. Only 10 per cent of its business is from India. The rest is from abroad. However, TCS is deeply committed to computerization within the country. It believes computerization in Indian languages will lead to unparalleled growth and prosperity.

- It developed links with the top companies worldwide— eighty of them—including IBM, Oracle, General Electric and Hewlett-Packard. Its first major foreign assignment was way back in 1971 for the Detroit police.

- It launched its own software products in 1980 with Addict, a data dictionary, to advanced systems like a system integration for the National Stock Exchange.

- It was the first Indian company to get contracts for foreign outsourcing in India way back in 1974.
- It dared to move fast at every opening—Japan in 1992, Africa in 1995, China in 2002.
- Accessibility: It gives first rate service with 149 offices in thirty-one countries.
- It invests heavily in training—Rs 200 crore ($41 million) per year—at its dedicated centre in Kerala.
- It has the largest staff of 20,000 software engineers, average age of 90 per cent is under thirty years. It spends 3 to 4 per cent of its revenue on training and continuing education programmes.
- It docs not rest on its oars. 'Unless we reinvent ourselves, we face the real prospect of becoming irrelevant,' says R. Ramadorai.
- TCS's decision to open thirteen global development centres to service its customers has catapulted it into a global player.
- Ramadorai is an electronic and telecommunication engineer from the Indian Institute of Science founded by Jamsetji Tata. When Kohli opened up the USA in the 1970s, it was Ramadorai who followed it through and opened new avenues.

When Kohli stepped down at seventy-five, Ramadorai succeeded him.

The I.T. industry, like telecom, moves at a hurtling pace. To survive it demands that you don't sit still for a day. It needs strong nerves apart from vision and know-how.

Having attained pre-eminence in its speciality, TCS has gone ahead in social fields too. Apart from the adult literacy project, it has expertise on Mumbai's transport system and its research wing has developed a water filter that uses agricultural waste water to deliver safe and clean drinking water in the rural areas.

TCS operates not by brains alone. Software can have a soft heart too.

Tata Teleservices

While all companies aim for growth, the most promising areas are I.T. and telecom. In both cases the path is ridden with risks.

At different times different industries hold the promise of growth. In the 1990s it was Information Technology. From 2000 onwards it is the telecom sector, though I.T. will grow along with it.

In March 2001 subscribers to the telecom sector were thirty-five million. By 2006 it is expected to touch eighty-five million. In terms of revenue it is expected to leap to Rs 66,000 crore.

Tatas have a strong presence in every aspect of the business—basic, cellular, internet, national long distance and, through its acquisition of VSNL, in international long distance.

The genesis of Tatas' involvement with the hi-tech and services field goes back to the 1980s when Ratan Tata outlined a plan to enter these areas. Telecom equipment was among the areas identified, but government's policy reserved this sector for the Department of Telecommunications (DOT).

Hesitantly the government took one step, paused; then took another step, paused and proceeded.

First the manufacture of telephone instruments and private automatic telephone equipment was opened up. Tatas formed a joint agreement with the government of Kerala and Tata Keltron was born. On Private Telephone Exchange (PABX) Tatas linked up with Oki in Japan and started manufacturing in Ahmedabad. When Oki's technology became outdated they linked up with Lucent Technologies, USA. Lucent Technologies transferred the manufacture of their system to a new company, Avaya, and Tatas entered into a joint venture with them.

With the onset of liberalization in the early 1990s, the government opened up the window wider and permitted multinationals to start joint ventures to manufacture public telephone exchanges and switch equipment. Tatas briefly joined Lucent in this venture but when the government changed its policy to permit 100 per cent foreign holding, Tatas got out.

In 1995 the government invited bids for cellular services all over the country. Tatas joined hands with Bell-Canada and started a joint venture company in 1997, Tata Teleservices. Later as part of their restructuring, Bell-Canada pulled out and Tatas took over.

Tata Teleservices got the licence to provide basic telecom services to Andhra Pradesh in 1999. By 2003 they had embraced five other 'A' telecom circles—Karnataka, Tamil Nadu, Delhi, Gujarat and Maharashtra including Mumbai. These five states yield 56 per cent of India's subscriber base and 65 per cent of its revenue.

Ratan Tata says: 'We have not created a lot of hype. We are very satisfied with Andhra Pradesh. We have chosen to stay in six states based on the business potential there. We have not built an all-India long-distance network because we believe it will be more effective to build part capacity and lease the rest from others. We need to have coverage all over India but we don't need to own it all or build it all.'

Tatas are determined but realistic. They have kept a low profile. If you have muscle you don't need to flex it all the time. Tatas are promising less but expect to deliver more.

When China went into telecom they started with a centralized system and when they found it was difficult to cope with it they opened up the industry into geographic circles. India was wiser and began with circles and started the industry by giving responsibility to various companies.

Many have seen the promise of telecom for the future. Quite a few have rushed in. But at the end of the day, only three or four big players are expected to survive. This will involve mergers and acquisitions.

With subscriber growth in cellular operations, Tatas decided to widen their wings and go beyond one circle. They decided to merge and grow. Joined by AT&T Wireless, USA, and Birla they formed Idea Cellular. Hughes Telecom was acquired for its land line service with a subscriber base of two lakh lines—two-thirds of them in Mumbai.

Tatas' strategic strike was to emerge as winners in the race to acquire the giant Videsh Sanchar Nigam Limited (VSNL), with its international link. It gave the Tatas the capability to offer every conceivable service under one umbrella even if it be through different Tata-linked companies.

Tatas believe in forming 'clusters of strength'. The group has concentrated in the South and the West, plus Delhi.

Tatas cover the entire spectrum of the telecom sector through different companies. Till 2003 March they have put in Rs 6,000 crore into this project and could do more.

'The Tatas,' says R. Gopalakrishnan, executive director of Tata Sons, 'are uniquely positioned compared to any other private telecom player. About 20 per cent of what TCS does falls under telecom. TCS moved from software in banking and financial services to software in telecom. From there the group has moved to telecom services. It always helps if you are moving into a new business from an adjacent point.'

22

SOME PERFORMERS

The Taj Group

Jamsetji had four pioneering schemes: steel, hydro-electric power, a 'university of research' (now the Indian Institute of Science, Bangalore) and a hotel the like of which hardly existed in Asia.

For steel he was very business-like. He studied the freight rates for iron ore and coal in America and Europe, and demanded concessions from the government. Business like too he was for hydro-electric power. The Indian Institute of Science occupied a special place in his heart and he left half his fortune for it. But it was only for the Taj he could physically work, buying its soda water plant, its laundry and other wherewithals from Germany. He wanted to give the Bombay of his days a world-class hotel. It was his gift to the city he loved and he never counted the cost. The Taj Mahal Hotel was his only grand scheme that came up in his lifetime. He was then about sixty-four years old. He died at sixty-five.

At the time of writing this book, the Taj is his only grand project to celebrate its centenary. Tata Steel will follow in 2007, the Indian Institute of Science in 2009 and Tata Hydro in 2010.

It would cheer his spirit to know that today the name 'Taj' is synonymous with the finest hospitality one can expect. The Taj group has 18,000 employees globally.

The group has benchmarked itself with the world's best for customer satisfaction. In an industry where how the staff interfaces with the public is crucial to success, it has established several centres of excellence for training its employees.

At the 8th World Travel Awards ceremony held at Kuala Lumpur, travel agents worldwide voted the Taj Mahal Hotel, Mumbai, as the leading hotel in the Asia Pacific region. The new Taj Exotica in Maldives also won the Best Opening Resort award from Harpers and Queen.

In Kerala, Taj has pioneered what is called green tourism—having expert ayurvedic treatment centres at five of its hotels there.

In 2002, it acquired a five-star presence in Mumbai's northern suburbs acquiring the 9-acre former Regent Hotel in Bandra. Strategically placed at the opening of the Bandra Worli sea-link due in the near future, this acquisition has reinforced its leadership position in the country.

The Taj group is looking for expansions and acquisitions globally.

Under R.K. Krishna Kumar, till recently its managing director, the Taj group and the Archaeological Survey of India joined hands to preserve and upgrade facilities at the Taj Mahal complex in Agra. The fifteen-month-long project will not only involve conservation of the monument but will also include development of some of the thirty-three lost Moghul gardens around the Taj complex, besides a collaborative study on long-term preservation of the structure itself. Indian Hotels will invest Rs 1.87 crore in the first phase of an upgrading of tourist facilities, putting up a new lighting system around the monument, developing the gardens, cleaning up the surroundings, pathways and the fountains.

Tata Tea

There are two ways to establish a global presence. One is to build your own brand, something both expensive and risky. The other, quicker route is to acquire an existing global brand. In 1995 Tata Tea made a bid for Tetley of UK, the world's second largest tea company, but was not successful. Fortunately, Tetley was up for sale again in 1999. This time

Tata Tea made a bid and acquired the company for £271 million (Rs 1,900 crore).

India has been the world's largest tea supplier for well over a century, but it had no control over the global market. Apart from Hindustan Lever, no tea-estate company could significantly sell its own teas as brands. They were dependent on tea auctions over which they had no control. The Tetley acquisition gave Tata Tea a global reach.

Tata Tea had earlier acquired Consolidated Coffee, the largest coffee producer in Asia, and, in 1996, it made its first foreign acquisition, Watala Tea Estate of Sri Lanka with its 11,000 million kilos of high quality tea leaves. It also controls Tata Tea Inc., which has significant presence in the instant tea market in the USA.

The Tetley acquisition created waves in the British media. Perhaps this was the first time an Indian company had bought over a British company that was a household name. Tetley buys teas from all over the world, Argentina and Turkey included.

Tetley is extremely good at innovation in packaging. It was the first company in the world to introduce tea bags. It also created the round tea bags and the drawstring tea bags.

Tata Tea's employee facilities are unequalled in the tea industry. To keep itself competitive it has to count on its efficiency and sharpen it all the time. Its facilities, as of 2003, include sixty-three hospitals and two large referral hospitals with 1,700 beds and eighty-seven doctors. It also runs 280 adult literacy centres and 173 childcare centres. The referral hospital in Assam is renowned in the region.

Success has its own price. In 1997 Tata Tea was accused of colluding with the Assamese extremist organization ULFA. The truth, as has been revealed in subsequent years by the courts, is that Tata Tea was the only company that refused to pay any money to the extremists. Its actions have been cleared by the Central government's Intelligence Bureau.

Mr R.K. Krishna Kumar, a Tata Administrative Services

244 THE CREATION OF WEALTH

(TAS) officer, who has played a significant part in the tea interests of Tata for two decades, says: 'The key task before the company now is to integrate all these subsidiaries. I see fusing of all these entities into one super global company: maybe, with a listing on the New York Stock Exchange, the London Stock Exchange, the Bombay Stock Exchange, and so on—seamlessly operating as one entity, deriving all the efficiencies of integration and imparting the necessary aggression in the marketplace to gain market share. It will be a very successful global tea company, owned by the Tatas, an Indian company, and very successfully run across the globe.'

Tata Power

Mumbai is the only metropolis in India that is free of electric power cuts. No one there keeps generators handy. Tata Power's unique 'islanding system' keeps Mumbai lights on at all hours of the day and night.

Until recently the Tata group's electricity operations were largely focussed on generation, transmission and bulk distribution in Mumbai. Currently it has two 500 MW thermal units providing power supply to Mumbai. The pride of Tata Power is the Load Despatch Centre with its state of the art Data Acquisition and Power Supply Security Management System. The system helps maintain reliable power supply at an economical rate to Mumbai city. The on-line data from all the generating and receiving stations is transmitted to this centre via a computer network for monitoring. This enables the operator on duty to control the continuously changing system load requirement. There is seldom any load-shedding in Mumbai city.

Apart from providing power to Mumbai, Tata Power has also set up power plants in Jojobera at Jharkhand, Wadi and Belgaum in Karnataka to supply power to Tata Steel, ACC and the Karnataka grid respectively, and a wind farm at Ahmednagar in Maharashtra.

Tata Power has also made a foray into retail distribution in Delhi in a joint venture with the Delhi government and into transmission business as a joint venture with the Power Grid Corporation of India Ltd, a public sector undertaking.

On 1 April 2000, Tata Hydro-Electric Power Supply Company and the Andhra Valley Power Supply Company merged with Tata Power Company to become the single largest private utility. The managing director at the time, Adi Engineer, said: 'The change in strategic thinking was mainly to eliminate the risks in Tata Power's business model as it was a couple of years ago. We had a one-stream revenue model—and a very reliable one at that—from the Mumbai licensee business. But however reliable a business model, it's too risky to have just one stream working. That's the thought that made us pursue streams of revenue for which we had the technical competence. The liberalization process helped, and the first thing we went into was captive power. We have two captive areas now, one in Wadi, Karnataka, and one in Jamshedpur.'

The company made history by signing the shareholders' agreement for construction, operation and maintenance of a 400 KV transmission line from Siliguri to Delhi with Power Grid Corporation, at an estimated cost of Rs 1,100 crore. This is the first joint venture company of its kind in India. Tata Power also took over the transmission construction business of Tata International and has orders worth Rs 200 crore for the construction of EHV lines.

With a view to expanding into the allied infrastructure business, Tata Power made a significant entry into the telecommunication business by initially utilizing its available optic fibre network for broadband communication. Tata Power Broadband (TPBB), a division of the Tata Power Company Ltd, is the first telecom player in India to commercially launch the state-of-the-art Dense Wave

Division Multiplexing (DWDM) based Metropolitan Optic Fibre Network (MAN) in Mumbai and Mumbai-Pune. The Tata Power Broadband's optic fibre network was completed in August 2001. The 600-km optic fibre network is designed with the best international networking standards covering the length and breadth of Mumbai. TPBB has positioned itself as a 'carrier's carrier', which means that it provides its services to other telecom service providers, such as internet service providers, cellular service providers, national and long-distance telephone operators, data centres, call centres, cable operators and video service providers. Currently the division has over fifty customers, among them some of India's best-known service providers.

In 2002 Tata Power made an investment of around Rs 1,350 crore, of which Rs 700 crore was in the power business, Rs 250 crore in energy and the balance Rs 400 crore in communications.

It could selectively move into other energy related businesses. Tata Petrodyne is a 100 per cent subsidiary of Tata Power and is engaged in the business/exploration and production of oil and gas. It is in consortium with leading oil and gas companies for exploration and development projects in three offshore blocks. At present these include two gas blocks in the Gulf of Cambay, Gujarat, and one oil block in the Cauvery basin, Tamil Nadu.

What does it take for a single-track company to diversify so much within a decade? Says Adi Engineer: 'We have been working on changing the mindset of our people. You can't run a large company like ours with totally new people, so the change comes from reorienting the mindset of the existing managers. We have some excellent senior managers, people who have adapted well to the shift in focus, from being totally operational to being both operational and commercial. We have seen a tremendous change here.'

Continuing its social commitment, in addition to the fingerlings and eco-restoration at its catchment areas in the

Western Ghats (covered in the earlier edition) a green belt of 1,00,000 trees has been raised round the thermal power plant in Mumbai.

Once the company guarded its lake water zealously but seeing the growing needs of nearby villagers it releases water to them and also at the government's request to drought-prone villages.

The Tata Power Company recently undertook the project of 'Lifeline Express' at Lonavla by sponsoring the world's first 'Hospital on Wheels', where almost 1,000 patients received surgical assistance and 10,700 patients were provided OPD facilities. In addition, Tata Power has regularly conducted family planning camps where laproscopic sterilizations are performed.

Tata Power has been providing alternate livelihood to people by donating trees and fingerlings to the villagers in the catchment areas.

The Titan Story

Strange encounters can sometimes result in new ventures. One day, in the mid-seventies, a recipient of the Jawaharlal Nehru scholarship one Mahadevan came to the then managing director of Tata Press, Xerxes Desai. He was researching the undeciphered Indus Valley script and using facilities at the Tata Institute of Fundamental Research. He wanted his computer generated tapes to be converted into a printed book. It so happened that the gentleman was a joint secretary in the ministry of industry. He suggested to Xerxes Desai that Tatas may want to look into the manufacture of watches as a possible area of diversification. Desai little realized where the trail would lead him.

Government policy in those days required that anyone wishing to enter the watch business should be able to make the movement—the mechanism that drives a watch. It took years to find a party willing to provide the technical know-how to make movements. The four major movement producers in the world: Seiko, Citizen, Timex and ASUAG (later the Swatch Group) were unavailable or unwilling to part with know-how. The scheme lay dormant till the joint secretary, Mahadevan, was transferred as chairman and managing director of the Tamil Nadu Industrial Development Corporation (TIDCO), where he discovered that TIDCO was in dialogue with a relatively unknown movement manufacturer in France about setting up a facility in India. Desai took the cue from Mahadevan and put together a technology transfer deal with the French company, France Ebauches. This was in the early 1980s.

The application was made by a newly formed company, Titan Watches Limited, which was a joint sector company with TIDCO as partner. The name Titan, was derived from Tata Industries and Tamil Nadu.

Titan entered the market in March 1987. Going against conventional wisdom, Titan chose not to make mechanical watches. It read the writing on the wall and chose the electronic, quartz analog route instead. It was to prove to be a wise decision. Within a decade, mechanical watches were virtually wiped out worldwide, save in a minuscule luxury segment.

Propelled by a wide choice of styles, good advertising, excellent quality and, marketed as a Tata product, Titan watches were an immediate success. When asked what was the secret of Titan's remarkable success Desai replies: 'The name Tata. We have no idea of the magic in that name.'

It undertook the manufacture of cases, bracelets, electronic circuitry and step motors. Capacity was progressively raised from 2 million watches per year to 6 million over a fifteen-year period. Know-how came from a variety of sources, including from the Citizen watch company for the case plant.

Titan soon became the dominant force in India's watch market accounting for about half of the watches that were produced in India. With Titan's meteoric rise came the sad decline of its two main competitors, Allwyn and HMT.

Another factor in its success was the accent on selection and training. Out of every 100 who applied only three got selected through a demanding test of aptitude and attitude. They were then put through months of carefully crafted and supervised training before being sent on to the shop floor. And training them for production was not the only knowledge imparted. Most of the young men and women came from poor rural and semi-urban backgrounds and had lived all their lives in the sheltered environments of their homes. These young men and women had to be prepared for life in countless other ways—how to take care of their minds and bodies, their relationships with each other, how to meet their obligations to their families and how to plan and prepare for the future. In the setting of Tamil Nadu's semi-rural area Titan became their foster parent.

A factor in Titan's marketing success has been its chain of owned and franchised outlets.

Titan's management instituted educational scholarships for students of the Dharmapuri district and won the national award for employment of the physically handicapped. It is an experience to see how well and speedily the blind can pack boxes. Titan embarked upon a project to develop and build a township, designed by Charles Correa, for its employees so as not to strain the resources of Hosur town and to develop a model township that others could emulate. Today an excellent physical and social infrastructure awaits its staff.

In 1994, Titan launched its range of jewellery and jewellery watches under the brand name 'Tanishq'—a word coined from Tata and Nishq (meaning a necklace of gold coins) and, again, from Tan, meaning body and Ishq, meaning love. Jewellery was a good fit with the watch business, both being in the personal adornment sector. Globally watchmakers were turning to jewellery and jewellers to watch making. Gold is often adulterated in India. Tanishq has brought the stamp of reliability with it. It has brought about a transformation in the manner in which jewellery is bought and sold in India.

Today Titan watches are sold in about forty countries. It has fared extremely well in the Middle East and moderately well in South-East Asia, but has yet to succeed in the European market where giants with large resources reign. The European foray resulted in a significant decline in Titan's profitability for a few years. The power of the giants was underestimated.

Titan has sought to create a work culture where each person, every group is driven by a burning desire to be outstanding, not only within the company, but in a much wider world. Titan's chairman is from the Tamil Nadu Industrial Development Corporation and its managing director is from Tatas. Its chairman says: 'The route to excellence is the route of endeavour. The route to satisfaction is the route of dissatisfaction. Everything that we do, every achievement, every decision is taken through a process of rational discussion—yet nothing is so final that it cannot be reviewed, discussed and revised, again and again. Reason, an enquiring mind, a scientific temperament are essentials for the achievement of excellence. Every proposal has to be thoroughly argued and defended, proceeding by logical steps from proven premises to credible conclusions. In this environment, there is no room for opinions that are not convincingly argued. There is no scope for hang-ups and predilections. At every discussion or brain-storming session everyone becomes instantly equal and is allowed to freely question or advise. This cerebral approach has become a corporate feature. Every agreed plan of action can be successfully challenged and displaced by a more convincing argument for a better way of doing things.'

Tata BP Solar

The energy crisis in India happened in the 1970s and Tatas were considering different avenues to meet this challenge. Syamal Gupta, who studied at the Imperial College of Science, Technology and Medicine in London foresaw the application of solar energy lighting up India's far-flung villages where electric power will probably not reach for decades. We have 300 days of sunlight and we have sufficient sand to obtain silicon for solar batteries. Tatas entered into a joint venture with British Petroleum(BP) Solar, the second largest producer of solar energy in the world.

While working on the previous edition of *The Creation of Wealth* the author visited Tata BP Solar in Bangalore in early 1990. At the time it had only two rooms in an industrial estate, separated from each other. Today, it is spread over ten acres and is a Rs 260-crore company. It has literally brought light and transformed the lives of a few lakh villages in India.

Deep inside Ladakh fossil fuel and wood are expensive and it is cumbersome to carry kerosene 11,500 ft above sea level. Each lantern replaced by a solar lamp saves an average 100 litres of kerosene. Gompa Tsering, who would otherwise have never known electricity, has her home lit up. Her village is cut off from the outside world for weeks in the freezing winter. Inhabitants of about 9,000 such villages in Ladakh and an equal number in Jammu and Kashmir have benefited like Gompa Tsering.

We take electricity for granted, but when electric power arrives afresh to a village it transforms the lives of these villages. It allows their children to study effortlessly at night. Women who sew need not strain their eyes to earn their livelihood and the inconvenience of a kerosene lamp, with its fumes, is averted.

It is more than lighting villages. Tata BP Solar does its own research and comes out with innovative products of great practical utility. For example, vaccine can be stored in refrigerators where there is no electricity and pumping systems are introduced for water heating and solar cookers. The research at Bangalore is so effective that Harry Shimp, CEO of BP Solar International, says, 'Today our technology is being developed here and exported to our other establishments worldwide. Indian engineers work at our global system engineering department in Bangalore.'

Renewable energy is a fledgling industry. Earlier solar lamps had to be recharged with automobile batteries which lasted for a short while only. Tata BP Solar has developed its own batteries which can go on for at least five years. Local technicians are trained to instal and maintain solar modules and thus find employment. Greenhouse emissions are cut down.

Tata BP Solar home lighting system can work for six hours a day on a four-light system and four hours a day on a six-light system. The performance will improve with time.

BP Solar exports its products to countries in Africa and, surprisingly, also to the USA.

A fledgling industry today, the sky is the limit for solar energy tomorrow.

*

Tata BP Solar is a child of Tata Exports, now Tata International (covered in the earlier edition under 'A Little Leaven'). India's largest solar thermal heating system is installed at Tata International's Dewas leather factory. Leather is known as a polluting industry. This company has a sophisticated effluent treatment plant that exceeds statutory requirements.

Tata AIG Life Insurance Company and Tata AIG General Insurance Company are offshoots of Tata International whose global turnover is $800 million.

23

TATA PHILANTHROPY—VISION, COMPASSION, ATTAINMENT

The longer I live the more I am convinced that the one thing worth living for and dying for is the privilege of making someone more happy and more useful. No man who ever does anything to lift his fellows ever makes a sacrifice.

—Booker T. Washington.

Jamsetji had a vision of an India resurgent as a technological and industrial power standing shoulder to shoulder with the West. To that end he planned to give India steel and hydro-electric power. He bequeathed half his fortune, fourteen buildings and four landed properties to start a 'University of Research', 'the likes of which England did not have' at that time.* It finally came up as the Indian Institute of Science, the fountainhead of technology for India for decades to come.

Sir Ratan Tata had the vision to support Mahatma Gandhi in his struggle in South Africa—he was the single main contributor—because, as he noted, if the struggle failed, 'it will be considered tantamount to an acknowledgement by us of our inferiority to the white races.'

Sir Dorab Tata's wife died of leukaemia in 1931 and he wanted to establish a radium institute in her memory in Bombay. He went to Europe to study this project in 1932 and died there—within a year of his wife's death. The substantial trust of Rs 1 crore that he left behind (today's about Rs 90 crore) finally set up the Tata Memorial Hospital,

* Said by Sir Dorabji Tata who was educated at Cambridge.

the Tata Institute of Social Sciences and the Tata Institute of Fundamental Research. At the Tata Memorial's opening in 1941 Sir Roger Lumley, Governor of Bombay, said: 'Of all of the philanthropic projects connected with the name of Tata, none would attain a greater importance, or reflect greater credit on its founders, than the Tata Memorial Hospital for cancer . . . This hospital is the first large contribution of India to the international fight against cancer.'

J.R.D. Tata had the vision to give India not only an airline but an institute that would produce the most brilliant administrators and bankers modelled on the lines of the four Grande Ecole Polytechniques of France. These produced the top 75 per cent of administrators and bankers of France. It did not happen in 1966 as he had wanted,* but it did come up as a multi disciplinary institute in Bangalore in 1992, the National Institute of Advanced Studies. In the last years of his life J.R.D. Tata started his second trust, the J.R.D. and Thelma Tata Trust, for the benefit of 'disadvantaged women and children.'

The late Minoo K. Tata who inherited two settlements of Jamsetji Tata also had his own trust which is run by his wife, Pilloo.

Modern organized philanthropy grew out of the considerable wealth gathered from the steel and oil industry of America. In 1889 the steel king Andrew Carnegie wrote an essay on wealth in the *North American Review*. He had netted an enormous fortune and spent the last twenty years of his life giving back to society what he had received from it. At a time when literacy was rising but books were difficult to obtain, he established 2,000 public libraries in North America and his beloved Scotland. 'The problem of our age,' he wrote, 'is the proper administration of wealth.'

Ten thousand miles away in India the administration of

---

* Details in *The Heartbeat of a Trust*, by R.M. Lala, Tata McGraw-Hill (1998), page 165.

wealth also exercised the mind of Jamsetji Tata though his wealth was far less than Carnegie's. The vision of Jamsetji was clear: that India take its place among the advanced countries of the world. For that the first need was excellent higher education. In 1892 he started the J.N. Tata Endowment for the higher education of Indians. He realized that vital as it was, something on a much bigger scale was required if his objective was to be achieved. He left half his fortune for his dream child, a research university. The Indian Institute of Science at Bangalore, started in 1911, was the fountainhead of scientific and technical manpower for India. From this institute were spin-offs like the National Aeronautical Laboratory, the Central Food Research Institute, the National Metallurgical Laboratory and others.

The steel plant was similarly to become the fountainhead of heavy engineering for India. He pioneered hydro-electric power to rid Bombay of the pollution of its textile mills which ran on coal generated power.

*

In 1910, Ratan Tata (later Sir), observing Gandhiji's struggle in South Africa, sent his second instalment of Rs 25,000 (equivalent to Rs 13 lakh in 2003). He perceived the importance of the struggle and wrote by hand to M.K. Gandhi on 18 November 1910, stating that the support Gandhiji had thus far received from India was 'not adequate.' Sir Ratan went on to add: 'We must recognize the significance of the issues involved, and see to it that the great sacrifices made, and the sufferings so willingly endured by the Indian community in South Africa, are not rendered useless by our supineness or neglect. We, in India, must not forget that you and your fellow-workers in the Transvaal have suffered much and have sacrificed much to maintain our country's . . . [illegible] in the Transvaal, and that though your spirit might be steadfast your resources would be considerably diminished in so prolonged a struggle. Unless I feel therefore ... [illegible] you receive renewed support it would be difficult for you to carry on so unequal a fight. Should you however be obliged to give up this struggle for want of due appreciation and support from us in India I fear it will be considered tantamount to an acknowledgement by us of our inferiority to the white races. What effect this would have in future in the treatment of our countrymen by the whites in various part of the world, could easily be imagined.

'Therefore I think it is the clear duty of all in India at this juncture to do what lies in their power—to give those who are engaged in this supremely important struggle the confident feeling that the vigorous sustained support, both material and moral, of their countrymen in India is behind them. If the cheque which I enclose herein will in any degree be instrumental in giving you and your fellow-workers this feeling, my object in sending it will have been accomplished.'

Gandhiji wired Gopal Krishna Gokhale:

PRAY THANK MR TATA FOR MUNIFICENT TIMELY HELP. DISTRESS GREAT. PRISONERS' LOT HARD. RELIGIOUS SCRUPLES DISREGARDED. RATIONS SHORT. PRISONERS CARRY SLOP-PAILS; FOR REFUSING, PUT ON SPARE DIET. SOLITARY CONFINEMENT. PROMINENT MOSLEMS, HINDUS, PARSIS IN JAIL.

The origin of the word philanthropy is the Greek word 'Fil-anthra-pi', meaning 'Love of fellowmen.' It is not only or necessarily in giving of money as we understand it today.

Since 1905 Ratan Tata was the main supporter of the Servants of India Society, a role G.K. Gokhale, its founder, was grateful for. Ratan Tata was touched that Gokhale could find volunteers sworn to poverty for the social, political and economic welfare of India. His father had earlier urged Swami Vivekananda to have ascetics engage in scientific research in India.

In 1913 Ratan Tata spelt out his vision on how his trust funds should be used:

> ... for the advancement of Education, Learning and Industry in all its branches, including education in economy, sanitary sciences and art, or for the relief of human suffering or for other works of public utility . . .
>
> To engage qualified and competent person to investigate into matters that pertain to the social, economic or political welfare of the Indian community, the object being to design schemes of a practical nature calculated to promote the welfare of the said community, care being taken that such work is not undertaken from the stereotyped point of view but from the point of view of fresh light that is thrown from day to day by the advance of science and philosophy on problems of human well-being . . .

Further, he also directed that:

> No experiment and no venture should be aided or undertaken unless the scheme thereof is carefully prepared . . .

The same year the 'Ratan Tata Department for study of the causes of poverty and its alleviation' was established at the London School of Economics. The professor chosen for the first appointment rose to be the prime minister of Britain. (See Section on 'Tata Trusts'.)

In March 1911 Ratan Tata (knighted in 1916) made an offer to the Government of India to conduct archaeological exploration at his own expense on certain conditions. He offered to pay all the expenses connected with the excavations. The director-general of the Archaeological Survey of India proposed Pataliputra or Taxila with the department's preference for Pataliputra, the ancient capital of the Maurya dynasty. The expenses were estimated at Rs 20,000 a year over some years.

Sir Harcourt Butler wrote to the education department that Mr Tata's offer 'will make it possible to carry out excavations on a scale hitherto impossible with the limited resources available.'

Though they expected Pataliputra to be the most promising, the extent of the site and the depth at which the most important remains lay buried, proved an expensive operation for those days. The site was identified as Asoka's classic capital.[*]

The Chinese monk Fa Hsien visited Pataliputra (Patna) in 407 AD with three followers, and has left an account of the palace of Asoka which was then standing. Fifteen hundred years later 'the long buried palace when it came to light was such as to suggest that the builder was Asoka's grandfather, Chandragupta, and that the plan was to some large extent copied from the famous palace of Darius at Persepolis,' notes Rev. Dr Hope Moulton. Persepolis was built of stone and torched by Alexander, though a few parts still stand. The Pataliputra palace was built of wood—but the base was of stone. They counted eighty stone stumps for columns and later ten more emerged, coming closer to the 100 columns of Persepolis.

In *The Parsis*, Volume 1, by Mlle. Delphine Menant,[**] she writes: 'Strangely enough the bounty of a Zoroastrian in the 20th century indicated his Persian forbears' influence on India. What is important is that it indicates a Zoroastrian influence in India which was stronger than imagined earlier.'

Sir Ratan's elder brother, Sir Dorabji, was preoccupied with fulfilling the great plans of his father. Even so, he found the time for philanthropic work. When he died *The Times of India* wrote (4 June 1932):

Sir Dorabji's fame, however, will not rest on his great (industrial) achievements, splendid as they were, or on his wealth, but it will rest solidly on the use he has made of his possessions.

[*] Archaeological Survey of India, Annual Report 1912–1913.
[**] Danai, 1994.

Three months before he died he created the two important trusts: the smaller one, Lady Tata Memorial Trust (for research primarily in leukaemia) and the larger Sir Dorabji Tata Trust. To the latter trust he bequeathed all his wealth, then totalling Rs 1 crore (nearly Rs 90 crore in 2003). This trust gave India its pioneering institutions:

1936—Tata Institute of Social Sciences
1941—Tata Memorial Hospital
1945—The Tata Institute of Fundamental Research
1966—National Centre for the Performing Arts.*

One of the last acts of J.R.D. Tata was to establish the National Institute for Advanced Studies in Bangalore. We live in a world of specialization. The NIAS builds bridges between the disciplines of arts and science, between science and religion, between man and the society he lives in. Sir Dorabji Tata Trust and a number of other Tata trusts and companies plus a generous grant of the Karnataka government, helped in its creation.

In his foreword to the last edition of *The Creation of Wealth*(1992) J.R.D. Tata wrote:

I believe that the social responsibilities of our industrial enterprises should now extend, even beyond serving people, to the environment. This need is now fairly well recognized but there is still considerable scope for most industrial ventures to extend their support not only to human beings but also to the land, to the forests, to the waters and to the creatures that inhabit them. I hope that such need will be increasingly

* More information is available on these and other developments from *The Heartbeat of a Trust—The Story of Sir Dorabji Tata Trust* by R.M. Lala, Tata McGraw-Hill, 3rd Edition (1998).

recognized by all industries and their managements because of the neglect from which they have suffered for so long and the physical damage that the growth of industry has inflicted, and still inflicts, on them.

In pursuance of his wishes, after JRD's death the Sir Dorabji Tata Trust enabled the M.S. Swaminathan Research Foundation to establish the J.R.D. Tata Centre for Ecotechnology, Chennai—harmonizing development with concern for environment.*

In 1912, Jamsetji Tata's eldest son Dorabji wanted a school of medical research into tropical medicine as his father had been very keen on that. It could not happen then. In 1999—almost a century after Jamsetji's death—the wish of Jamsetji and his son came true. The Sir Dorabji Tata Centre for Research in Tropical Diseases was established at the Indian Institute of Science, Bangalore.

And so the saga continues to unfold.

Of the significant institutions established by the Sir Dorabji Tata Trust earlier (covered in the 1992 edition) all have grown in the last decade. The Tata Institute of Social Sciences (TISS) Rural Campus at Tulzapur is nearing completion for operation in 2004. Furthermore, the TISS had the windfall of a gift of land just behind its Mumbai campus. The land originally belonged to the grandson of Dadabhai Naoroji. His wife, Malati Naoroji, bequeathed it to the institute. It is called the Jal Naoroji Campus. Sir Dorabji Tata Trust and other Tata trusts have contributed substantially to its infrastructure as they have to a major extension of the Rural Campus in Tulzapur.

The Tata Memorial Hospital started with one large building put up by Tatas. The Atomic Energy Commission has added two buildings nearby and is spending nearly Rs 100 crore on an Advanced Centre for Treatment, Research

* Further facts in *The Heartbeat of a Trust*.

and Education in Cancer (ACTREC) in Navi Mumbai at Khargar. It will have all the research facilities and eighty beds for research cases only.

The TIFR has now three national centres, each of which has added a new dimension to its academic outreach. One is the Department of Biological Sciences which has branched out into a separate national centre with a base in Bangalore. The Homi Bhabha Centre for Science Education has also its own setup now in Chembur and has done pioneering work. Its seed grant came from the Sir Dorabji Tata Trust. The National Centre for Radio Astrophysics was spun off of TIFR and former Tata scholar Dr J.V. Narlikar headed it for eleven years. It came under the University Grants Commission (UGC) to promote the study of astronomy. A beautiful centre has come up at the Pune University complex. In America and Europe a good deal of research is done in universities. We do it in national laboratories. The potential of universities needs to be tapped.

Dr Narlikar was pleasantly surprised to find that the best department of astronomy was at the Indore University. The task of this centre is to nurture others in India.

The prize project of the TIFR is the Giant Metrewave Radio Telescopes (GMRT) which has aroused considerable interest in the world. The California-based Centre in Search for Extra-terrestrial Intelligence (SETI) is interested in collaborating with it to find out about life in outer space. GMRT is better equipped to do so than other astronomical laboratories in the west because Pune, near where it is based, is closer to the equator than telescopes in Europe and North America.

The talent at this complex at Narayangaon in Pune is entirely Indian. The giant telescope consists of thirty remote controlled dishes, 140 feet wide, of stainless steel mesh, each the size of a football field. Each weighs 80 tonnes. It covers a frequency range of the sky as no other telescope and if any one can pick up a signal from space it will be an indication of life beyond the earth.

Scientists from the US-based SETI held a conference in 2003 with the world's scholars at the Tata-founded National Institute of Advanced Studies in Bangalore.

The Tata companies in addition to working around their areas of location like Jamshedpur and Mithapur also take an interest in bringing succour to other parts of India.

Tatas have responded to distress from the times of the Quetta earthquake of 1934. The tradition of Tatas is not to give money to general funds, which is much easier and quicker but less productive. Instead they put in resources of men and funds to undertake the difficult task themselves, be it of relief or rehabilitation. They give of themselves.

In 1993 the Latur earthquake took place at about 4 o'clock in the morning and by 4 o'clock the same evening, 1 October, J.R.D. Tata was presiding over a Tata Relief Committee meeting. It was heartening to see that even before the meeting was summoned that morning, three busloads of Telco workers on their own initiative had gone with adequate equipment to relieve those who were trapped at Latur. Meanwhile, other Telco workers volunteered to donate blood. Tata Chemicals from its Gujarat base flew in blood from the Rajkot blood bank for the victims. The Lifeline Express, which originated at the initiative of Voltas—a Tata company—was barely twenty-four hours away and was expected at 6.00 the next morning in Latur.

On such occasions the tradition of the Tata group is that the workers and officers of its major companies take the initiative of donating their salary of one or two days and the companies match that donation. There is a Tata Relief Committee for eastern India but it has not restricted itself to the east and was among the first to give relief to Gujarat during the Gujarat earthquake with Tata Steel at the fore. Meanwhile the Tata Relief Committee of the western region undertook an elaborate programme which included construction of dwelling units, schools and one primary health centre building in three villages in the Saurashtra region of Gujarat. Far from leaving after relief work it went on to rehabilitation. In addition Sir Dorabji Tata Trust moved in with a major grant towards development of water infrastructure and improvements in agriculture and livestock. The Centre for Environment Education in Ahmedabad is to undertake the work over the next two years.

When Latur and the Kargil War took place it was fashionable to present a cheque and get a photograph taken and published, and then forget all about it. Tatas, as per their policy, wanted a part in doing the job themselves for our armed forces. This took time. Tatas negotiated with the defence ministry and had a special Tata Defence Welfare Corpus Fund set up at the defence ministry. Tata companies and workers joined together to contribute Rs 12 crore to be kept in a corpus fund.

This allocation was not only for the Kargil victims and their families, who by that time were reasonably well looked after. The benefits were extended to those who had fought for India in earlier wars, including the Sri Lanka conflict of 1984. There are today mechanized wheelchairs, three-wheeler scooters, prostheses, etc. for the disabled personnel. For widows and children of the army personnel killed in operation, counter insurgencies, peace-keeping operations and army conflicts, grants are given for higher education in the fields of engineering, medicine, management studies, computer sciences, legal studies, technical and vocational skills and training. The maximum tenure of the educational grant would be for a period of five years.

Tatas and defence officials meet every six months to make the necessary allocations.

*

The holding pattern of the parent company Tata Sons on 31 March 2003 was as follows:

Tata Trusts	65.89%
Corporate Bodies	31.24%
Individuals	2.87%

The Tata trusts from the holdings of Tata Sons and from its dividends plus other income expend between all the trusts over Rs 75 crore a year for philanthropic purposes. In addition to these two major trusts, Sir Dorabji Tata Trust and Sir Ratan Tata Trust, other holders of Tata Sons shares are:

J.R.D. Tata Trust
Tata Education Trust
Tata Social Welfare Trust
R. D. Tata Trust
M. K. Tata Trust

*

Sir Ratan Tata Trust concentrates on five broad fields:

Education
Health
Rural Livelihood
Arts and Culture
Public Initiatives

Sir Dorabji Tata Trust is more widespread in its coverage and is renowned for the institutions it has established.

A trust has to meet with the emerging needs of a nation. When institutes were needed, they were pioneered. Today the need is to conserve natural resources, to create livelihood opportunities, water harvesting, relief of distress and of course education and health.

The trusts are not occupied in big schemes alone. The individual in need is not forgotten. In 2002-03 the two major trusts plus the J.R.D. Tata Trust gave assistance to individuals:

Individual Grants

Medical: 1,761 cases - totalling Rs 523.75 lakh
Education: 5,402 cases - totalling Rs 731.50 lakh

The ultimate test of any philanthropy is what happens in the lives of people—a patient at the Tata Memorial who has recovered; a villager who rejoices at the first sight of drinking water in his village; the excitement of a radio-astronomer as a new pulsar comes within his ken; the thrill of a mountaineer standing atop a Himalayan peak; or the quiet thanksgiving of a mother whose child, after heart surgery, first opens his eyes and recognizes her face.

If today someone somewhere is walking, is seeing, or is healthy with a pacemaker ticking away, it is because of the grace of the Creator and because of the vision of the Tata family members who left their wealth in trusts that have been professionally managed with care and consideration for decades. Was it Tolstoy who said: 'Not till here and there, someone is thinking of us, someone is loving us, does this waste earth become a peopled garden'?

In March 1992 J.R.D. Tata was decorated with the Bharat Ratna. At a reception in his honour, two thousand of the Mumbai Tata staff sat on the open grounds of the NCPA at Nariman Point. A gentle breeze blew from the Arabian Sea. The eighty-seven-year-old patriarch, rose to speak. At one point he said: 'You are my family, my friends.' He stopped, then added: 'My children.' Many an eye was wet. And as he neared the end of his talk he said:

> An American economist has predicted that in the next century India will be an economic super power. I don't want India to be an economic super power. I want India to be a happy country.

EPILOGUE

When I reflect on the ten-odd years that I have been chairman of the group, I cannot help but recall the day Jeh told me that he was stepping down and that he was appointing me in his place as group chairman.

I remember it was a Monday afternoon at 12:30, on 23 March 1991, which is the appointed time that I met him every week, and it was the Monday following a week he had spent in the hospital recovering from an angina attack which he had in Jamshedpur. I had been in to see him every day in the hospital and we had talked mostly of non-business issues. On this afternoon he confronted me with his usual 'Well, what's new?' which was his standard greeting to me every Monday. I said, 'Nothing Jeh, we only met on Friday. There's nothing new since then.' He smiled and said, 'I have something new. I've decided to retire as chairman and to appoint you in my place as Tata Sons' chairman.' Needless to say I was overwhelmed—and a bit speechless. He went on to say, 'I haven't decided the day because I have to consult Ajit Kerkar.' That sort of jolted me a bit. He then clarified that Ajit was very good at picking auspicious dates and he wanted the day to be an auspicious one.

So on that presumably auspicious day decided on by Ajit Kerkar, the momentous board meeting was held at which time he very eloquently and touchingly spoke about his years as chairman, how much he'd enjoyed them, what he felt he had tried to contribute during his time, what he thought his achievements were and his frustrations. He talked a great deal about the firm and what it stood for. And then his reason for 'passing the baton', as he put it, to a younger person.

Obviously my response to his eloquence was absolutely lost to the winds. I was nervous, awe-struck and therefore quite ineloquent. As we left the meeting, I walked him back to his office and with his very characteristic humility he turned to me and said, 'Do you want me to move out of my office?' I said 'Of course not Jeh—don't even think about that. That office is yours. It's your space and nothing is really going to change. I look to you as somebody I will always turn to.' And although I said that and I meant it, I did have some concerns that Jeh would be in the office every day, that he would interfere and that he would forget that he was not any longer the chairman, that he would be irritable and render somewhat impotent the moves that I was hoping to make.

All these fears I had were unfounded because he was just fantastic. He was indeed in the office every day, but he never interfered. He acted as the senior statesman. He was available for counselling, he was available for advice, he was available for guidance. He was my best adviser. When I turned to him he was supportive of many of the moves I tried to make. He was an encouragement to me in my early days and he had become like a second father to me, which he continued to be till the end. I often told him that I wished that both of us were ten years younger so that we could have enjoyed the relationship that we had developed for a longer period in time.

And it's known to many that Jeh and I shared many views, but that we also differed in many of our views, or had differences in terms of approach. More often than not, Jeh was right, and I was wrong. But he allowed those differences to exist. We agreed to disagree very often. But most of the time we were on the same path, maybe the route to the end might have been different. The short period of time that we worked together in our new roles was a wonderful and a very worthwhile experience. I truly am sorry that he passed away (29 November 1993) so soon as he did after the change.

After the initial period of basking in the glory of this new change I settled down to trying to figure out what was required and what I should do. I had a series of dinner meetings with my friends at McKinsey where I discussed some of the thoughts I had and some of the issues which I thought needed to be addressed. We debated on what we believed were some of the changes that the group needed to make. Broadly we agreed that the group should be restructured to become more competitive, to provide better returns to the shareholders, to be more nimble-footed or more proactive to the changing scene than it had been in the past.

All of which would reflect positively on the fast changing scene in India—when India would be open to competition from both within and overseas—when the consumer would have far greater choice, and when the shareholder would demand a good return on his investment.

These meetings led to McKinseys being commissioned to articulate what we had discussed in the form of a set of discussion papers which were jointly worked on in my office and in theirs and presented to the Tata Sons board.

Broadly the plan was to critically look at various companies through a group mechanism which in fact did not exist. And so the Group Executive Office (GEO) was born. The intention was that the Group Executive Office would consist of a group of executive directors of Tata Sons who would have the responsibility of overseeing the performance of various operating companies. The Group Executive Office would also look critically at restructuring the group by way of mergers, acquisitions of our core businesses, as also divestments in companies that were in businesses that we did not consider to be our core businesses or where our market position was not predominant.

Also critically important was the need to review our human resource activities so as to ensure that the bright stars in the Tata group who were identified were rewarded both monetarily and also recognized by being given diverse enriching exposure in different organizations in different functional responsibilities to equip them to undertake senior management responsibility in the future.

The GEO has been in existence now for around ten years. It has served an important function in terms of bringing the group into focus. Perhaps in some ways I feel it could have been more effective than it has been. I must share the onus of any shortcomings that there may be in the GEO as it has been under my leadership, but there have been a great many distractions caused by the changing economic scene and some major disruptions within the house.

Other important 'welding' mechanisms that were introduced after I took over were:

- The creation of a common, unified brand with a common logo which would be used and displayed by all the companies.
- A code of conduct was written to embody the value systems within the Tata group, which had never been codified before.
- A set of operating requirements for companies that use the brand.

A series of other mechanisms were also created to get people of our various companies together to dwell on common issues and a significant stress was laid on improving the quality of our products, and the quality of manner in which our companies operated.

All these are major changes for an organization to undertake which has been traditional and in a manner has had no major internally imposed change or restructuring in its entire history. Therefore any view that this change could be overnight, I think, would be erroneous. Quite often, when you are undertaking major changes, there is a tendency to have what appears to be a negative effect for a period of time, following which there is an upturn and the benefits of what you have done start to be realized. Some call it the hockey stick effect, based on the shape of the curve. I believe the group really did seem to go down the slope of the hockey stick and we are now starting to see some of the benefits of what we have put in place. My hope is that we will start to see the group come together. We are seeing a greater awareness of returns on the part of the managements of various of our operating companies and we are starting to see a new focus on the future, both from existing companies and also in our new businesses, like telecom and information technology in which we are placing an enormous amount of our future destiny.

If I reflect on what these ten years have been for me personally—they have been a mixed bag. There is some satisfaction that I've seen the group come together in many ways. I've seen some of the younger elements of the group understand the changes and support the changes we are trying to make. But at the same time there is also a sense of frustration at the resistance to change from many of my colleagues that I have seen through this period of time. Some resistance is open, which I can deal with, but some resistance, in the form of undercurrents, has been very destructive.

What I would like to leave behind is a group which is more institutionalized rather than personalized like it was in Jeh's time. And a group which could continue to operate and grow effectively, irrespective of who the leader might be. Jeh and I argued on this point many many times. I expressed the view that the group was in jeopardy after him because he ran it in a very patriarchal way. People respected him and looked up to him but much of the consonance was a measure of his long-tenured leadership and his personal charisma rather than his control through financial or legal means. He disagreed with this. He felt that this was not the case. I was quite convinced it was. I therefore set myself the task to institutionalize the operating structure to provide the chairman of the group with more powers than Jeh ever needed to have in a legal or financial way.

I did this by increasing the group ownership in each of our major companies. I re-established Tata Sons as the focal point of the group with a level of equity holding to enable it to exercise some degree of control over the individual operating companies while honouring their autonomy. This was not a pleasant development for many of the operating companies that had operated on their own, with no central group oversight. A central mandate was an imposition because there were multiple companies in the same business competing with each other; these were companies that had operating styles which reflected the personal style of their chief executives; and there were companies that imbibed the Tata values as also companies that flouted them.

We were rightly called a loose confederation of companies. Therefore the task was to transform this loose confederation into a synergetic group of companies with a unified direction. And that's the task I have undertaken in the years that I have been in this position. Very often in undertaking this kind of role, your objectives are not well understood. You are seen to be disruptive just for the sake of change. You are seen to be trying to exert your will when for forty to fifty years individual companies operated entirely independently.

So all in all it has been a hard and sometimes unrewarding experience. All I can say is that I have genuinely worked hard to create an integrated, strong, well-performing Tata group driven and motivated to be predominant in the business areas in which we operate in the Indian scene and, it is hoped, overseas.

The people within the Tata group have displayed enormous spirit over the many decades that we have been in existence. I hope they will remain totally committed to making the Tata group what I think all of us would like it to be—the predominant business house in India, which amidst fast-eroding values, will continue to stand out as being a well-integrated, growth-oriented group with market leadership, operating with a high level of integrity, a great value system and uncompromising in its goal to achieve results without partaking in corruption, bribery and/or political influence.

If this is what the group looks like in the future, I would believe that I would have achieved the task I undertook. I would hope that my successors would never compromise and turn to soft options to meet their ends, and never allow the Tata group to join the growing number of companies in India which have shed their values, forgotten about their integrity, and closed their eyes to maintaining ethical standards. If Mr J.R.D. Tata was able to uphold the values of the firm and if I have been able to carry on that tradition through my tenure, I hope the future generations in Tatas will recognize these traditions as being critical to the fabric and the fundamentals on which our group was built and grew so successfully for over a century.

Bombay

Raian T. Tata

September 5, 2003

Appendices

Appendix A

TATAS AT A GLANCE

Tata Steel is India's largest integrated steel company in the private sector with a 13 per cent market share and a strong presence in international markets.

Tata Motors (Telco), India's largest commercial vehicle manufacturer, is rated among the top six manufacturers of commercial vehicles in the world, and is among the top three passenger car manufacturers in the country.

Tata Consultancy Services is Asia's largest I.T. consulting services and solutions company.

Indian Hotels operates India's largest hotel chain.

Tata Chemicals is one of the world's largest producers of synthetic soda ash.

Tata Tea is India's largest integrated tea company and had a 16.1 per cent share in the branded packet tea segment.

The Tetley Group is the world's second largest tea bag company.

Tata Coffee is Asia's largest integrated coffee company.

Titan, the world's sixth largest manufacturer of brand watches, is the market leader, having a 65 per cent share by value and 50 per cent share by volume of the organized domestic watch market.

CMC is India's second largest software developer for the domestic market.

Tata Interactive runs the world's largest development team for custom e-learning applications.

VSNL is India's leading international telecommunications service provider.

Appendix B

Chairmen of Tatas from 1887

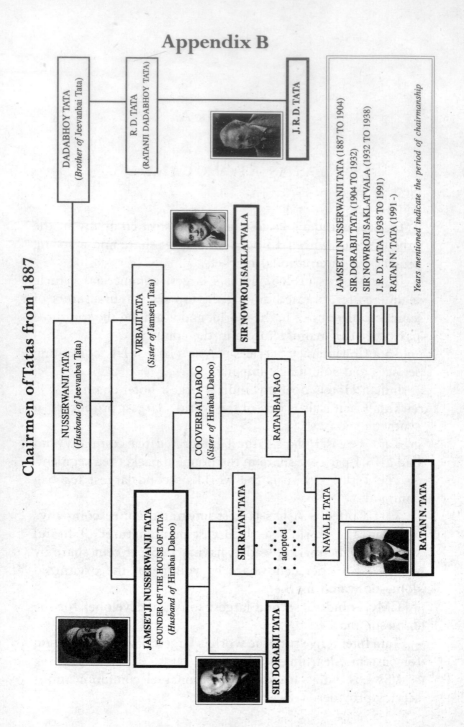

DADABHOY TATA
(Brother of Jeevanbai Tata)

R. D. TATA
(RATANJI DADABHOY TATA)

J. R. D. TATA

NUSSERWANJI TATA
(Husband of Jeevanbai Tata)

VIRBAIJI TATA
(Sister of Jamsetji Tata)

SIR NOWROJI SAKLATVALA

COOVERBAI DABOO
(Sister of Hirabai Daboo)

RATANBAI RAO

JAMSETJI NUSSERWANJI TATA
FOUNDER OF THE HOUSE OF TATA
(Husband of Hirabai Daboo)

SIR RATAN TATA

· · · adopted · · ·

NAVAL H. TATA

SIR DORABJI TATA

RATAN N. TATA

JAMSETJI NUSSERWANJI TATA (1887 TO 1904)
SIR DORABJI TATA (1904 TO 1932)
SIR NOWROJI SAKLATVALA (1932 TO 1938)
J. R. D. TATA (1938 TO 1991)
RATAN N. TATA (1991 -)

Years mentioned indicate the period of chairmanship

Appendix C

J . R . D . TATA

Guiding Principles

Nothing worthwhile is ever achieved without deep thought and hard work;

One must think for oneself and never accept at their face value slogans and catch phrases to which, unfortunately, our people are too easily susceptible;

One must forever strive for excellence, or even perfection, in any task however small, and never be satisfied with the second best;

No success or achievement in material terms is worthwhile unless it serves the needs or interests of the country and its people and is achieved by fair and honest means;

Good human relations not only bring great personal rewards but are essential to the success of any enterprise.

Source: From a letter dated 13 September 1965, by J.R.D. Tata to K.C. Bhansali, a schoolteacher in Calcutta.

RATAN N. TATA

My Business Values

Integrity: We must conduct our business fairly, with honesty and transparency. Everything we do must stand the test of public scrutiny.

Understanding: We must be caring, show respect, compassion and humanity for our colleagues and customers around the world and always work for the benefit of India.

Excellence: We must constantly strive to achieve the highest possible standards in our day-to-day work and in the quality

278 THE CREATION OF WEALTH

of the goods and services we provide.

Unity: We must work cohesively with our colleagues across the group and with our customers and partners around the world, building strong relationships based on tolerance, understanding and mutual cooperation.

Responsibility: We must continue to be responsible, sensitive to the countries, communities and environments in which we work, always ensuring that what comes from the people goes back to the people many times over.

Source: The Times of India, 27 October 2002.

Appendix D

Promoter Companies

1. Tata Sons Limited
2. Tata Industries Limited

Engineering

Automotive

3. Tata Engineering & Locomotive Company Limited
4. Telco Construction Equipment Company Limited
5. Tata Cummins Limited
6. Tata Holset Limited
7. HV Transmissions Limited
8. HV Axles Limited
9. Tata Autocomp Systems Limited

Joint Ventures Promoted in Auto Components

10. Tata Johnson Controls Automotives Systems Limited
11. Tata Toyo Radiators Limited
12. Tata Auto Plastic Systems Private Limited
13. Tata Yazaki Autocomp Private Limited
14. Tata Ficosa Automotive Systems Private Limited
15. TC Springs Private Limited
16. JBM Sungwoo Limited
17. JBM Tools Limited
18. Automotive Composite System
19. Tata Yutaka Autocomp Private Systems Limited

Engineering Products

20. Voltas Limited
21. TRF Limited
22. TAL Manufacturing Solutions Limited

Engineering Services

23. TCE Consulting Engineers Limited
24. Tata Projects Limited
25. Stewarts and Lloyds of India Limited
26. Tata Korf Engineering Services Limited
27. Tata Construction and Projects Limited

Materials

28. The Tata Iron and Steel Company Limited

Joint Ventures Promoted in Materials

29. Tata Ryerson Limited
30. Tata SSL Limited
31. Tata Sponge Iron Limited
32. Tata Metaliks Limited
33. Tata Yodogawa Limited
34. The Tinplate Company of India Limited
35. Tata Refractories Limited
36. Tata Advanced Materials Limited

Communications & Information Systems

Communications

37. Videsh Sanchar Nigam Limited
38. Tata Teleservices Limited
39. Idea Cellular Limited
40. Tata Telecom Limited
41. Tata Internet Services Limited

Information Systems

42. Tata Consultancy Services (a division of Tata Sons Limited)
43. Tata Infotech Limited
44. CMC Limited
45. Tata Elxsi (India) Limited
46. Tata Technologies Limited
47. Tata Interactive Systems (a division of Tata Industries Limited)
48. Nelito Systems Limited

Industrial Automation

49. Tata Honeywell Limited
50. Nelco Limited

Consumer Products

51. Tata Tea Limited
52. The Tetley Group Limited
53. Tata Tetley Limited
54. Tata Coffee Limited
55. Titan Industries Limited
56. Trent Limited
57. Tata Infomedia Limited
58. Tata McGraw-Hill Publishing Company Limited
59. Tata Ceramics Limited
60. Concorde Motors Limited
61. ITel Industries Private Limited

Energy

62. The Tata Power Company Limited
63. Tata BP Solar India Limited

Chemicals

64. Tata Chemicals Limited
65. Rallis India Limited
66. The Tata Pigments Limited

Services

Hotels and Property Development

67. The Indian Hotels Company Limited
68. Information Technology Park Limited
69. Tata Housing Development Company Limited

Financial Services

70. Tata AIG General Insurance Company Limited
71. Tata AIG Life Insurance Company Limited
72. Tata Finance Limited

Joint Ventures Promoted in Financial Services

73. Tata TD Waterhouse Securities Limited
74. Tata Finance Amex Limited
75. Tata Finance Merchant Bankers Limited
76. Tata Home Finance Limited
77. Tata Investment Corporation Limited
78. Tata TD Waterhouse Asset Management Private Limited
79. Tata Share Registry Limited
80. Tata AIG Risk Management Services Limited
81. TT Forest Limited

Other Services

82. Tata Economic Consultancy Services (a division of Tata Sons Limited)

83. Tata Financial Services (a division of Tata Sons Limited)
84. Tata Quality Management Services (a division of Tata Sons Limited)
85. Tata Strategic Management Group (a division of Tata Industries Limited)
86. Tata Services Limited
87. Megapode Airlines Limited
88. Sitel India Private Limited

International Operations

89. Tata International Limited
90. Tata Limited
91. Tata Incorporated
92. Tata International AG/Tata AG
93. Tata Enterprises (overseas) AG
94. Tata Tea Inc.
95. Tata Precision Industries Pte. Ltd.
96. Tata Technologies Pte. Ltd.

Appendix E

FIRSTS IN LABOUR WELFARE

Tata Steel has been the pioneer in introducing a number of firsts in the field of labour welfare. All of these measures listed below were ahead of Indian legislation and several benefits like the eight-hour working day were incorporated by Tatas before they were implemented by law in many western nations.

	Tisco Introduction	Enforced by law	Legal Measure
Eight-hour working day	1912	1948	Factories Act
Free Medical Aid	1915	1948	Employees State Insurance Act
Establishment of Welfare Department	1917	1948	Factories Act
Schooling facilities for child	1917		
Formation of Works Committee for handling complaints concerning service conditions and grievances	1919	1947	Industrial Disputes Act
Leave with pay	1920	1948	Factories Act
Workers' Provident Fund Scheme	1920	1952	Employees Provident Fund Act
Workmen's Accident Compensation Scheme	1920	1924	Workmen's Compensation Act
Technical Institute for Training of Apprentices, Craftsmen & Engineering Graduates	1921	1961	Apprentices Act

Maternity Benefit	1928	1946	Bihar Maternity Benefit Act
Profit sharing Bonus	1934	1965	Bonus Act
Retiring Gratuity	1937	1972	Payment of Gratuity Act
Ex-Gratia Payment—road accident while coming to or returning from duty	1979		

Appendix F

TATAS AND SPORTS

The tradition of Tatas supporting sport began with Jamsetji Tata who, in a letter to his son, Dorab, envisaged a steel city before the site was found—and instructed him to: 'Reserve large areas for football, hockey, and parks.' He had even chosen Tatas' colours, blue and gold, now familiar in the sports fields of India.

India's participation in the Olympic arena came through Sir Dorabji Tata, himself a good athlete and an excellent horseman. In his time he rode from Bombay to Kirkee in eighteen hours. Before India had an Olympic body, he chose and financed four athletes and two wrestlers for the Antwerp games in 1920. He secured for India a place for the 1924 Paris Olympics and he was chosen to be a member of the International Olympic Committee. Come the 1928 Olympics at Amsterdam, India won the gold at hockey.

Sir Dorabji had scouted for talent and arranged for the then director of the YMCA to tour the country and bring home to the people of India the importance of the Olympic movement. As early as 1893 Sir Dorab encouraged the formation of athletic associations in Bombay's high schools with the help of principals. Sport was of abiding interest to him. When he died, his successor as chairman of Tatas, Sir Nowroji Saklatvala, was instrumental along with some others, in bringing into existence the Cricket Club of India, where the main J.N. Tata pavilion was financed by Tatas.

The next chairman, J.R.D. Tata, in his early twenties was seen driving round Bombay in his Bugatti. A skier and a patron of sports, J.R.D. Tata was offered membership to the International Olympic Association but declined because of pressure of other work. JRD encouraged sports as a 'profession'. Some Tata employees did nothing but play games and excel in them. They were encouraged to go for practice or training, because this was how they developed and brought laurels for their state or country.

Jawaharlal Nehru appointed Naval Tata as the first president of the All-India Council of Sports. He was also president of the Indian Hockey Association. During his term India won the Olympic gold for hockey on three consecutive occasions.

Tata companies have fielded over 400 sportsmen of renown including cricket captains of the past, Nari Contractor, Dilip Vengsarkar, Ravi Shastri; Olympic hockey players who won the gold medal for India: R.S. Gentle, L. Pinto, L. Fernandes, G. Perumal; Olympic football players: S.S. Narayan, F.A. Franco; five world championships in billiards have gone to Tatas sportsmen—Michael Ferreira three times and Geet Sethi twice so far. Prem Chand was crowned Mr Universe for body-building in 1988. Edward Sequeira's record for the 1500 metres run stood unbeaten in India for twenty-five years.

The Tata Sports Club was formed in 1937 and Tatas were the first industrial house to encourage sporting talent in India.

Over the years the Tata group has spawned academies for different sports, sponsored events and individuals, and supported countless talented sportsmen and women. No other corporate house in the country has done as much for the cause of Indian sport, and for as long.

For the group, backing Indian sport does not mean hitching its wagon to the big-ticket names and games. Rather, its endeavours have been directed at spotting and then nurturing potential, at providing an early platform for those who deserve no less. Take the case of Ajit Agarkar, who provided a silver lining to India's performance at the test against England at Lord's in 2003.

Agarkar was a skinny kid of sixteen, who looked more like a jockey than the international fast bowler he was aspiring to be, when he was granted a scholarship in 1997 by the Tata Sport Club, established in 1937 to encourage sports and sports people within and outside the group. In 1999, as soon as he turned eighteen, Agarkar was absorbed as an employee at Tata Steel, where he is today an officer in the corporate communications department.

Morad Ali Khan, who won the gold for India in the double trap shooting event at the 2003 Commonwealth Games, is another example of the group giving talented athletes the opportunity to blossom. The forty-one-year-old Khan, who joined Tata Steel as an administrative trainee, has been with the company for two decades, a period during which he has had the unstinted backing of his employers.

'Supporting sport has been a tradition with the Tatas, not for any return but as a policy,' says Milind Rege, in his prime a stalwart of the Mumbai cricket scene: 'Saurav Ganguly was a nobody when we took him on board (Ganguly is currently a manager in the marketing department at Tata Steel). Dilip Vengsarkar joined Tatas before he played international cricket.' Most of the sports people targeted are not readymade champions. For instance, Morad was helped from day one. He was sent all over the world. The support to him has been long term.

Leander Paes is only too glad to recognize the support he received from the group when he was but a child in tennis terms. And Pullela Gopichand, when he was rewarded with a Rs 5-lakh cheque by the group for winning the All-England badminton crown, said: 'The first people to give me a break were the Tatas.'

The Tata group has considered every sport as worthy of support; so long as people excelled in a particular field, we supported their talent. Two world billiards champions, Geet Sethi and Michael Ferreira, were Tata employees.

A sampling of what the group has done in other sporting disciplines explains why:

- The Tata Football Academy, set up in Jamshedpur in 1987, selects boys of fourteen and under and trains them for a four-year period in world-class facilities, while taking care of their every need.
- The Tata Archery Academy, established in Jamshedpur in 1996, has produced a long list of archers who have gone on to win national and international honours.
- The Tata Adventure Foundation, headed by Bachendri Pal, the first woman to climb Mount Everest, has rock climbing, river rafting and para-sailing on its alternative sports agenda.

The group has also created some of the finest infrastructure for sports and recreation in India. Conspicuous among these is the J.R.D. Tata sports complex in Jamshedpur, a 40,000 capacity area with facilities for athletics, archery, boxing, basketball, volleyball, boxing, tennis and more. Also in Jamshedpur is the Keenan Stadium, a regular venue for international cricket. Tata Power is another company that has created an infrastructure and encouraged individuals.

Champions don't show up in a hurry on the Indian sports horizon, but it helps to have a group backing the quest to find them. And the earlier you start the search, the better the prospects of unearthing these elusive diamonds.

Appendix G

DIRECTORS OF TATA SONS LIMITED— JANUARY 2004

R.N. Tata, Chairman

N.A. Soonawala, Vice-Chairman

P.S. Mistry

F.H. Kavarana

B.G. Deshmukh

Syamal Gupta

J.J. Irani

R. Gopalakrishnan

Ishaat Hussain

R.K. Krishna Kumar

A.R. Gandhi

INDEX

100 Great Modern Lives, 140

AT & T Wireless, USA, 240
Avaya, 238
Advanced Centre for Treatment, Research and Education in Cancer (ACTREC), 261
Agarkar, Ajit, 287
Air-India International, 77, 82
Air-India Ltd., 77, 81 84, 110, 195, 215
Alexander, 258
All India Council of Sports, 203, 287
Allwyn, 249
Amarjeet Singh, 172
American Tenth Air Force in India, 82
Andhra Pradesh cyclone, 177-78, 186
Andhra Valley Power Supply Company, 49, 245
Andrews, C.F., 126-27
Anjuman-i-Islam, 141
Apprentices Act, 116
Apsara (nuclear system of reactor), 152
Arakal, Xavier, 63
Archaeological Survey of India, 242
Asha Singh, 172
Associated Cement Companies (ACC), 70, 90, 100
Atomic Energy Commission, 51, 144, 151, 160, 260
Attlee, Clement, 140
Autopolis, 225

BHEL, 119

Bangladesh crisis, 177
Bapa, Thakkar, 132
Bari, Abdul, 128-29
Bell-Canada, 238
Bhabha, Homi, 43, 141, 147, 150-52
Bhabha, Hormusji, 8
Bhabha, Jamshed, 141
Bhabha Atomic Research Centre (BARC), 44, 123
Bharucha, Pesi, 180-81
Bhatnagar Prize, 44-45
Bhoothalingam, S., 139
Bihar Relief Committee, 177
Bleriot, Louis, 75
Bombay Plan, 107-08
Bombay University, 37-38, 146
Bombay's Horniman Circle Gardens, 52
Born, Max, 43
Bose, P.N., 23
Bose, Subhas Chandra, 126-28
Brand Equity and Business Promotion (BEBP) agreement, 217-19
Brilliant, Larry, 179-82
British Petroleum (BP), 251
Bromfield, Louis, 57
Brown, Michael, 107
Burroughs Corp., 235
Butler, Harcourt, 258

CIDCO, 160
Calcutta Botanical Museum, 8
Calcutta University, 37
Cama, Freny K.R., 138
Camillia Assamica, 102

Camillia Sinensis, 102
Cancer Research Institute of Tata Memorial, 160
Candy, 39
Canning, John, 140
Carnegie, Andrew, 254-55
Catholic Relief Services, 167
Central Bank of India, 70
Central Food and Technological Research Institute, Mysore, 43
Central Food Research Institute, 255
Central India Spinning, Weaving and Manufacturing Company, 6
Centre for Environment Education, Ahmedabad, 263
Centre for the Advancement of Philanthropy, Bombay, 143
Centre in Search for Extra-terrestrial Intelligence (SETI), 261-62
Chambers, W.A., 55
Chandragupta, 258
Charan Singh, 234
Chaukar, K.A., 217
Child Guidance Clinic, 164
Chirney-Pawley, Charles James, 61
Choksi, J.D., 35, 57, 107, 109-10
Choksi, Rustom, 143
City Rover, 224
Clibborn, J., 39
Clibborn-Masson Committee, 39
Colaba Woods, 52
Computer Maintenance Corporation (CMC), 219, 275
Computer Society of India, 234
Consolidated Coffee, 243
Contractor, Nan, 287
Correa, Charles, 249
Cosmic ray air shower project, 154
Council of Scientific and Industrial Research, New Delhi, 43
Coyaji, J.C., 138
Cray Research, 119
Creation of Wealth, The, 251, 259
Cricket Club of India, 286

Curzon, Lord, 17, 19-21, 26-27, 38-41

Daewoo, 224
Daftary, Dinesh, 155
Daimler-Benz A.G., 94, 119
Dalal, A.R., 138
Dalal, Ardeshir, 106-10
Dalton, Hugh, 140
Dange, S.A., 126
Daniel Guggenheim Medal Award, 84
Das, C.R., 126
De Havilland Mosquito, 79
Dehejia, V.T., 139
Delhi School of Economics, 146
Demographic Research Institute, 109
Dense Wave Division Multiplexing (DWDM), 245-46
Department of Scientific Research, 125
Department of Telecommunications (DOT), 238
Desai, Armaity S., 166
Desai, Praful, 161
Desai, Xerxes, 247-48
Deshmukh, B.G., 290
Devapur project, 167, 171
Dhawan, Satish, 43
Dinshaw, F.E., 72
Directorate of Civil Aviation (DCA) of India, 79
Discovery of India, 3
Douglas Aircraft Corporation, 84
Dr. Borges Memorial Home, 160
Drought Maharashtra, 177
Dwivedi, Sharada, 54

East Asiatic Corporation of Denmark, 35
Eastern and the United Airlines, 84
Economic Times, 204
Edison, Thomas Alva, 47

Elphinstone Club, 8
Empire Mail Service, 79
Employees, technical and management development of, 115-19
Empress Mills, 5-6, 11, 13, 183
Engineer, Adi, 245-46
Engineer, Aspy, 77
Engineering Research Centre, Pune, 97
Eravikulam National Park, 100-01
Estate, 98-99
Eucalyptus Globulus, 103
Eucalyptus Grandis, 103
Excel Industries, 90

FICCI Award, 125
Fa Hsien, 258
Factory Bill of 1911, 129
Fernandes, L., 287
Ferreira, Michael, 287-88
Food for Work programme, 167
Ford Foundation, 147
Fort Aguada, Goa, 58
France Ebauches, 248
Franco, F.A., 287
Fraser, Lovat, 57

Gandhi, Indira, 68
Gandhi, Mohandas Karamchand, 66, 75, 126, 137, 139-40, 253, 255-56, 229
Gandhi, Rajiv, 229, 235
Ganguly, Saurav, 288
Gateway Hotels, 61, 200
Gateway Resorts, 61, 200
General Electric, 236
General Motors, 94, 222
Gentle, R.S., 287
Ghandy, Jehangir, 31
Giant Metrewave Radio Telescope (GMRT), 155, 261
Giri, V.V., 126, 128
Gokhale, Gopal Krishna, 139-40
Gokhale Institute of Politics and

Economics, Pune, 169, 171
Goodlass Nerolac, 214
Gopal, V.G., 129-30
Gopalakrishnan, R., 217, 221, 240, 290
Gopichand, Pullela, 288
Gore, M.S., 164, 166
Government Training Centre, Singapore, 119
Grande Ecole Polytechniques, France, 254
Grasset, Nicole, 179
Greenwood, Arthur, 140
Grey, C.G., 77
Group Corporate Centre (GCC), 217
Group Executive Office (GEO), 268-69
Gujarat floods, 175, 177
Gupta, Sujit, 180
Gupta, Syamal, 251, 290
Gurukula system, 143
Guzder, Nusserwanji, 47

HMT, 249
Haldia Petrochemicals Project, 200
Hamilton, George, 21, 39, 41
Hammarskjöld, Dag, 179
Hanspal, Arjun Singh, 122
Hari, Viyogi, 133
Harris, F.R., 106
Harvey-Jones, John, 115
Hewlett-Packard, 236
Hindustan Lever, 243
Hindustan Lever Chemicals Ltd., 227
Hitech Drilling System, 199
Homi, Manek, 127
Homi Bhabha Centre for Science Education, 261
Homi Bhabha Fellowship Council, 147
Honda Accord, 98
Hospital on Wheels project, 247

Hoyle-Narlikar theory, 139
Hughes Telecom, 240
Hunt, 191
Hussain, Ishaat, 217, 290
Hydro-electric power projects, 17, 29, 47, 49-53

IBM, 119, 214, 236
Idea Cellular, 240
Illustrated Weekly of India, 107
Imperial Airways, 78-79, 81
Imperial Bank of India, 72
India Cements, 70
Indian National Congress, 6
India Today, 214, 220
Indian Academy of Sciences, 44
Indian Airlines, 83
Indian Cable Company, 31
Indian Cancer Society, 160
Indian Companies Act of 1937, 14
Indian Express, 175, 178
Indian Hockey Federation, 203
Indian Hotels Company Limited, 59, 194, 200, 216, 242, 275
Indian Institute of Science, Bangalore, 36, 42-46, 57, 141, 146, 150, 237, 241, 254-55, 260
Indian Institute of Technology (IIT), 43
Indian Journal of Social Work, 164
Indian Space Research Organization, 44
Indian Steel and Wire Products, 31
Indian Steel Rolling Mills Limited, 34
Indian Tube Company, 31
Indica car project, 222-24
Indica V2, 99, 224
Indigo, 99
Institute of Metallurgical Technology, 116
Institute of Electric Engineers, USA, 233
International Cancer Congress, 160
International Chamber of Commerce, 202
International Institute for Population Studies, Bombay, 109
International Labour Organization (ILO), 128, 164, 202-03
International Olympic Committee, 286
International Organization of Employers, Geneva, 203
Investment Corporation of India, 203
Ipitata Sponge Iron Limited, 34
Irani, J.J., 217, 229-31, 290
Iron and Steel Committee, ILO, 129

J.N. Tata Auditorium, 46
J.N. Tata Endowment, 138-39, 147, 231, 255
J.N. Tata Memorial Centre, Navsari, 144
J.N. Tata Scholar, 37, 139, 147, 231
J.N. Tata Scholarship, 107
J.R.D. and Thelma Tata Trust, 254
J.R.D. Tata Centre for Ecotechnology, Chennai, 260
J.R.D. Tata Sports Complex, Jamshedpur, 289
Jail Reforms Committee, 165
James Finlay tea company, 100-02
Jamsetji Nusserwanji Tata: A Chronicle of His Life, 106
Jamsetji Tata Trust, 147
Jamshed Bhabha Theatre, 143
Jamshedpur, 29, 31
Jamshedpur Labour Association, 126
Jamshedpur Labour Federation, 128
Jenks, Wilfred, 202
Jha, Prem Shankar, 148
Jhanda Singh, 172
Jinnah, M.A., 110
John, Michael, 128-29
Jussawalla, D.J., 160

Kadir, Abdul, 186-87

Kaiser Engineers, 31
Kalimata Investments Company Limited, 34
Kant, Ravi, 225
Kargil War, 263
Karnad, Girish, 148
Kartar Singh, 172
Kavarana, F.H., 290
Keenan, John, 31, 33
Kelavkar, Krishnabai, 138
Keltron Telephones, 199
Kennedy, Julian, 21, 132
Kerkar, A.B., 59, 61
Khan, Liaquat Ali, 110
Khan, M.A. Wadud, 110
Khan, Morad Ali, 288
Khan, Nur, 84
Khanderao, Sitaram, 55
Khatau Mills, 163
Kohli, Faqir Chand, 233-37
Kothari, Rajni, 134
Kotwal, S.P., 134
Koyna earthquake, relief work at, 176
Kripa Foundation, 143
Krishnamachari, T.T., 94
Kumar, R.K. Krishna, 217, 242, 244, 290
Kumardhubi Metal Casting and Engineering Limited, 35

Lac Research Institute, Ranchi, 43
Lady Meherbai D. Tata Education Trust, 147
Lady Tata Memorial Trust, 61, 147, 259
Lake Palace Hotel, Udaipur, 59
Lakmé, 69, 214
Lala, R.M., 254, 259
Latur earthquake, relief to, 262-63
Life of Sir Phirozeshah Mehta, 112
Lifeline Express project, 247, 262
London School of Economics, 140, 257

Lord Mayor's Fund, London, 176
Lotus Development Corporation, 119
Lucent Technologies, USA, 214, 238
Lumley, Roger, 157

M.K. Tata Trust, 203, 264
M.S. Swaminathan Research Foundation, 260
Macaulay, Lord, 3
Madras University, 37
Mahatre, Bhupendra, 135
Mahon, R.H., 20
Malcolm Baldrige Model, 218
Management Development Centre, Jamshedpur, 116
Managing Agency System, 194-95, 198
Manshardt, Clifford, 163
Masson, David Orme, 39
Matrix Materials, 199
Matthai, John, 107
Matthai, M.O., 67, 69
Maugham, W. Somerset, 57
Mavalankar, P.G., 134
Maxton, Graeme, 225
Mazda, 98
McDonnell Douglas Information Systems, 119
Medical Services in the Welfare Work, Sakchi, 127
Mehta, Fali, 155
Mehta, Goverdhan, 44
Mehta, Jivraj N., 138
Melbourne University, 39
Menant, Delphine, 258
Menon, Prasad, 226, 228
Merind, 214
Metals Workers' Union, 128
Metropolitan optic fiber network (MAN), 246
Mirza, D.N., 55
Mistry, P.S., 290
Mithapur 85, 87-90

Mitsubishi, 91
Miyake, Sabura, 154
Mody, Homi, 111-12
Mody, Russi, 35, 180, 187
Mohammed, Ghulam, 110
Mohammed, Noor, 173
Monghyr (Munger) earthquake, relief work at, 176
Monopolies and Restrictive Trade Practices (MRTP) Act, 212, 233
Monopolies Inquiry Commission, 195
Moolgaokar, Sumant, 94, 96, 98-99, 111, 231-32
Morvi floods, relief work at, 175
Moulton, Hope, 258
Muslim League, 110
Muthuraman, B., 231
My Days with Nehru, 67
Mysore Soap Factory, 43

NELCO, 209
Nagpada Neighbourhood House, Bombay, 163
Nanavatty, Savak, 231
Naoroji, Dadabhai, 260
Naoroji, Jal, 67
Naoroji, K.A.D., 8, 129
Naoroji, Malati Jal A.D., 165, 260
Napier, General, 4
Narayan, Jayaprakash, 126, 131, 137
Narayan, S.S., 287
Narayanan, K.R., 138
Narielwala, P.A., 66
Narlikar, J.V., 139, 261
Narlikar, V.V., 139
National Aeronautical Laboratory, Bangalore, 43, 255
National Centre for Radio Astrophysics, 261
National Centre for the Performing Arts, 143-44, 146, 259
National Chemical Laboratory, 43

National Institute for Advanced Studies (NIAS), Bangalore, 144, 254, 259, 262
National Institute of Health, Washington, 155
National Metallurgical Laboratory, 43, 146, 255
National Police Commission, 165
National Sports Institute, Patiala, 133
National Thermal Power Corporation, 51
Navsari, park for exotic animals at, 12
Nawaz, Shah, 173
Nawaz, Shamsh, 173
Nehru, Jawaharlal, 3, 33, 67, 126, 128, 152, 159, 16, 203, 247, 287
Nehru, Motilal, 28
Nehru Plan, 108
New India Assurance Company, 70-71
New York's Memorial Sloan-Kettering Cancer Centre, 157
Nicco Corporation Limited (Steel Division), 35
Nirmal Singh, 172
Nissan, 98
North American Review, 254

OXFAM, 180
Oda, Minoru, 154
One Night in Bombay, 57
Online Systems International, 119
Oracle Corporation, 119, 236

P & O Line, 17
Padmanaban, G. 44
Padshah, B.J., 64
Padshah, Burjorji, 106
Paes, Leander, 288
Pakistan International Airlines, 84
Pal, Bachendri, 289

Palkhivala, N.A., 99
Palkhivala, Nani, 235
Pandit, Y.S., 169, 171
Panshet Dam disaster, 177
Parsis, The, 258
Peck, Gregory, 57
Pegoud, Adolph, 75
Perin, Charles Page, 21-22, 26
Perumal, G., 287
Peterson, John, 79, 106, 191
Philanthropy by Tatas, 38, 137-38,
    141, 188, 253-65
Philips of Holland, 119
Pinto, L., 287
Pithampur, 90
Power Grid Corporation of India
    Ltd., 245
Power Supply Security Management
    System, 244
Prabhu, S.S., 46
Prasad, Rajendra, 126, 128
Prem Chand, 287
Prince of Wales Museum, Bombay,
    12, 146
Proton Decay Project, 154

R.D. Tata Trust, 264
Raffles Hotel, Singapore, 57
Rallis India, 90, 214, 220
Ram, Jagjivan, 82
Ramadorai, R., 236-37
Raman, C.V., 43
Ramanna, Raja, 138, 144
Ramsay, William, 39
Ranganathan, S., 138
Rao, B.N., 138
Rao, C.N. R., 44
Rao, V.K.R.V., 138
Ratan Tata Department, London
    School of Economics, 140, 257
Ratan Tata Foundation, 140
Ratan Tata Industrial Institute, 146
Reay, Lord, 37, 45
Redford, Norman, 9

Reed, Stanley, 8
Rege, Milind, 288
Regent Hotel, 242
Rollei, West Germany, 119
Roorkee Engineering College, 39
Rossi, Bruno, 154
Rover, UK, 224
Royal Commonwealth Society, 109
Royal Society of England, 39, 150
Rural Welfare Board, 144, 167-68
Ruskin, John, 47

Sabavala, S.A., 212
Safari-India, 97
Saklatvala, Nowroji, 70-71, 157,
    193, 197, 276, 286
Saklatvala, Shapurji, 22
Sandalwood Oil Factory, 43
Sarabhai, Vikram, 43
Sayaji Rao, 87
School of Hope, Jamshedpur, 134
Schumacher, E.F., 136
Schwartz, Ritter von, 20
Seiko, 248
Sen Gupta, A.K., 118
Sequeira, Edward, 287
Servants of India Society, 132, 139-
    40, 256
Seth, Darbari, 88-90, 103
Sethi, Geet, 287-88
Sethna, H.N., 51
Shahabad Cement, 70
Shastri, Ravi, 287
Shepherd's Hotel, Cairo, 55, 57
Shimp, Harry, 252
Shourie, Arun, 148
Shroff, A.D., 107
Singapore Airlines, 214
Singh, Indra, 31
Singh, Manmohan, 76-77, 212
Singh, S.N., 187
Singhbhum workshop, 93
Sinha, T.P., 107

298 INDEX

Sir Dorabji Tata Centre for Research
in Tropical Diseases, 260
Sir Dorabji Tata Graduate School of
Social Work, 163-64
Sir Dorabji Tata Trust, 61-62, 109,
141, 143-44, 146, 151, 157-58,
163, 167, 169, 171, 176, 186,
203, 259-61, 263-64
Sir Ratan Tata Trust, 61, 141, 144,
146, 176, 203
Small is Beautiful, 136
Smallpox epidemic at Chotanagpur,
179-82
Soonawala, N.A., 217, 290
Special Steel Limited, 34
Spies, John, 157
Sports and Tatas, 286-89
Sreekantan, B.V., 154
Srinivas Rao, 24
Srinivasan, M.N., 44
St. James Court, London, 61
Steel Authority of India Limited
(SAIL), 110
Strategic Plan for Tatas, 210-11
Sugar Corporation, 71
Sumantran, V., 222, 225
Sumitomo, Yoshiteru, 91
Suratwala, S.R., 168
Suresh Press Works, 120
Svadeshi Mills, 13-14
Swadeshi movement, 66
Sydenham, Lord, 49

TATA MAN GHH Limited, 35
TISCO, 28
TOMCO, 214
Tagore, 6
Taj Exotica, Maldives, 242
Taj Group, 61
Taj Inter-Continental, 57
Taj Mahal complex, Agra, 58, 242
Taj Mahal Hotel, Bombay, 12, 54-
62, 241-42
Talaulicar, J.E., 99

Tamil Nadu Industrial Development
Corporation (TIDCO), 248, 250
Tanishq, 249-50
Tariff Commission, 73
Tata, Cooverbai, 202
Tata, Cooverbai Daboo, 276
Tata, Dadabhoy, 191
Tata, Dorab, 14, 22-23, 27, 41, 49,
70, 72, 77, 106, 116, 127, 141,
145-47, 157, 186, 193, 197,
253, 258, 260, 276, 286
Tata, Ervard Jamsheed, 191
Tata, Hirabai, 202
Tata, Hirabai Daboo, 276
Tata, J.R.D., 27, 35, 58-59, 61, 64,
91, 94, 97, 99, 110-11, 141,
191, 193-94, 196-98, 200-02,
204, 209, 211-12, 231-32, 262,
276, 286
Bharat Ratna award to, 265
Chairman of various Tata
companies, 193-95
establishment of NIAS, 259
guiding principles, 277
joined Tata Steel, 191
on functioning of Tata
companies, 195-99
on house of Tata, 201-02, 205
on human relations, 193-94
on role of chairman, 194-95,
200-01, 212
set up Tata Industries, 196-98
step down as chairman, 204-05
style of operation as chairman,
200-01, 212
Tata Sons and, 193-95, 204
tributes to, 204
vision for an airline, 254
Tata, Jamsetji Nusserwanji,
apprenticeship system, 14
as Green Scholar, 4
birth, 3
care for workforce, 13-14, 127
Chairman Tata Sons, 197

collaboration with Japan, 91
death, 17, 24
desire to manufacture cotton
    goods, 4
early successes, 13
experiment in sericulture, 12
experiments in technology and
    labour welfare, 13
exploration for iron ore, coal and
    fluxes for steel plant, 21-23
fund endowed for higher
    education abroad, 37
idea of building steel plant, 20-
    22, 230
in Bombay, 4, 6
in oil and cosmetic sector, 63-69
introduction of foreign trees and
    plants to India, 12
Jawaharlal Nehru on, 33-34
last days advice to cousin, 17
love for literature, 4
man of ideas and vision, 4-19
nationalism, 6
Norman Redford on, 9
on his dream city of steel, 14, 17
on interest of shareholders, 215
on object of science institute, 46
on philanthropy, 38, 137-38
on practice of commission
    charged by managing agents,
    14
on social responsibilities, 183-84
passion to train young Indians,
    138
scholarships by, 138
significance of industrial
    revolution of India, 6
steel and hydro-electric projects,
    17, 19, 49, 253
steel saga, 20-35
Taj Hotel venture, 54-62
three imperatives of industry, 6,
    8
trading adventures in Far East
    and Europe, 4

travel document of, 10
university of science project, 17,
    19, 37-41, 141, 237, 253, 255
vision of, 4-19
visits abroad, 4, 12
Tata, Jeevanbai, 276
Tata, Jehangir R.D., 75-85, 87-88
Tata, Meherbai, 147, 157
Tata, Minocher Kaekobad, 203
Tata, Minoo K., 254
Tata, Navajbai, 146
Tata, Naval, 51, 106
Tata, Naval H., 276
Tata, Naval Hormusji, 202-03
Tata, Nusserwanji, 191, 276
Tata, Pilloo, 203, 254
Tata, R.D., 17, 27-29, 75, 106, 126,
    191, 193, 276
    address to shareholders, 28-29
    on building Jamshedpur, 29
    on steel company, 28-29
Tata, Ratan N., 99, 139-41, 145-
    46, 197-99, 203-04, 209-20,
    239, 276, 290
    birth, 203
    business values, 277-78
    Chairman Tata Group, 266-72
    Chairman Tata Industries, 203,
    211
    Chairman Tata Sons, 204, 211-
    12, 216
    contribution towards social
    causes, 139-40
    Indica project, 222-24
    measures taken to meet challenges
    of liberalization, 216-20
    on J.R.D. Tata, 266-67, 72
    on politics, 214-15
    on use of trust fund, 257
    Strategic Plan for Tatas, 210-11
    support to Mahatma Gandhi
    struggle in South Africa, 253, 255
    support to Servants of India
    Society, 256

Tata Plan, 209-10
Tata, Ratanbai Rao, 276
Tata, Simone N., 69
Tata, Thelma, 202
Tata, Virbaiji, 203, 276
Tata AIG General Insurance Company, 252
Tata AIG Life Insurance Company, 252
Tata Administrative Service (TAS), 119, 224
Tata Adventure Foundation, 289
Tata Agricultural and Rural Training Centre for the Blind, 109
Tata Air Lines, 79, 81
Tata Aircraft Limited, 81
Tata Aquatic Farms Orissa Limited, 35
Tata Archery Academy, 289
Tata Aviation, 202
Tata B.P. Solar, 251-52
Tata Burroughs, 194
Tata Business Excellence Model, 217, 227
Tata Chemicals Limited, 67, 73, 85-90, 108, 148, 185, 194, 196, 198, 200, 216, 225-28, 262, 275
Tata Coffee, 275
Tata Construction, 71
Tata Consultancy Services (TCS), 119, 218, 220, 233-38, 240, 275
Tata Consulting Engineers, 233
Tata Davy Limited, 34-35
Tata Defence Welfare Corpus Fund, 263
Tata Economic Consultancy Engineers, 233
Tata Education Trust, 264
Tata Electric, 123, 216
Tata Electric Companies, 109, 233
Tata Electric system, 50-51
Tata Electro-Chemicals, 71
Tata Electronic Development Services, 124

Tata Elxsi India, 199
Tata Energy Research Institute (TERI), 148
Tata Engineering, 71
Tata Engineering and Locomotive Company, see, Telco
Tata Engineering's Commercial Vehicle Business Unit, 218
Tata Exports (now Tata International), 220, 252
Tata Finance, 199, 215
Tata Financial Services, 233
Tata Finlay, 104
Tata Football Academy, 187, 289
Tata Group, 69, 90
Tata Honeywell, 199
Tata Hydro-Electric Agencies Ltd., 72
Tata Hydro-Electric Companies, 196
Tata Hydro-Electric Power Supply Company, 49, 245
Tata Industrial Bank, 70
Tata Industries, 88, 175, 185, 194, 196, 198-99, 203, 211, 215
Tata Infomedia, 216
Tata Infotech, 216
Tata Institute of Fundamental Research (TIFR), Bombay, 62, 141, 144, 149-52, 251, 254, 259, 261
Tata Institute of Social Sciences, Bombay, 62, 141, 143-44, 162-66, 168, 253, 259-60
Tata Interactive, 275
Tata International, 220, 245, 252
Tata Iron and Steel Company, 25, 29, 31-35, 57, 72-73, 108, 115-16, 183, 187
  accident incident, 31, 33
  expansion, 31
  Golden Jubilee, 33
  industrial relations in, 126-32
  J.D. Choksi on, 35
  JRD Tata and, 191, 193-95

labour welfare measures in, 284-85

Mahatma Gandhi visit to, 229

manpower, 33

modernization of, 34, 229

planning for success of, 229-32

protest against nationalization of, 34, 195

response to distress, 176-77, 262-63

response to smallpox epidemic at Chotanagpur, 179-82

social responsibilities, 183-84, 186-88

social welfare and community development programme, 132-36

sports foundation, 187

value appreciation, 29

workers, 172-73

Tata Keltron, 238

Tata Kisan Kendras, 226, 228

Tata Korf Engineering Services Limited, 34

Tata Korf Metals West Bengal Limited, 35

Tata Line, 17

Tata Management Training Centre, Pune, 117-18

Tata Memorial (Cancer) Hospital, Bombay, 62, 110, 158-61, 253-54, 259-60

Tata Memorial Centre for Cancer Research and Training, 141

Tata Metals and Strips Limited, 34

Tata Motors, 224-25, 275

Tata Oil Mills Company (TOMCO), Tatapuram, 63-67,70, 72, 110, 125, 194, 203

Tata Petrodyne, 246

Tata Pigments Limited, 34

Tata Plan, 209-10

Tata Power Broadband (TPBB), 245-46

Tata Power Company Ltd., 49, 219, 231, 244-47

Tata Press, 247

Tata Refractories, 31

Tata Relief Committee, 176-77, 186, 262

Tata-Robins-Fraser, 31

Tata Salt, 226

Tata Scholars, 138-39

Tata Sierra, 98-99

Tata Social Welfare Trust, 264

Tata Sons, 25, 64, 71, 77, 81, 87-88, 93, 157, 193-98, 202, 204, 211, 215, 217, 235

directors of, 290

holding pattern, 263-64

Tata Spice Centre, 103

Tata Sports Club, 287-88

Tata Steels Rural Development Society, 134

Tata Steels Technical Training School, 116

Tata Sumo, 97

Tata Tea, 67, 90, 101-05, 216, 242-44

Tata Tea-Tetley, 220

Tata Telecommunications, 199

Tata Teleservices, 238-40

Tata Textiles, 196

Tata Theatre, 142-43

Tata Timken Limited, 34

Tata Trusts, 61

Tata Workers' Union, 34, 107, 128-30

Tatamobile, 98-99

Tatanagar, 29

Tatapuram, 63

Tata-Yodogawa, 31

Tatas / Tata groups of companies,

Articles of Association of, 185

at a glance, 275

aviation project, 75-84

business sectors, 279-83

challenges and responses, 209-20

chemicals sector, 282

commercial vehicle venture, 91-99

communication and information system sector, 280-81

consultants, 132-36

consumer product sector, 281

creating industrial culture, 183-88

cult of excellence in, 91-99

during inter-war years, 70-73

electric companies, 49-53

energy sector, 281

engineering sector, 279-80

environmental development, 52-53

foundations for future, 216-20

founder and chairmen of, 276

framework for reconciliation, 174

functioning of, 191-205

future of, 233-40

growth of, 212-14

heavy chemical industry, 85-90

holdings, 216

hotel projects, 54-62

hydro-electric project, 17, 19, 47, 49-51

impulse to learning, 37-46

in sports, 286-89

individual grants by, 265

industrial relations, 126-31

international operations sector, 283

land transport project, 91-99

liberalization and, 211

life in, 106-12

losses, 215-16

Maharaja of Mayurbhanj and, 25

major acquisitions, 219-20

oil and cosmetics project, 63-68

on social responsibilities, 183-88

performers in, 106-12

philanthropy works by, 38, 137-38, 141, 188, 253-65

public parks in Bombay, 52

raising capital for steel project, 24-25, 27-28

research and technology development, 123-25

response to distress, 175-78, 262-63

response to smallpox epidemic at Chotanagpur, 179-82

see also, under specific company

services sector, 282-83

shareholders' interest, 215-16

social welfare and community development programmes, 132-36

struggle for survival of steel plant, 28-29

suppliers, 120-22

tea production, 100-05

technical and management development of employees, 115-19

tradition of dealing with labour, 126-31

trusteeship/ trusts, 137-48

vision and contribution to,

atomic energy, 150-56

cancer treatment, 158-61

rural development, 167-71

social work, 163-66

workers, 172-73

World Bank relations, 110

Tawney, R.H., 140

Telang, Prakash, 222

Telco, 71, 91, 93-99, 108, 115-16, 118, 181, 186-87, 196, 200-01, 203, 216, 221-25, 229, 262, 275

diversification, 94

material supplier to, 120-22

Telco Management Centre, 116

Tetley, 219-20, 242-4
Thackeray, 4
Thakkar, A.V., 132
Thompson, Edward P., 64
Thurlow, Baron Edward, 185
Times of India, 8-9, 41, 57, 99, 258
Timex Industries, 214, 218, 248
Tinplate Company of India, 31
Tiscon bars, 125
Titan Watches Limited, 185-86, 247-50, 275
Tony Jannus Award, 84
Toyota, 98
Trans-Continental Airways, 78
Trent Ltd., 216
Trivedi, C.M., 139
Trusteeship concept, 137
Tsering, Gompa, 251
Tutwiler, T.W., 31
Twain, Mark, 4

UNICEF, 164
US Atomic Energy Commission, 159
US Steel Corporation, 128
Union Medical College, Peking, 157
University Grants Commission (UGC), 261
Upcott, Frederick, 20

VSNL, 219, 238, 240, 275
Vakil, Kapilram, 87

Vengsarkar, Dilip, 287-88
Vintcent, Nevill, 77, 79, 81
Visvesvaraya, M., 43
Vivekananda, Swami, 137, 256
Voltas, 216, 262

Wadhekar, Dattu Tukaram, 120-21
Walwhan dam, 47, 49, 52-53
Washington, Booker T., 253
Watala Tea Estate of Sri Lanka, 243
Wavell, 43, 107
Webb, Beatrice, 127, 132, 183
Webb, Sydney, 127, 132, 183
Weld, C.M., 22-24
Westinghouse, George, 12
Whittle, Frank, 84
Willcock, William, 49
Willingdon, 176
Wittet, George, 118
Woods, George, 110
World Bank, 50, 110, 118, 164
World Health Organization (WHO), 164, 179-82
World Travel Awards, 241
World War I, 70, 106, 132
World War II, 29, 31, 79, 87, 91, 150
Wright, Orville, 84